Communications
in Computer and Information Science   62

Dominik Ślęzak   Tai-hoon Kim
Jianhua Ma   Wai-Chi Fang
Frode Eika Sandnes   Byeong-Ho Kang
Bongen Gu (Eds.)

U- and E-Service, Science and Technology

International Conference, UNESST 2009
Held as Part of the Future Generation
Information Technology Conference, FGIT 2009
Jeju Island, Korea, December 10-12, 2009
Proceedings

 Springer

Volume Editors

Dominik Ślęzak
University of Warsaw and Infobright Inc., Poland
E-mail: slezak@infobright.com

Tai-hoon Kim
Hannam University, Daejeon, South Korea
E-mail: taihoonn@hnu.kr

Jianhua Ma
Hosei University, Tokyo, Japan
E-mail: jianhua@hosei.ac.jp

Wai-Chi Fang
National Chiao Tung University, Hsinchu, Taiwan
E-mail: wfang@mail.nctu.edu.tw

Frode Eika Sandnes
Oslo University College, Norway
E-mail: frodes@hio.no

Byeong-Ho Kang
University of Tasmania, Hobart, Australia
E-mail: bhkang@utas.edu.au

Bongen Gu
Chungju National University, South Korea
E-mail: bggoo@cjnu.ac.kr

Library of Congress Control Number: 2009940120

CR Subject Classification (1998): C.2, H.3, J.1, J.4, K.6, K.8, C.3

ISSN   1865-0929
ISBN-10   3-642-10579-3 Springer Berlin Heidelberg New York
ISBN-13   978-3-642-10579-1 Springer Berlin Heidelberg New York

springer.com

© Springer-Verlag Berlin Heidelberg 2009
Printed in Germany

Typesetting: Camera-ready by author, data conversion by Scientific Publishing Services, Chennai, India
Printed on acid-free paper   SPIN: 12807116   06/3180   5 4 3 2 1 0

Foreword

As future generation information technology (FGIT) becomes specialized and fragmented, it is easy to lose sight that many topics in FGIT have common threads and,
because of this, advances in one discipline may be transmitted to others. Presentation
of recent results obtained in different disciplines encourages this interchange for the
advancement of FGIT as a whole. Of particular interest are hybrid solutions that combine ideas taken from multiple disciplines in order to achieve something more significant than the sum of the individual parts. Through such hybrid philosophy, a new
principle can be discovered, which has the propensity to propagate throughout multifaceted disciplines.

FGIT 2009 was the first mega-conference that attempted to follow the above idea of
hybridization in FGIT in a form of multiple events related to particular disciplines of IT,
conducted by separate scientific committees, but coordinated in order to expose the most
important contributions. It included the following international conferences: Advanced
Software Engineering and Its Applications (ASEA), Bio-Science and Bio-Technology
(BSBT), Control and Automation (CA), Database Theory and Application (DTA), Dis-
aster Recovery and Business Continuity (DRBC; published independently), Future Generation Communication and Networking (FGCN) that was combined with Advanced
Communication and Networking (ACN), Grid and Distributed Computing (GDC), Multimedia, Computer Graphics and Broadcasting (MulGraB), Security Technology
(SecTech), Signal Processing, Image Processing and Pattern Recognition (SIP), and
u- and e-Service, Science and Technology (UNESST).

We acknowledge the great effort of all the Chairs and the members of advisory
boards and Program Committees of the above-listed events, who selected 28% of over
1,050 submissions, following a rigorous peer-review process. Special thanks go to the
following organizations supporting FGIT 2009: ECSIS, Korean Institute of Information Technology, Australian Computer Society, SERSC, Springer LNCS/CCIS,
COEIA, ICC Jeju, ISEP/IPP, GECAD, PoDIT, Business Community Partnership,
Brno University of Technology, KISA, K-NBTC and National Taipei University of
Education.

We are very grateful to the following speakers who accepted our invitation and
helped to meet the objectives of FGIT 2009: Ruay-Shiung Chang (National Dong
Hwa University, Taiwan), Jack Dongarra (University of Tennessee, USA), Xiaohua
(Tony) Hu (Drexel University, USA), Irwin King (Chinese University of Hong Kong,
Hong Kong), Carlos Ramos (Polytechnic of Porto, Portugal), Timothy K. Shih (Asia
University, Taiwan), Peter M.A. Sloot (University of Amsterdam, The Netherlands),
Kyu-Young Whang (KAIST, South Korea), and Stephen S. Yau (Arizona State Uni-
versity, USA).

We would also like to thank Rosslin John Robles, Maricel O. Balitanas, Farkhod Alisherov Alisherovish, and Feruza Sattarova Yusfovna – graduate students of Hannam University who helped in editing the FGIT 2009 material with a great passion.

October 2009

Young-hoon Lee
Tai-hoon Kim
Wai-chi Fang
Dominik Ślęzak

Preface

We would like to welcome you to the proceedings of the 2009 International Conference on u- and e- Service, Science and Technology (UNESST 2009), which was organized as part of the 2009 International Mega-Conference on Future Generation Information Technology (FGIT 2009), held during December 10–12, 2009, at the International Convention Center Jeju, Jeju Island, South Korea.

UNESST 2009 focused on various aspects of advances in u- and e- Service, Science and Technology with Computational Sciences, Mathematics and Information Technology. It provided a chance for academic and industry professionals to discuss recent progress in the related areas. We expect that the conference and its publications will be a trigger for further related research and technology improvements in this important subject.

We would like to acknowledge the great effort of all the Chairs and members of the Program Committee. Out of around 80 submissions to UNESST 2009, we accepted 25 papers to be included in the proceedings and presented during the conference. This gives an acceptance ratio firmly below 30%. Two of the papers accepted for UNESST 2009 were published in the special FGIT 2009 volume, LNCS 5899, by Springer. The remaining 23 accepted papers can be found in this CCIS volume.

We would like to express our gratitude to all of the authors of submitted papers and to all of the attendees, for their contributions and participation. We believe in the need for continuing this undertaking in the future.

Once more, we would like to thank all the organizations and individuals who supported FGIT 2009 as a whole and, in particular, helped in the success of UNESST 2009.

October 2009

Dominik Ślęzak
Tai-hoon Kim
Jianhua Ma
Wai-chi Fang
Frode Eika Sandnes
Byeong-Ho Kang
Bongen Gu

Organization

Organizing Committee

General Chairs	Jianhua Ma (Hosei University, Japan)
	Wai-chi Fang (National Chiao Tung University, Taiwan)
Program Chairs	Frode Eika Sandnes (Oslo University College, Norway)
	Byeong-Ho Kang (University of Tasmania, Australia)
Publicity Chair	Tai-hoon Kim (Hannam University, Korea)
Publication Chair	Bongen Gu (Chungju National University, Korea)

Program Committee

Alexander Loui	H.-D. Zimmermann	Regis Cabral
Antonio Coronato	Helmar Burkhart	Sajid Hussain
Biplab Kumer	Hiroshi Yoshiura	Seng W. Loke
Birgit Hofreiter	Hongli Luo	SeongHan Shin
Bok-Min Goi	Hongxiu Li	Sheng Zhong
Ch. Chantrapornchai	Igor Kotenko	Simone Fischer-Hübner
Chao-Tung Yang	Irene Krebs	Stefano Ferretti
Chengcui Zhang	J.H. Abawajy	Tomasz Janowski
Costas Lambrinoudakis	Jianhua He	Tony Y.T. Chan
David Taniar Monash	Kuo-Ming Chao	Weijia Jia
Dorin Bocu	Ling-Jyh Chen	Yao-Chung Chang
George Kambourakis	Mei-Ling Shyu	Young Jin Nam
Hai Jin	Nguyen Manh Tho	Zhaohao Sun Hebei
Hakan Duman	Rami Yared	Zhenjiang Miao
Hans Weigand	Raymond Choo	Zhuowei Li

Table of Contents

Mobile Manufacturer or Service Provider? An Empirical Study on Consumers' Adoption Intention

Feng Hu[1], Xiao-Yi Du[2], and Yong Liu[3]

[1] School of Business Administration
Zhejiang Normal University, Jinhua 321004, China
Hufeng@zjnu.cn
[2] Zhejiang Normal University, Jinhua 321004, China
Duxy@zjnu.cn
[3] IAMSR, TUCS,
Åbo Akademi University, Turku 20520, Finland
Yong.liu@abo.fi

Abstract. As mobile manufacturers today seek to attract consumers by increasingly integrating mobile services into their products, little research is available regarding whether and to what degree this new feature of mobile phone would motivate consumers' purchase intention. Concerning m-learning, this study investigates the relationship among users' intentions to adopt mobile service, service-enabled-phone as well as intention to pay for the new phone functionality. Based on 209 useful responses, this study suggests that users' intention to adopt m-learning would impact their intention to acquire facilitating conditions (specific m-learning enabled mobile phones). Theoretical and practical implications are discussed in the present paper as well.

Keywords: Mobile services, mobile phone, m-learning, adoption intention.

1 Introduction

In recent years, more and more mobile manufacturers integrate new mobile services into their handheld devices. This appears to be a market strategy increasingly adopted by mobile manufacturers to acquire market share and to generate new revenue. Taking Nokia for example, it has been back in retail services and launched its own online platform in order to compete with iTunes in 2007. The platform offered is termed as 'Ovi', a word meaning 'door' in Finnish. In this platform, a large amount of fantastic music and mobile games are provided to Nokia phone users. Google is also interested to integrate its service to handheld devices, such as in T-Mobile. Similarly, mobile manufacturers in China play a central role in offering m-learning products and services with an expectation to attract consumers' purchase of m-learning enabled phones. Currently, there are a number of online m-learning platforms with a wide range of m-learning services are offered to phone users. As technology-mediated education, such as e-learning, is mostly initiated by educational institutions, it is of practical significance to investigate consumers' responses to the m-learning service offered by mobile manufacturers.

D. Ślęzak et al. (Eds.): UNESST 2009, CCIS 62, pp. 1–5, 2009.

As mobile manufacturers in general hold an expectation that consumers' intention to adopt a mobile service would impact their intention to acquire facilitating conditions, such as a new phone with required functionalities, this paper serves as a first important step to investigate the consumers' responses to this market strategy. The paper is structured as follows: after introducing the theoretical background in the next section, research methodology and results are presented in section 3. Finally, conclusions and implications of the paper are discussed in section 4.

2 Theoretical Background

Current adoption research relating to mobile industry is mostly targeted on mobile services or physical mobile phone respectively. There is limited research offering insights on the relationship between the adoption of mobile phone and mobile services. A number of studies potentially viewed the possession of a mobile phone as a kind of facilitating condition to adopt a particular mobile service. Based on eight previous adoption models, Venkatesh et al. proposed the Unified Theory of Acceptance and Use of Technology (UTAUT), and defined facilitating condition as the availability of resources needed to engage in a behavior [1]. For instance, a consumer's ownership of a mobile phone enables the access to mobile services. It is well understood that behavior can not occur if objective conditions in the environment prevent it [2]. Lu et al. found that facilitating condition is a significant variable impacting perceived usefulness, which in turn influences consumers' intention to accept wireless mobile data services [3]. Regarding ICT adoption in the government organization, facilitating conditions were found to positively impact the use of the ICT [4]. In addition, facilitating conditions were found to significantly influence the use of health information technology [5].

Nonetheless, little research has been found to investigate a reversed impact. In other words, there is little understanding regarding whether consumers' willingness to use a mobile service would motivate them to adopt the facilitating conditions required, such as a new mobile phone. It is self-evident that people today no longer accept mobile phone merely for making and receiving calls. Instead, consumers intend to acquire advanced mobile phone with respect to a number of new functionalities, such as MMS, GPS and wireless connection. Consumers' preference of advanced mobile phone indicates that there might be a relationship from mobile service adoption to the adoption of corresponding mobile phone which enables the new mobile service. In addition, as mobile manufacturers add new value to their products by integrating new functionalities, it is important that consumers in general would perceive the value delivered and therefore would like to pay for the new phone functionality. In this light, we proposed following hypotheses:

H1: Users' m-learning intention is positively related to the (m-learning enabled) phone purchase intention.

H2: Users' m-learning intention is positively related to payment intention of the m-learning functionality.

H3: Users' (m-learning enabled) phone purchase intention is positively related to the payment intention of m-learning functionality.

Table 1. Definitions of variables

Variables	Definitions
M-learning intention (MLI)	Consumers' behavioral intention to adopt m-learning.
Phone purchase Intention (PPI)	Consumers' behavioral intention to purchase m-learning enabled phones.
Payment intention (PI)	Consumers' behavioral intention to pay for m-learning service or functionality offered by mobile manufacturers.

3 Research Methodology

To assess our research model, a survey was carried out in Zhejiang Normal University in China in November 2008. A total of 220 responses were collected from 230 undergraduate students giving a response rate of 95.7%. However 11 questionnaires were discarded as they were partially incomplete. More females (144) than males (65) took part in the survey. These respondents range from 18 to 23 years old. The questionnaire utilized a seven-point Likert-scale ranging from strongly disagree (1) to strongly agree (7) to measure each item. The scales for variable measurement were adapted from the instrument developed by Davis' [6].

Partial least square path modeling (SmartPLS 2.0) was used to evaluate the predictive research model. All the factor loadings are found to above threshold of 0.6 as shown in Table 2. The values of composite reliability (CR) and Cronbach's alpha

Table 2. Results of convergent validity and reliability test

	Factor loading	T Statistics	α	CR	AVE
MLI1	0.9384	86.5259	0.8676	0.9379	0.8830
MLI2	0.9410	97.5852			
PPI1	0.9005	46.5348	0.9467	0.9617	0.8625
PPI2	0.9306	73.5123			
PPI3	0.9546	114.8402			
PPI4	0.9285	71.2163			
PI1	0.7971	13.8936	0.8323	0.8872	0.6645
PI2	0.8424	26.9103			
PI3	0.7114	13.4114			
PI4	0.8982	64.3354			

Table 3. Correlation Matrix and Discriminant Assessment[1]

Variables	Mean	SD	MLI	PPI	PI
MLI	4.80	1.37	**0.939**		
PPI	4.73	1.32	0.811	**0.928**	
PI	4.30	1.21	0.606	0.627	**0.815**

---

[1] The bold items on the diagonal represent the square roots of the AVE, off-diagonal elements are the correlation estimates.

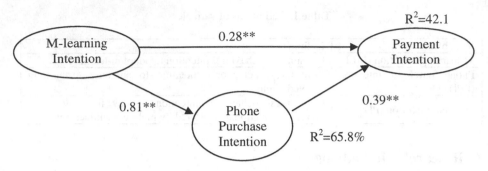

Fig. 1. Results of PLS path modeling analyses

(α) of all the constructs are greater than 0.7, indicating good reliability of the structures. The values of average extracted variance (AVE) satisfy the cutoff value 0.5 (Fornell and Larcker, 1981). In addition, the shared variances among the constructs are less than the square roots of AVE [7], as shown in Table 3. These values indicate that the convergent and discriminant validity of constructs are supported.

The findings provide significant support of all hypotheses. M-learning intention significantly influences both phone purchase intention (β=0.81, *t-value*=29.27) and payment intention (β=0.28, *t-value*=2.97). Phone purchase intention positively relates to payment intention (β=0.39, *t-value*=3.95). Furthermore, m-learning intention accounts for 65.8 percent of variance of phone purchase intention, which together explain 42.1 percent of variance of payment intention.

4   Conclusion and Implications

Our results provide evidences that a provision of mobile service would help mobile manufacturers to attract consumers to purchase mobile phone and to pay for the new functionality accordingly. In theory, this study provides evidences that there is a reversed relationship from service adoption intention to facilitating condition. In other words, a user's intention to adopt a mobile service would motivate them to adopt corresponding facilitating conditions, such as a proper mobile phone, even when the mobile service is offered by mobile manufacturers. Also this would increase consumers' evaluation of the whole value of mobile phone.

Further, even if consumers in general prefer new services for free, this study suggests that m-learning is a service that would lead to a new resource of revenue for mobile manufacturers, as the intention to adopt m-learning significantly motivate the intention to pay for the new m-learning functionality. Also the results indicate that it should be a feasible method to prosper m-learning by encouraging mobile manufacturers to offer m-learning products and services.

As this research only assesses the influence of m-learning on the mobile phone purchase, future research would take impacts of other mobile services, such as mobile music and mobile games, into consideration.

References

1. Venkatesh, V., Morris, M.G., Davis, G.B., Davis, F.D.: User Acceptance of Information Technology: Toward a Unified View. MIS Quarterly 27(3), 425–478 (2003)
2. Triandis, H.C.: Values, Attitudes, and Interpersonal Behaviors. In: Nebraska symposium on motivation, in Beliefs, attitudes and values, pp. 159–295. University of Nebraska Press, Lincoln (1979)
3. Lu, J., Liu, C., Yu, C.S., Wang, K.: Determinants of accepting wireless mobile data services in China. Information & Management 45, 52–64 (2008)
4. Gupta, B., Dasgupta, S., Gupta, A.: Adoption of ICT in a government organization in a developing country: An empirical study. Journal of Strategic Information Systems 17(2), 140–154 (2008)
5. Kijsanayotin, B., Pannarunothai, S., Speedie, S.M.: Factors influencing health information technology adoption in Thailand's community health centers: Applying the UTAUT model. International Journal of Medical Informatics 78, 404–416 (2009)
6. Davis, F.D.: Perceived usefulness, perceived ease of use, and user acceptance of information technology. MIS Quarterly 13(3), 319–340 (1989)
7. Fornell, C.D., Larcker, F.: Evaluating structural equation models with unobservable variables and measurement errors. Journal of Marketing Research 18, 39–50 (1981)

The Development of Software Pricing Schemata and Its Application to Software Industry in Korea

Youngsik Kwak[1], Yunkyung Lee[2], and Yoonsik Kwak[3]

[1] Jinju National University
yskwak@jinju.ac.kr
[2] Korea Culture & Tourism Institute, Seoul
yunky@hanmail.net
[3] Dept. of Computer Engineering, Chungju National University
yskwak@cjnu.ac.kr

Abstract. The purpose of this this research is to suggest a comprehensive pricing schemata that software developers can use in the integrated state of software uses. To do so, we have reviewed the pricing criteria that the current fields of business administration treat and offered the basis of pricing systems. Then we have applied the prices of software products in Korea to the systems and earned abundant price payment units.

As for the research works of software pricing at the present, however, it seems that they are mainly focused on the uses and functions of some specific software rather than on general variables that affect the software pricing policies of PC and Client/Server environment. There have been many researches on individual consumption features such as on the case of upgrade, on the case of outsourcing like ASP, on the case of pricing package items, or on the case of ERP software.[1-5] In other words, there have been few researches on the schemata of pricing that software developers can use.

This paper aims to suggest a comprehensive pricing schemata that software developers, sellers, and distributers can use regardless of the state of software uses. To do so, first, it reviews the criteria of pricing that are frequently discussed in the current fields of economics and management and thereby establishes the basis that leads to a pricing schemata. Then the prices of software in Korea will be applied to the schemata, which will eventually make it possible to produce the complete pricing schemata unique in Korea.

Keywords: Software Pricing, Industry.

1 Introduction

Since IBM introduced a policy that was to take off the software price from the hardware price of the computer in the early 1970s, the software was a different, independent item from the computer. The pricing of the software has been an important factor directly related to the sale and revenue management of the company.

As for the research works of software pricing at the present, however, it seems that they are mainly focused on the uses and functions of some specific software rather

D. Ślęzak et al. (Eds.): UNESST 2009, CCIS 62, pp. 6–12, 2009.
© Springer-Verlag Berlin Heidelberg 2009

than on general variables that affect the software pricing policies of PC and Client/Server environment. There have been many researches on individual consumption features such as on the case of upgrade, on the case of outsourcing like ASP, on the case of pricing package items, or on the case of ERP software.[1-5] In other words, there have been few researches on the schemata of pricing that software developers can use.

This paper aims to suggest a comprehensive pricing schemata that software developers, sellers, and distributers can use regardless of the state of software uses. To do so, first, it reviews the criteria of pricing that are frequently discussed in the current fields of economics and management and thereby establishes the basis that leads to a pricing schemata. Then the prices of software in Korea will be applied to the schemata, which will eventually make it possible to produce the complete pricing schemata unique in Korea.

2 Literature Review

2.1 Linear vs. Nonlinear Pricing

The most frequently treated topic on pricing in economics is the decision on the price scheme. [6] In economics, the price scheme is divided into the linear pricing and the nonlinear pricing. The linear pricing refers to the case that the unit price does not change although the quantity the customer purchases changes. On the other hand, in the nonlinear pricing the unit or service price changes when the quantity changes. [7] In the nonlinear pricing, the provider of the unit or service suggests different prices for different quantities in advance, and the customer adjusts the quantity of purchase to the pre-noticed list of prices as he or she wishes. In other words, in the nonlinear pricing the customer him- or herself chooses the price scheme that best suits his or her purpose. Because the nonlinear pricing offers the heavy user discounted prices, it gives more benefits to loyal customers, who in turn benefit the company, and enhances the level of customer satisfaction. In this regard, the nonlinear pricing is the most effective policy for digitalized cases such as on-line business or service-offering cases such as ASP.

Many researches that deal with nonlinear pricing offer in common 1) the two-part tariff system, 2) n-block tariff system, and 3) all-unit quantity discount system. The two-part tariff system refers to a system of applying a certain price for a certain unit that has been purchased additional to the fixed fee; the n-block tariff system, a system of pricing the unit expensively to its certain amount and discounting the price in case of outnumbering the purchase volume. For example, if when there are four purchasers, $10 is charged for one unit or service, when there are five purchasers, for the additional one purchaser only $8 is charged. The all-unit quantity discount system is a system of applying a discount to all units when the amount of purchase goes over a certain purchase volume. Generally, it is reported that the nonlinear pricing system produces more profits and sales volume than the linear pricing system [8-9].

2.2 Pay-First and Product-Second vs. Product-First and Pay-Second

The decision making issue that has been recently discussed most in management is the payment timing decision making. When the customer pays first and then the product or service is provided, it is called the pay-first & product-second system; when the customer uses the product or service first and then pays later, it is called the product-first & pay-second system.[10-11]

For the company, the pay-first & product-second system is preferable. Since it is paid in advance, its cash inflow enhances. Also, the customer receives many benefits such as discounts for paying in advance, and the company does not have to worry about losing its customers to other companies.

However, the product-first & pay-second system leads the customer to use the product or service in advance and thereby get used to the software. It also leads to the increase of trials of the product because it allows the customer to pay later after he or she uses the product. So it is very useful for a company that develops new software. It is a representative example that recently security corporations receive fees after one-month of future and option transaction on home trading system as one of ASP systems.

2.3 Price Unit Criteria

While not treated often in economics or business administration, the price unit criteria is an issue that is much discussed in the software industry. Table 1, suggested by Jung Hongjin (2000), shows the companies that offer pricing by license unit criteria.[12] In this Table, it is shown that as the list moves downward, the price unit criteria relying on hardware is offered; on the other hand, when moving upward, it is decided by the number of users. Well-known general purpose computer companies such as DEC and IBM rely more on hardware.

Table 1 shows that some companies such as Oracle and IBM use multi price unit criteria instead of just one. It is said that such cases have complexity, while cases of using one have simplicity. According to the current researches, as the complexity of the price unit criteria is higher, the customer's right for preference gets higher and the

Table 1. Variety of C/S License Contract Model (Jung Hongjin 2000)

Price unit criteria	Companies
Product/Step Newwork/User	D&B, SAP, Lawson
Application/ module network/ user	D&B, SAP, Lawson
Network/ user+ uniform server price	Microsoft
Network/ user+ nonlinear server price	Oracle
Uniform user price per server	Oracle, IBM
Nonlinear price	Novell, IBM, MS
Process Size	DEC, HP, IBM

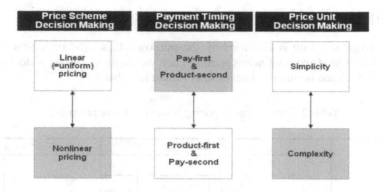

Fig. 1. Topical classification of researches on pricing

company's profits increase.[11] Various price unit criteria are also found in other industries as the license models of software are various. For example, in security business, the customer can make different prices according to the amount of transaction money, the number of transaction, transaction channel, transaction items, or the period of possession. Therefore, there could be some price unit criteria unique only for software industry. Figure 1 shows the software pricing systems that have been discussed so far in the previous researches. This will be the basis for producing our software pricing schemata.

3 Experimental Model

At this stage of positive research, the prices of software in Korea are applied to the pricing systems that are deductively earned in the previous chapter. It is expected in this process that we could find a new pricing schemata not detected in the earlier systems and that we could get the unique price unit criteria for the industry.

For the data collection, the researchers decide the scope of software. The target software is decided upon the classification for the purpose of use. It is because the price of the software upon the classification of industry can be decided by the "deal" that researchers cannot approach. The Korean government reports that there are two software by the classification of the purpose of use.[13] The first classification is the system software which supports the operating system and application. This classification is divided into system management software, system support software, and system development software. The other classification is the application software which treats the operations that users are interested in. It is divided in the general purpose application software and the special purpose application software.

The data by the classification of software have been collected among the software that can be purchased in the on-line software shops that were searched by the explorer engine such as naver.com or yahoo.com from January to May, 2008. As a result, the price schemes, the price levels and price unit criteria of 153 companies could be earned. The number of software products and prices earned on line was relatively lower than in the statistics that says 7,067 software companies were recorded on line in 2006.[13]

4 Analysis of the Model

After the target software is classified by the purpose of use, the price schemes are divided in the linear and nonlinear systems. Then the payment timing is decided and the price unit criteria is studied. The result is shown in Table 2.

Table 2. Current state of pricing Korean software products

| | | price scheme | | | | payment time | |
| | | linear | nonlinear | | | pay-first | product-first |
			two-part tariff	n-block tariff	all-unit discount		
system software	system management software	linux, Window, Asianux, Hancomlinux, Igetlinux, Mizilinux, MySQL, Nitix, Red Hat, Tirbo Linux, WebTrend, Oracle, Ispector	Ipswitch	Hancom office, Ipswitch, Red Hat, Suse, Window, Oracle, Ispector, Semantec		linux, Window, Asianux, Hancomlinux, Igetlinux, Mizilinux, MySQL, Nitix, Red Hat, Tirbo Linux, WebTrend, Oracle, Ispector, Hancom office, Ipswitch, Red Hat, Suse, Window, Oracle, Ispector, Semantec	
	system support software	namo, hauri, Alzip, Fineprint, DISKEEPER, RarLab, Winzip, ZipNall, ACDsee, Nero Burning, EditPlus, CuteFTP, DaOffice, IpswitchFTP, Easy CD, Patition, Vandyke, Virobot, Ahnlab Policy Center, V3, V3 Plantium, Spyzero, V3netserver, V3pro, V3firewall, Norton,	Virobot	Alzip, Fineprint, Quest, RarLab, Winzip, paperPort, Snalgt, Ultra Edite32, virobot, Ahnlab Policy Center, V3, Semantec antivirus, norton, virus chaser, terrace		namo, hauri, Alzip, Fineprint, DISKEEPER, RarLab, Winzip, ZipNall, ACDsee, Nero Burning, EditPlus, CuteFTP, DaOffice, IpswitchFTP, Easy CD, Patition, Vandyke, Alzip, Fineprint, Quest, RarLab, Winzip, paperPort, Snalgt, Ultra Edite32, Virobot, Ahnlab Polic	
	system development software	C++		EditPlus2.12, Ultra Edit-32		C++, EditPlus2.12, Ultra Edit-32	
application software	general application software	hangul 2007, hangul PDF, hangul Office, MS Office, Wordperfect, Acrobat, Hunminjungum, Namo, Adobe, Corel, streamauthor, paintshop, micromedia, fontpage		hangul 2007		hangul 2007, hangul PDF, hangul Office, MS Office, Wordperfect, Acrobat, Hunminjungum, Namo, Adobe, Corel, streamauthor, paintshop, micromedia, fontpage	
	specific application sftoware	autodesk, Dreamweaver, SPSS, Sketchup, Nase, mainz, softclass, iquest, snsoft, zounsoft, Mymailer, jointinfo, Transcat, Easyman, Armi, IRIS, Yoondesign, Nova, Quark, junjajang		SPSS, Softcity, inbi.com	Mymailer	autodesk, Dreamweaver, SPSS, Sketchup, Nase, mainz, softclass, iquest, snsoft, zounsoft, Mymailer, jointinfo, Transcat, Easyman, Armi, IRIS, Yoondesign, Nova, Quark, junjajang, SPSS, Softcity, inbi.com, Mymailer	ASP (Home trading system)

Table 2. (*continued*)

		price unit					
		product differentiation	client/server	upgrade(repeat purchase)	person/org	Bundling	usage time
system software	system management software	linux	linux, Ipswitch, MySQL, Nitix, Red Hat, Suse, Turbo linux, Webtrend, Window, Oracle, Ispector	linux, Window, Semantec	Window, Asianux, Hancom Office		
			Quest	Finprint	Finprint, ACDsee		
	system support software	V3 Plantium, V3firewall, final data	virobot, V3NetServer, final data	V3, V3 Plantium, Spyzero, V3netserver, Semantec Antivirus, casperski	virobot, casperski, safezone	V3+Xkeeper, V3+final data, v3pro+spyzero, Anti virus+antispyware	caspersky anti virus Linux/Unix File Servers, casperski anti virus 6.0 for Windows Servers, Gikimi, safezone
	system development software			C++		Toad(Quest)	C++
application software	general application software	MS Office, Adobe, Corel, Micromedia	Adobe	hangul 2007, hangul Office, MS Office, Wordperfect, Acrobat, Hunminjungum, Namo, Adobe, Corel, paintshop, mixromedia, fontpage	hangul PDF, MS Office, Adobe, Corel, paintshop, micromedia, frontpage	Adobe Design Bundle, CorelDRAW Graphics Suite 12 + Corel KnockOut 2	
	specific application sfotware	iquest, snsoft, zounsoft, jointinfo, eTran, Easyman, Yoondesign, Nova, Qurk, junjajang	Mymailer	Dreamweaver, Sketchup, armi, Yoondesign	sketchup, By voice, Armi, junjajang	Easyman, Armi, Yoondesign	Create Adobe PDF Online, sketchup

First, as for the price scheme, more companies prefer the linear pricing system to the nonlinear. This shows that the software companies do not make use of the theory that the nonlinear pricing system produces more profits for the company than the linear pricing system. In the nonlinear pricing system, the n-block tariff system is more often used than other systems. The n-block system is usually used in the client/server environment by the number of users. It is necessary to use the two-part tariff or all-unit discount systems more often in the future.

Second, as for the payment timing, the pay-first & product-second system is usually used in software industry. Only the home trading system that the security companies adopt uses the product-first & pay-second system in the form of ASP. It is urged to introduce the product-first & pay-second system more positively.

Third, as for the price unit criteria, there are various criteria such as product differentiation, clients/server, upgrade, person/organization, bundling, or usage time horizon. Also, major companies use complexity of various price unit criteria, while small and medium companies use simplicity of few price unit criteria.

Fourth, the price payment unit differs on the character of software. Among the system software, the system support software shows the most various payment units while the application software shows more various payment units than the system software.

5 Conclusion and Suggestions

The purpose of this research is to suggest a comprehensive pricing schemata that software developers can use in the integrated state of software uses. To do so, we have reviewed the pricing criteria that the current fields of business administration treat and offered the basis of pricing systems. Then we have applied the prices of software products in Korea to the systems and earned abundant price payment units.

Software developers and sellers have seen the chances to increase the profits of their companies by making use of the above systems. According to our research, Korean software companies have not made full use of price payment systems, payment timing, and payment units to maximize their profits. Therefore, it is suggested that they seek to adopt various nonlinear pricing payment systems. In addition, they may have to offer their customers various payment opportunities, like a cafeteria, instead of offering one payment unit.

References

[1] Hedtke, J.: Small Business Accounting Software: Low-cost accounting software features increasing power at an affordable price. Accounting Technology 15(4), 37–44 (1999)
[2] Lee, K.: Competitive upgrade pricing of PC software. Journal of Management Sciences in China (2006)
[3] Wang, W.: An Economical Study of the Mechanism in Pricing Software Products. Collected Essays on Finance and Economics 320 (2004)
[4] Yoon: Implementation of Software License Management Agent System. Research Bulletin 51(2), 191–196 (2000)
[5] Stauffer, D.: Price-optimization software is helping companies come up with better prices for their products. There's one catch: the price of the software has been optimized, too. CFO Publishing Corporation 20(3), 27–30 (2004)
[6] Wilson, R.B.: Nonlinear Pricing. Oxford University Press, Oxford (1993)
[7] Simon, H.: Price Management. North-Holland, New York (1989)
[8] Tacke, G.: Nichtlineare Preisbilding: Theorie, Meassung and Anwendung. Gabler (1988)
[9] Holden, N.T.: The Strategy and Tactics of Pricing, Englewood Cliffs (1995)
[10] Dolan, R., Simon, H.: Power pricing. Free Press (1997)
[11] Kwak, Y., Hong, J., Lee, Y.: Strategic Pricing. Benet (2007)
[12] Jung, H.: Pricing software on client/server environment. Industrial Management Study 14 (2000)
[13] Korea SW Industry Promotion Agency (2008), http://www.software.or.kr

The Determinants of Home Shopping Sales in Korea from the Producer Perspectives

Hyuntae Lim[1], Youngsik Kwak[2], and Jisoo Kim[3]

[1] Hyundae Home Shopping, Seoul, Korea
[2] Jinju National University, Korea
[3] Ogilvy Korea, Seoul, Korea
yskwak@jinju.ac.kr

Abstract. Research on CATV homeshopping as focused on the perspective of the customer, mainly using consumer buying behavior. We believe that further research on producer planning factors is urgently needed. This research aims to isolate variables relating to producers for homeshopping and empirically analyze the impact of those variables upon sale.

Keywords: Homeshopping, CATV.

1 Introduction

CATV homeshopping has contributed to the rapid growth of the domestic on-line shopping industry. Current research on CATV homeshopping, however, has been performed on the basis of the customer's perspective which mainly uses consumer buying behavior as its variable. It clearly shows that further research on the planning factors of production is urgently needed.

This research aims to clarify the variables affecting homeshopping sales from producer's perspectives and empirically analyze the impact of those variables upon sale. Academically, it could complement current homeshopping research which tends to neglect the perspectives of manufacturers and competitiveness; and practically it could help the manufacturer to check the best state of the controllable variables according to broadcasting or product conditions and to participate in the product planning and exposure strategies of the TV homeshopping producer, which will eventually enhance the sale.

2 Literature Review

2.1 Demographic Traits of Homeshoppers

Research on the demographic characteristics of homeshopping consumers has been conducted since the 1970s in the United States, Europe and in Korea[1]-[6]. Previous research outcomes comparing the demographic variables of TV Homeshopping and Internet Shopping show that TV Homeshopping consumers generally have a higher

D. Ślęzak et al. (Eds.): UNESST 2009, CCIS 62, pp. 13–18, 2009.

income and come from an older age group. In comparison, Internet Shopping consumers are generally younger and earn less. This shows the need for demographic variables to be controlled when conducting research on sales effectiveness. That is, the purchase behavior for Homeshopping products changes depending on demographic characteristics. Therefore, it is easier for TV Homeshopping to contact the selected target audience compared to a regular off-line store. Moreover, demographic variables should be closely observed prior to conducting product sales at TV Homeshopping.

2.2 Clothing Homeshoppers

Previous research on clothing purchase behavior through homeshopping channels show the following traits.

First of all, research was conducted based on various variables such as motivation, clothing purchase, criteria in selecting certain clothing, place of order, frequency of purchase, purchase price, payment method, satisfaction or dissatisfaction, etc. These variables can be largely divided based on questions such as time of purchase (when), route of purchase (where), reason for purchase (why), frequency of purchase and quantity (what), etc [7].

Secondly, the variables used in previous research focused only on the variables that consumers consider upon purchase. Variables based on producer perspectives such as program rating or viewing method were found to be rare [6].

Thirdly, clothing sales comprise the largest component of TV homeshopping. Therefore, most of variables from the previous research had focused on clothing. So, the variables relating to another industry have not been investigated deeply.

Lastly, a lot of research had been exploratory research that aimed to find related variables for purchase behavior and descriptive research such as market segmentation. It is rare to find causal research related to homeshopping sales [7]-[8].

3 Method

3.1 Research Questions

This research examined the variables that homeshopping marketers believe to affect on-the-spot sales, and checked the extent to which each variable influences the sale. The first variable is the audience rating that shows the rate of houses among those with TVs watching a certain homeshopping channel. It has been widely argued whether the audience rating reflects sales of products. For homeshopping broadcasting, the reach rate could be a more effective variable that measures how many viewers have watched a certain program. Considering the process of purchase after listening to the description of a product, it can be a critical point how long the act of watching lasts. For this reason, we examined the effect of the audience rating upon sale first and then the effect of the reach rate upon sale.

Research Question 1: The audience rating will affect the sale positively.
Research Question 2: The reach rate will affect the sale positively.

There is a saying in the homeshopping industry that the sales go up on a rainy day. It means that if it rains, people tend to stay inside their houses and watch TV, which leads to the increase of sales.

Research Question 3: The precipitation will affect the sale positively.

The last issue that this research deals with is sales promotion. The main patterns of promotion are free gifts, payments by installment with no interest, reserve fund, and ARS(Automatic Response System). ARS is a type of promotion that when a customer calls to buy a product, the automatic response system answers instead of an agent, and that the customer gets a discount for it. This research is focused on the effects of ARS and free gifts.

Research Question 4: The ARS discount will affect the sale positively.

ARS is a very practical type of promotion that aims to reduce the redundant expense required when agents answer all the calls from customers. However, the ARS discount should be within 10 percent of sales price of a product. It is law. So it is more effective to approach this type of promotion by discount percentage for the sales price rather than discounted price.

Research Question 5: The ARS discount will affect the sale more positively when discount percentage for the sales price is higher.

In addition, people often think that free gifts can affect the sales, and many free gifts are offered on many TV homeshopping programs. Its authenticity will be examined.

Research Question 6: Free gifts will affect the sale positively.

3.2 Sampling and Analysis

The data for this research are sampled from business results over a period of three months from June 1, 2008 to August 31, 2008. The broadcasting time covers from seven in the morning to one the next morning, which could be considered common for a homeshopping broadcasting company. All data are limited to the weekday programs for a coherent analysis of a variable under similar circumstances because customers' viewing pattern on weekdays is different from that on weekends. 781 products in total are analyzed for this research. The sales in this research are counted with pure orders that except cancellation and return from all orders, to use data that are realistically close to the real sales for each product.

Audience rating, reach rate, precipitation, ARS price, ARS discount percentage, and free gifts are used as independent variables, and the sale per minute of a product as a dependent variable. And the multiple regression analysis is performed to see how each independent variable affects the dependent variable.

4 Results

Table 1 shows the results of the multiple regression analysis with the sale per minute as the dependent variable and with audience rating, reach rate, precipitation, ARS

Table 1. Results of the Multiple Regression Analysis

Variables	Beta	Standardized beta	t	p
Audience rating	-1254548.8	-0.102	-1.437	0.152
Reach rate	559462.6	0.388	5.128	0.000
Precipitation	7582.1	0.124	2.207	0.028
ARS Price	15.9	0.085	0.938	0.349
ARS % for list	-5989897.9	-0.186	-2.068	0.040
price	159559.4	0.072	1.310	0.191
Free gift				

R^2=0.242, adjust-R^2=0.219, F= 10.621 (p=0.0001)

price, ARS discount percentage for the sales price, free gifts, and sales price as independent variables.

Independent variables of audience rating, reach rate, precipitation, ARS price, ARS discount percentage for the sales price, free gifts, and sales price account for the dependent variable of the sale per minute by 24.2%. And the value of F is 10.621(p=0.0001), which indicates this regression equation is significant. Therefore, the explanation of regression coefficients is possible.

Research question one analyzes if the audience rating can affect the sales positively. According to the results of the regression analysis, the t value of the regression coefficient 1254548 of the audience rating is -1.437(p=0.152), which means that it does not significantly affect the sale per minute on the 95% of significant level. Therefore it is not true that a program with a high audience rating makes a high sale per minute, and a homeshopping producer should not have such a falsely-conceived concept.

Research question two analyzes if the reach rate can affect the sale positively. According to the results of the regression analysis, the t value of the regression coefficient 559462 of the reach rate is 5.128(p=0.0001), which means that it significantly affects the sale per minute on the 95% of significant level. The regression coefficient is also positive. Therefore, the research question two can be accepted. It is also confirmed that the reach rate is a more significant variable than the audience rating to explain the sale per minute.

Research question three analyzes if precipitation can affect the sale positively. According to the results of the regression analysis, the t value of the regression coefficient 7582 of precipitation is 2.207(p=0.028), which means that it significantly affects the sale per minute on the 95% of significant level. Therefore research question three can be accepted, too. The homeshopping producer's experience that the sale goes up on a rainy day is positively true.

Research question four analyzes if the ARS price can affect the sale positively. According to the results of the regression analysis, the t value of the regression coefficient 15.998 of the ARS price is 0.938(p=0.349), which means that it does not significantly affect the sale per minute on the 95% of significant level. In other words, even if the ARS price is discounted more, it still does not lead to the increase of the sale per minute. So research question three is not positively significant.

Research question 5 analyzes if the higher ARS discount percentage can affect the sale positively. The t value of the regression coefficient 5989897.944 of the ARS discount percentage is -2.068(p=0.04), which means that it significantly affects the sale per minute on the 95% of significant level. Here the coefficient has a minus sign, which means that the lower the ARS discount percentage for the sale price gets, the higher the sale per minute goes.

To understand this result, we need to see the original limitations of the ARS discount promotion. That is, for those products that record a normal sale, promotions such as ARS discount are not applied. Therefore, it is concluded that the ARS discount, which is applied within 10% to those products that are not selected by customers, cannot affect the sale positively.

Research question six analyzes if free gifts can affect the sale positively. The t value of the regression coefficient 159559 of free gifts is 1.310(p=0.191), which means that it does not significantly affect the sale per minute on the 95% of significant level. In other words, although free gifts are offered, it does not necessarily leads to an increase of the sale per minute.

5 Conclusion

The homeshopping industry is a mixture of two on-line characteristics, circulation and broadcasting, which is different from the off-line product sale. Since homeshopping is based on broadcasting, it has been often argued whether the audience rating of a certain program is higher or lower. In addition, rather than the audience rating that is usually used by broadcasting companies, the reach rate that counts the cumulative number of viewers for a certain program is often discussed as a more efficient way to explain the relationships of the viewers and the sale for homeshopping programs. It is generally agreed that precipitation affects the sale positively, but the preposition has not been practically verified. At present many programs use promotions such as ARS discount or free gifts to increase the selling conditions of a product without specific analysis of their effectiveness. For these reasons, this research sets up six questions as independent variables and analyzes how those independent variables affect sales.

According to the results, the reach rate accounts for the sale per minute more effectively than the audience rating. Also it is verified that precipitation affects sales. However, it is shown that the most commonly used promotions such as ARS discount and free gifts do not affect sales significantly. Therefore, the homeshopping marketers have to maintain a high-level reach rate for their program and be more careful about the exposure of their products when it rains. Also they should exercise restraint in their use of ARS discount or free gifts because they do not significantly affect the homeshopping sales.

References

1. Berkowitz, Eric, N., John, R., Walton, Waker Jr., O.C.: In-Home Shoppers: The Market for Innovative Distribution (1979)
2. Darin, J.C.: In-home shopping:Are There Consumer segment? Journal of Retailing (1987)
3. Gillette, P.L.: In-home shoppers-An overview. Journal of Marketing (1976)
4. Reynolds, F.D.: An Analysis of Catalog Buying Behavior. Journal of Marketing (1974)

5. Chang, J.: Internet Shopper Demographics and Buying Behavior in Australia. The Journal of American Academy of Business, Cambridge (2004)
6. Ku, Y., Kim, J.: Apparel purchasing behavior of cable TV home-shopping viewer. Journal of Korean Society Clothing Industry 1(3), 231–238 (1999)
7. Ko, E., Kim, S.: A qualitative study about the purchase behavior of internet shoppers. Journal of the Korean Home Economics Association 42(1), 153–166 (2004)
8. Kim, Y., Son, Y., Koo, B.: A study on the characteristics and satisfaction level comparison in the use of home-shopping media. Journal of Business Research 17(2), 63–88 (2002)

The Scanner Data Shows Size Elasticity at Package Food Category?

Jae Soon (Jason) Byun[1] and Youngsik Kwak[2]

[1] The Nielsen Company,
Beijing, China
[2] Jinju National University,
Korea
Jason.Byun@nielsen.com

Abstract. The purpose of this research is to identify whether pack-size elasticity exists within Fast Moving Consumer Goods (FMCG). If this is found to be existed, for brand or trade marketing manager may consider doing more price promotion for pack-size with high elasticity to maximize its return-on-investment (ROI) and/or doing less price promotion for pack-size with less elasticity in order not to waste Below-The-Line investment. In-store price promotion will be more effective if brand or trade marketing managers focus its investment on pack-size with high-elasticity. This research is conducted, using scanner data in Instant Noodle category in China to understand pack-size elasticity.

Keywords: Scanner data, pack-size elasticity, pricing.

1 Introduction

In Webhard service, the service fee for one gigabyte should charge more for less frequently user, while charge less for more frequently users, if considering optimizing the pricing.

In instant rice category, for 300g pack instant rice is sold at cheaper price for 200g pack. Would it be the right pricing decision?

In Carbonated drinking category, the price for 350ml coke comes different when it is sold in retail outlet and vending machine. Would these pricing differences be suitable?

In automotive industry, the price is different between Grandeur 3000c and 2500c. Would this price difference be optimized?

At what price point should it be made for pricing, if a manufacturer is about to re-launch the product by reducing 25% pack from original one.

As described in above case studies, we have observed the different pricing decision, dependent upon the difference in pack-size. At the same time, even with same pack-size, the pricing decision is made for different usage pattern. However, existing pricing research appears to overlook the price elasticity on size or pack-size, where there is no normative guideline for brand or trade managers at the marketplace(Simon 1989; Kwak et al. 2007).

D. Ślęzak et al. (Eds.): UNESST 2009, CCIS 62, pp. 19–24, 2009.

This is the research domain of cognitive psychology theory on different value being imposed on different size(Wheeler 2003). If consumers value differently, the pricing should be made differently. In this context, marketer should consider no pricing promotion for pack-size with less elasticity while do more for the one with more elasticity, resulting in increasing the chance of maximizing profit.

Using scanner data, being collected from Instant Noodle in China, price elasticity by pack-size be measured. This research contributes to pricing research through introducing cognitive psychology theory. Practically, it does provide fundamental theory and insights in making price & promotion decision to brand / trade marketing managers.

2 Literature Review

2.1 Traditional Pricing Schemata

Price is an important topic in economics and marketing. Price is viewed and determined differently depending upon the approach. Simon (1989) suggests a taxonomy of pricing using economics and marketing classifications. He categorizes pricing into three approaches; economics, qualitative/descriptive, and quantitative/methodology-based. The economic based approach deals with the relationship between price and quantity. The qualitative/descriptive approach is for the studies including the pricing decision making process and results within company. The quantitative/methodology-based approach deals with measurement issues associated with optimal price and price response. Because the purpose of the study is to calibrate a price elasticity in a food product, the quantitative/methodology-based approach is employed.

Table 1. Pricing Research in Economics and Marketing

	Approach	Issues	Researchers
Economics	Macroeconomics, Microeconomics	The Determination of Prices by Supply and Demand, Economic Efficiency of the Price System, Problems of Market Equilibrium.	Cournot, Chamberlin, Krelle, Stackelberg.
Marketing	Qualitative/ Descriptive	Directional Recommendation for Pricing.	Shapiro, Monroe, Oxenfelt
	Quantitative/ Methodology-based	Pricing Oriented from Econometric Analysis, Measurement Issues (the Conjoint Measurement).	Rao, Nagle, Simon, Kucher.

Note. From Price management (p. 8). by H. Simon, 1989, New York; North-Holland. Copyright 1989 by North-Holland. Adapted.

Yoo (1989) reviews the historical development of pricing research in marketing in Europe and the United States. According to Yoo's (1989) classification, pricing issues can be divided into three areas; normative, descriptive, and behavioral.

Table 2. Yoo's (1989) Pricing Classification

Approaches	Topics
Normative	Defensive Pricing Strategy, Pricing a Product Line, Price Determination Via Conjoint Analysis, Quantity Discount, Price Bundling.
Behavioral	Price Awareness, Price Consciousness, Price as an Indicator of Quality, Perceived Price, etc.
Descriptive	Decision Process of Price, Determinants for Price.

Note. From <u>Pricing research in marketing: The integration of European and American literature.</u> by P. H. Yoo, 1989, <u>Korean Marketing Review, 4</u>(1). Adapted.

Researchers utilizing the normative approach have dealt with the setting and measurement issue of price. Descriptive studies have explored the process of determining price, while behavioral studies have examined the psychological issues associated with price: price awareness, price consciousness, price as an indicator of quality, perceived price, etc.. Based on Yoo's classification scheme, the current study utilized a normative approach as a price elasticity via scanner data.

Conclusively, in measuring price elasticity, by Simon (1989) and Yoo's (1989) classification this study utilized both the quantitative/methodology-based approach and the normative approach. However, in pricing research, there is not many case, where cognitive psychology factors (e.g. pack-size) be employed. This research is to introduce this psychology factor in pricing research.

2.2 Topic of Cognitive Psychology

In cognitive psychology, it is suggested that consumers recognize as an order of shape - color – content(Wheeler 2003). This can be further interpreted as follows. For example, in recognizing Samsung Logo, following shape-color-shape order can be further described as follows. First of all, once people sees Samsung Logo, oval shape is recognized with comfortable and soft impression. Second, blue background color is recognized. Third, white-colored Samsung characters are recognized, resulting in that Samsung logo is finally recognized. In this regards of recognizing products, software and service, consumers put a value based on Shape, Color and Contents.

Shape ⟶ color ⟶ content

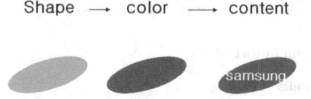

Fig. 1. Perception process of cognitive psychology

In existing pricing research, there appears to have no attention in different pricing methodologies, as the product shape is being changed. There is a study on different pricing scheme dependent upon the different color of products, yet the mechanism to what degree the price dependent upon different colors be adjusted has not been researched. An attention has been drawn to researches on the pricing impact from different service or quantity of purchased goods from cognitive psychology viewpoints. There seems to have a lot of rooms in understanding the pricing mechanism in shape and color. In this research, we focus on pack-size, which is one of subtopics of shape attribute through the cognitive psychology's point of view.

The following research question was developed to guide the study:

1. Are there differences in the price elasticities among size at a given product category in China?
2. Are there differences in the price elasticities among size at a given product category among brands in China?

3 Empirical Research

3.1 Sample

Scanner data was processed to understand price elasticity by pack-size. The weekly scan data from one of major retailers in China is used with the period from June 2006 to September 2008 in three major cities in China. Major six brands and multi pack-size has been used.

3.2 Data Analysis

In order to identify price elasticity on pack-size, the analysis is conducted as follows. For pricing factor, the weekly average price index is used for respective pack-size items. If the average price index is higher than 1.0, it indicates that a SKU has higher price than market average price. If the average price index is lower than 1.0, it indicates that a SKU has lower price than market average price. Market average weekly price from six major brands are used. Weekly sales data is used as dependent variables and average price index is used as independent variables so as to measure price response function. Using price response functions, the sales per respective SKUs of pack-size is estimated, using min & max price points over two years. A percentage of change in price between minimum and maximum price is used as a denominator and a percentage of change in estimated sales in minimum price and maximum price is used as a numerator in order to calculate the price elasticity.

4 Findings and Future Study

4.1 Size Elasticities

In this research, 80g pack-size is used as smaller pack-size, while 150g pack-size used as larger pack-size. Table 3 shows that the price elasticity appears to be highest in between 88g and 105g. Figure 2 shows its result in diagram. Mid-sized pack shows Zero price elasticity and smaller and bigger pack appears to be higher in price elasticity. Key implications are summarized as follows. First, the price elasticity by pack-size is clearly existed, suggesting that mid-size pack should avoid the price

Table 3. Price elasticities by pact size

Product size	Beijing	Shanghai	Guangzhou	Average
5 * 80 g	-3.40	-3.33	-1.73	-2.82
5 * 88 g	-2.76	-3.44	-0.42	-2.21
5 * 89 g	-1.79			
5 * 90 g	-2.78	-2.71	-1.69	-2.39
5* 91 g	-2.75	-0.31	-1.61	-1.50
5 * 100g	-1.82	-2.82	-2.63	-2.42
5 * 105 g	-2.30	-2.18	-1.92	-2.13
5 * 110g	-4.21	-2.43	-2.50	-3.05
5 *115 g	-7.06			-7.06

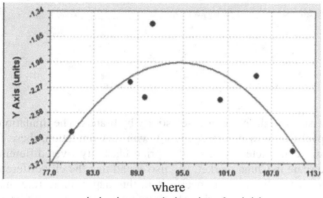

where

x axis is size, y axis is price elasticities

Fig. 2. Plot of price elasticities by brand

promotion. Second, the fact that different pack-size has different price elasticity indicates that size is also part of Shape factor in cognitive psychology. Therefore, marketers should consider pack-size factor in pricing decision making process.

4.2 Size Elasticities for Brand

The brand impact on price elasticity over pack-size is also reviewed as follows. Table 4 shows that strong price elasticity is found in smaller or lager pack-size across brand A, B and C, which are major players in the market place.

There is some different price elasticity found for the same pack-size in different brands, suggesting that marketers should understand the price elasticity of their own products by pack-size, before making a price decision.

4.3 Future Studies

This research reveals that pack-size is part of cognitive psychology factor (esp. Shape) and has price elasticity in different pack-size. Also, within the similar

Table 4. Size elasticities for brand

brand in BJ	5X80 GM	5X88 GM	5X89 GM	5X90 GM	5X91 GM	5X100 GM	5X105 GM	5X110 GM	5X115 GM
a	-3.37	-3.70	-1.79	-1.90	-3.78			-7.25	-7.06
b				-4.39		-1.82		-2.16	
c	-4.44	-1.82		-4.89	-2.66				
d	-2.38			-0.27	-1.80		-4.48	-4.85	
e							-1.20		
f				-2.44			-2.41		
average	-3.40	-2.76	-1.79	-2.78	-2.75	-1.82	-2.70	-4.76	-7.06

brand in SH	5X80 GM	5X88 GM	5X89 GM	5X90 GM	5X91 GM	5X100 GM	5X105 GM	5X110 GM	5X115 GM
a									
b				-2.76			-2.96	-2.88	
c	-3.33	-3.44					-2.67		
d				-4.47	-0.13			-1.99	
e							-2.18		
f				-0.91					
average	-3.33	-3.44		-2.71	-0.13	-2.82	-2.18	-2.43	

brand in GJ	5X80 GM	5X88 GM	5X89 GM	5X90 GM	5X91 GM	5X100 GM	5X105 GM	5X110 GM	5X115 GM
a									
b				-1.78		-2.53			
c	-1.73	-0.42				-2.72			
d				-1.53	-1.61			-2.50	
e							-1.92		
f				-1.74					
average	-1.73	-0.42		-1.69	-1.61	-2.63	-1.92	-2.50	

pack-size, there shows a different price-elasticity by brands. The limitation lies in that we use multi-packs only in our study. Even with this limitation, these findings are expected to inspire marketers to consider price elasticity over different pack-size. Also, given the scale in China market, we also found that the city difference exists in this topics, though we did not yet specify it in this paper, indicating that marketers should further analyze impacts of price-elasticity over pack-size in different cities.

References

1. Dolan, R., Simon, H.: Power pricing. Free Press (1997)
2. Geurts, M.D., Whitlark, D.: Forecasting market share. Journal of Business Forecasting 11(4), 17–22 (1993)
3. Kwak, Y., Hong, J., Lee, Y.: Strategic Pricing. Benet (2007)
4. Holden, N.T.: The Strategy and Tactics of Pricing, Englewood Cliffs (1995)
5. Simon, H.: Price Management. North-Holland, New York (1989)
6. Tacke, G.: Nichtlineare Preisbilding: Theorie, Meassung and Anwendung. Gabler (1988)
7. Wheeler, A.: Designing brand identity. Wiley, NY (2003)
8. Yoo, P.H.: Pricing research in marketing: The integration of European and American literature. Korean Marketing Review 4(1), 168–200 (1989)
9. Yoo, P.H.: Pricing Policy. Pakyoungsa, Seoul (1991)

OpenTide China's Pricing Decision-Making Support System 2.0 for Digital Industry in China

Yeisun Lee[1], Wonsang Youn[1], Jongwook Lim[1], Yongsik Nam[1], and Youngsik Kwak[2]

[1] OpenTide China, Beijing, China
[2] Jinju National University, Korea
{wyeth.lee, kane.youn, frontier, namys118}@opentide.com.cn,
yskwak@jinju.ac.kr

Abstract. The purpose of this research is to develop a comprehensive pricing decision-making support system that marketers in digital industry can use to set price level and quantity for digital products including mobile phone, TV, computer, mp3 and monitor. The OpenTide Pricing Decision-making Support System (OTC's PDSS) consists of the price response function for each product, the promotion response function, the cost function, mixture modeling, Kane's regency modeling and Brian's competitive algorithm. Then we have applied the OTC's PDSS to the digital industry and yielded the profit maximization price point, revenue maximization price point, and their quantity level for each product category.

Keywords: Pricing, price response function, mixture model.

1 Introduction

A consultant is like a doctor. As a doctor examines a patient and suggests a remedy, a consultant examines clients' situation and tries to lead them to a better situation. A doctor and a consultant share in common that they can determine their clients' future. For this reason, a sound consulting should be scientific, systematic, analytic, and strategic because it is concerned with the fate of a company.

OpenTide China has consulted various industries for 10 years in China. The MCG (Management Consulting Group) of this company has developed support systems to help their clients with strategic decision-making. This is the result that OpenTide China strategically made to help their clients' decision-making fundamentally and consistently rather than to help just one-time.

The support system introduced in this paper suggests measurable effects of various alternatives to the client's marketing mix (product, price, promotion, and place), which enables the marketers of the client to achieve specific purposes such as to maintain positioning and maximize profits and sales and protect the brand, etc. OpenTide China has the price-measuring system by product spec for electric home appliances, the advertisement effect measuring system for IT products, the distribution (place) decision-making system for off-line industries, and the pricing decision-making system for IT products. This research introduces the pricing

D. Ślęzak et al. (Eds.): UNESST 2009, CCIS 62, pp. 25–32, 2009.

decision-making system developed for digital industry among those systems. The OpenTide Pricing Decision-making Support System (OTC's PDSS) is based on the price response function for product lines, the promotion response function by products, and the cost function by each product. In order for these functions to reflect the recent market situation, we calibrated adjustment coefficients by Kane's regency modeling and applied them to PDSS. Also, we integrated Brian's competitive algorithm to reflect the competitiveness of the market. The reservation price, brand preference, and cost structure of the same product are all different from region to region in China, different sale DBs of one product by region should be made. And different PDSSs should be constructed according those different DBs by region. For this reason, the project database (PDB) by region and product is necessary to construct.

This paper shows the structures and functions of OTC's PDSS to calculate the production, sales, and profit by various prices and promotion types, and it also shows the methods of deriving coefficients. For this purpose, we used 32-inch TVs in TianJin Region and monitors in Beijing.

2   System Modeling

2.1   Step1: Price Response Function (PRF)

The relationship between alternative prices and the resulting sales quantity is called the price response function (PRF) (Simon, 1989). The price response function of a product or a brand is a tool to understand the effect of price on sales for a product or a brand. Many researchers have recommended calibrating the price response function for a product or a brand to find the optimal price for the product or the brand based on conjoint analysis (Kucher et al., 1993; Simon, 1989, 1992; Yoo, 1991).

There are two approaches to obtaining the price response function. The first approach is to calibrate the price response function with prices and types of promotion as independent variables and with the sales as a dependent variable when there are real sales data. The other approach is to ask customers' purchase intention through consumer research. The conjoint analysis is appropriate for the research on customers' purchase intention to obtain the price response function.

Conjoint analysis has been recommended as an effective tool for determining the value of a product deriving price response functions and optimal prices (Geurts & Whitlark, 1993; Simon, 1989; Weiner, 1994). This conjoint measurement uses individual customer's preference, which also satisfies the condition of setting the prices from the customers' viewpoint.

Therefore OTC's PDSS uses two types of PDB. If the client has already constructed sales DBs, they will be used; if not, we have to construct DBs after collecting customers' purchase intention DBs by separate market researches. Then the price response function will be derived on the basis of those PDBs.

The most systematic way to represent a price response function is by means of a mathematical equation. There are four types of price response function model in OTC's PDSS: linear, multiplicative, attraction, and Gutenburg models. These four basic models are expanded into 21 transformed models. Figure 1 shows some of those

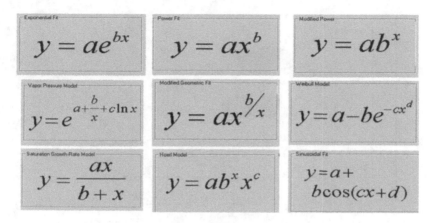

Fig. 1. Some of the Price Response Functions in PDSS

expanded models. PSDD applies the 21 expanded models to the PDB and seeks for the function to best explain the price and sale and uses it to predict the future.

2.2 Step 2: Dividing PRF into High-Demand and Low-Demand Seasons

On Chusok (Korean Thanksgiving Day) and the Lunar New Year's Day, customers feel different about brands or promotion. So if we construct PDB that is based on the sales DBs of the year and make just one price response function or sales promotion response function on the basis of it, we are likely to neglect the different aspects of dull and active seasons, promotion and non-promotion seasons, normal and abnormal seasons, and high-demand and low demand seasons. To reflect differences in customers' responses to price and promotion in these different seasons, we applied mixture modeling to the price response function.

For example, there were three linear price response functions as for the 32-inch TVs in TianJin. The first price response function explains the price and promotion during the first week of the year, the Lunar New Year's Day, the Labor Day, and national holidays; the second explains those of the low-demand season; and the third, those of the normal season.

Mixture model is to unmix the sample, to identify the segments, and to estimate the parameters of the density function underlying the observed data within each segment. Therefore in the first stage of PSD, we find the most appropriate price response function.

Then in the second stage, we apply the mixture model within the price response function and divide it into several price response functions that explain differences produced by products and regions. Mixture modeling has the following algorithm. Therefore the price response of the first stage can be seen as an aggregated price response function, and that of the second stage, as a disaggregated price response function.

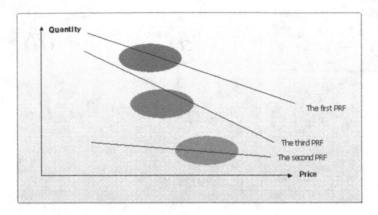

Fig. 2. PRF derived from the high-demand and the low-demand seasons

Data $y_n = (y_{nk})$ where k= no. of variables n= no of observations

S Classes with: $\sum_{s=1}^{S} \pi_s = 1$ where S= no of segment

Conditional density $f_s(y_n | \theta_s)$

Unconditional density $f(y_n | \phi) = \sum_{s=1}^{S} \pi_s f_s(y_n | \theta_s)$

Choice probabilities

Mixture model $p_n = \dfrac{\pi_s f_s(y_n | \theta_s)}{\sum_{s=1}^{S} \pi_s f_s(y_n | \theta_s)}$

Mixture regression model $\eta_{nk} = \sum_{p=1}^{p} X_{nkp} \beta_{sp}$ where beta= estimated coefficients

The above procedure enables us to understand the sales by prices. Clients can obtain the revenue by prices through multiplying the sale by the price.

2.3 Step 3: Promotion Response Function

Marketers try to increase the sales by various types of promotion other than the price. The sales reflect the effects of promotions toward the consumers or the middleman or the local dealer. To reflect it on OTC's PDSS, we inserted dummy variables that reflect promotion when deriving the price response function. As a result we could get differences by products and regions that affect the sales by each type of promotion. And it enabled the marketers to choose and execute the most effective type of promotion within the budget for marketing.

2.4 Step 4: Cost Function

The cost function traces the changes in cost by unit when the sales increase. It is generally known that the cost function has four types shown in Figure 3. Since each industry or company has a different cost function, we have to derive a different cost function when measuring the profits (Yoo, 1991). So the marketers keep the cost function appropriate for their brands, apply it together with the price response function, and achieve the profit function to find the prices that could maximize the profit. OTC PDSS offers a special pane where clients can choose the cost function and insert it by themselves. This is because the client usually does not want to show its own cost to other companies.

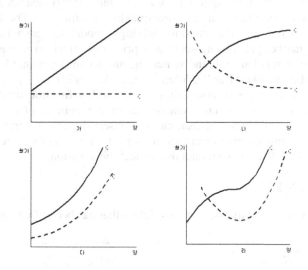

Fig. 3. Types of Cost Function

Through this procedure we could get the cost by unit for the sales achieved by prices. In step 3, we could measure the sales volume, the total cost and the profit by prices.

2.5 Step 5: Kane's Regency Model

Since PDB is basically the data of the sales in the past, it could be possible not to be able to reflect the recent sales trend. So we need an adjustment of the sales volume according the situation of the market. To do so, we integrated Kane's Regency Model based on time series model into PDSS.

This model adjusts assumed periods of the price response function and the promotion response function. Based on the moving average model, Kane's Regency Model adjusts periods by which the data of PDB are periodically applied to the price response function. For example, when the marketer uses PDSS, it can be possible that the functions of PDSS cannot reflect the recent situations of the market because of the time lapse. For this reason, Kane's Regency Model adjusts the assumed periods and derive Kane's adjustment index. This adjustment index changes the values of the price response function and the promotion response function. By this process, we could get the system that reflects the recent situation of the market.

2.6 Step 6: Brian's Competitive Algorithm

Steps one to four enable us to predict the sales and profit of our product when we change prices and types of promotion. However, our changes in price and promotion can make changes of our competitors in price and promotion. To reflect this aspect, we applied Brian's Competitive Algorithm to PDSS to derive our price adjustment and sale change in advance.

The Competitive Algorithm suggested by Brian Nam (1999) measures the extents of struggling among the brands in the corresponding positioning. The basic model takes on multinomial logit. The multinomial logit model has also been used to examine various market phenomena such as a price cut effect on a market, market segmentation, choice set change, brand switching, and so on (Bucklin, Gupta, & Han, 1995; Buckiln & Lattin, 1991; Hardie, Johnson, & Fader, 1993).

There are prices and types of competitors in the utility function used by Brian's Competitive Algorithm. So the cross-elasticities of competitors can be measured. Since PSDD has this algorithm, the marketer can insert the changes in price and the type or degree of promotion of competitors in user interface, and then get the sales by prices and the profits of our new product that reflect the situation.

2.7 Step 7: OTC's PDSS

Figure 4 shows the system expressing the modeling that has been discussed.

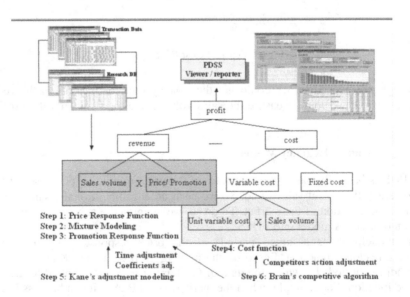

Fig. 4. OTC's PDSS

Table 1. PDSS Step-by-Step Algorithm and Its Outputs

Step	Title	algorithm	Output
1	Aggregate Price response function	21 mathematics functions	Sales volume for price points Revenue maximization price point
2	Disaggregated price response function	Mixture modeling	Sales volume for normal periods Sales volume for abnormal periods Revenue maximization price point
3	Promotion response function	21 mathematics functions	Sales volume for promotion types
4	Cost function	4 types	Cost for price point Profit Maximization price point
5	Kane's regency model	Time series model	Regency adjustment index Adjusted Sales volume for normal periods Adjusted Sales volume for abnormal periods Adjusted Revenue maximization price point Adjusted Profit Maximization price point
6	Brian's Competitive algorithm	Multinomial logit formation	Adjusted sales volume, Revenue maximization price point, Profit Maximization price point incorporating competitors' price and promotion action
7	Application to region and product		PDSS for each region and product line

3 Application to Digital Industry

The user interface and the results of the case that was applied by OTC's PSDD to 32-inch TVs in TianJin and monitors in Beijing, China, will be reported in the conference. However, they are not printed in the proceedings because of confidentiality of data of the clients.

4 Findings and Future Study

The outcomes earned by designing this price support system can be summarized as follows. First, different price response functions are derived by different aspects of high-demand and low-demand seasons and active and dull seasons. Marketers can trace the sales changes that appear differently in a low-demand season and in a certain period that all promotion concentrates.

Second, different price response functions are derived by regions in China. In other countries such as Korea, the sales change by prices is almost consistent. Therefore, PDSS should be made for each region.

Third, different price response functions are derived by size and type even in the same group of product. For example, as for the sizes of TV like 32 inches or 40 inches, different degrees of brand loyalty and different price and promotion elasticities are derived in the same market. Therefore, PDSS should be applied to product line as well as product category.

References

1. Bucklin, R.E., Gupta, S., Han, S.: A brand's eye view of response segmentation in consumer choice behavior. Journal of Marketing Research 32, 66–74 (1995)
2. Bucklin, R.E., Lattin, J.M.: A two-state model of purchase incidence and brand choice. Marketing Science 10, 24–40 (Winter 1991)

3. Dolan, R., Simon, H.: Power pricing. Free Press (1997)
4. Geurts, M.D., Whitlark, D.: Forecasting market share. Journal of Business Forecasting 11(4), 17–22 (1993)
5. Hardie, B.G., Johnson, E.J., Fader, P.S.: Modeling loss aversion and reference dependence effects on brand choice. Marketing Science 12, 378–394 (Fall 1993)
6. Kucher, E., Hilleke, K.: Value pricing through conjoint analysis: A practical approach. European Management Journal 11(3), 283–290 (1993)
7. Kwak, Y., Hong, J., Lee, Y.: Strategic Pricing. Benet (2007)
8. Nam, Y.: Defensive Strategy Adopting Consumer Heterogeneous Perception and Dynamic Preference, Structure. In: Proceeding of marketing Science Conference. Univ. of Syracuse (1999)
9. Holden, N.T.: The Strategy and Tactics of Pricing, Englewood Cliffs (1995)
10. Simon, H.: Price Management. North-Holland, New York (1989)
11. Tacke, G.: Nichtlineare Preisbilding: Theorie, Meassung and Anwendung. Gabler (1988)
12. Yoo, P.H.: Pricing Policy. Pakyoungsa, Seoul (1991)
13. Weiner, J.: Forecasting demand: Consumer electronics marketer uses a conjoint approach to configure its new product and set the right price. Marketing Research: A Magazine of Management & Applications 6(3), 6–11 (1994)

Application Service Program (ASP) Price Elasticities for Korean Home Trading System

Wanwoo Cho[1], Jaewon Hong[2], Ho Jang[3], and Youngsik Kwak[4]

[1] Daewoo Securities, Seoul, Korea
[2] Dongseo University, Pusan, Korea
[3] Benet Co. Seoul, Korea
[4] Jinju National University, Korea
yskwak@jinju.ac.kr

Abstract. Although the price elasticities for off-line industry are well documented in academic field, the report of price elasticities for on-line to a given brand or industry in practice have been relatively rare. The researcher aims to try to full this gap by applying a price response function to Home Trading System's on-line transaction data for the first time in Korean securities market. The different price elasticities among seven brands were found from -0.819 to -1.811. These results suggested that marketers should understand the price elasticity of their own HTS, before making a price decision.

Keywords: ASP, Stock market, Online trading system, pricing.

1 Introduction

The study for pricing elasticity is not a new subject. If we look at previous studies by four criteria: "Who", "Where", "What", and "How" for price elasticity, we are easily recognize that a number of study materials have been accumulated.

Firstly, in terms of "Who", so many studies for identifying high and low price elasticity groups have been conducted (Darin 1987; Ku and Kim 1999). The main purpose of these studies implements different pricing policy; price discount for a high price elasticity group and price increase for the low (Simon 2009).

Secondly, study with respect to "When"is associated with product life cycle and price elasticity. As a product reaches from introductory to growing or mature period, price elasticity is getting lower. Finally, at decline period, price elasticities is getting higher. Therefore, this study is useful to derive an optimal period of pricing strategy like price increase or decrease, when time goes by. In addition, study about price elasticity gap between a slack time and prosperity has been executed. And in a depression season price elasticity is usually high. Furthermore, there is a dynamic price response function derived by tracing price sensitivity with time variable (Simon 1989).

Thirdly, study in light of "Where" is that price elasticity is different by country or region. Mainly, price elasticity is different by urban and rural or area despite same products (Darin 1987; Ku and Kim 1999).

D. Ślęzak et al. (Eds.): UNESST 2009, CCIS 62, pp. 33–38, 2009.
© Springer-Verlag Berlin Heidelberg 2009

Fourthly, study for "What" is that price elasticity is different by product cluster and brand, which is to report difference of price elasticity between durables and non-durables (Simon 1989).

Fifth, study of "How"is about size of price elasticity in itself. The study has been carried out that in spite of same products, price elasticity between expensive and cheap price is different (Kwak, Hong, and Paik 2001). Also, changes in sales volume at the same level of price increase or decrease are different.

A newly initiated subject among these prior researches about price elasticity hardly finds out, especially researches regarding subjects mentioned above have mainly implemented in German-spoken areas, yet in recent the number presented as research outcomes in German has been declined.

However, the new study subjects for price elasticity have been made by the development of recent online industry. Numerous platforms generating revenue through on-line have been set up and developed. For instance, consumers pay mobile bill for use of their service in mobile industry, and contrarily companies make revenue. Online communication sales like TV home-shopping has been occurred and costumers trade stock or bond on-line by using Home Trading System, provided by securities companies. The HTS is ASP (application service program) that costumers pay fees for use of service of a company program. Furthermore, a company sometimes receives lending fees for a web-hard.

Even though there are a variety of online prices and revenues biz model, the relation between the price and revenue or price and sales volume, price elasticity, haven't been yet reported for on-line. The researcher aims to try to full this gap by applying a price response function to Home Trading System's on-line transaction data for the first time in Korean securities market. Through that, we can not only academically accumulate researches of price elasticity, but also practically get information about price elasticity for each brand manager in industry field.

2 Modeling

Price elasticity is defined as change in price in comparison to change in sales volume. For this measurement data of price changes is needed as a denominator and data of sales changes as a numerator. Depending on which price points are measured, price elasticity is different. Accordingly, price response function is introduced so that significant sales volume should be gauged for price elasticity measurement.

The relationship between alternative prices and the resulting sales quantity is called the price response function (PRF) (Simon, 1989). The price response function of a product or a brand is a tool to understand the effect of price on sales for a product or a brand (Kucher et al., 1993; Simon, 1989, 1992; Yoo, 1991).

There are two approaches to obtaining the price response function. The first approach is to calibrate the price response function with prices and types of promotion as independent variables and with the sales as a dependent variable when there are real sales data. The other approach is to ask customers' purchase intention through consumer research. The conjoint analysis is appropriate for the research on customers' purchase intention to obtain the price response function. In this study the first approach, using real data is employed as transaction data of HTS is analyzed.

Table 1. Four Basic Price Response Functions

model	equation
linear	$q = a - b\,p_i + p'$
multiplicative	$q = a\,(\,p_i/p')^b$
attractive	$q = a_0 + a_i\,p_i^{\,b_i} / \sum_j a_j p_j^{\,b_j}$
Gutenberg	$q_i = a - b\,p_i - c_1 \sinh(\,c_2(\,p_i - p_i'))$

p_i = company's price
p_j = competitors' price
p' = average competitors' price
$a, b, c1, c2$ = estimated variable

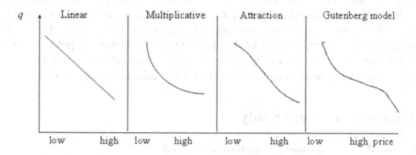

Fig. 1. Four basic Price Response Functions

The most systematic way to represent a price response function is by means of a mathematical equation. There are four types of price response function model: linear, multiplicative, attraction, and Gutenburg models. These four basic models are expanded into 21 transformed models. Table 1 shows four basic models. We apply the 21 expanded models to the transaction data and seek for the function to best explain the price and sale and use it to predict the future.

3 Methods

3.1 Sample

Online transaction data was processed to generate price elasticity by brand. The data was used with the period from January 2007 to May 2008 in Korea. Major seven brands in Korea securities market have been used as research subject.

3.2 Data Analysis

In order to identify price elasticity on ASP for 7 brands, the analysis is conducted as follows. For pricing factor, the monthly market average price index is used for each brand and monthly average fees of 7 brands have been followed up every month. In order to calculate market average ASP price, the value yielded by average brand fees times market share by brand is divided by total market share of 7 brands.

In the second stage, we need sales volume data for the study. We regard monthly transaction volume of 7 brands as sales volume.

Market share of brand on May 7th, 2008 for seven brands is 21 percent. On May 2008 the number of securities firms which have entered a Korean securities market is 53, so major seven securities firms are the subject of this research.

The third stage is to yield price response function. For that, dependent variable of price response function is monthly sales volume and independent variable is the size of average fees of each brand, compared to monthly market average ASP price. This independent variable is defined as relative ASP Price by brand.

If the relative ASP price index is high than 1.0, it indicates that a brand has higher price than market average price. If the ASP price index is lower than 1.0, it indicates that a brand has lower price than market average.

The fourth stage is to yield price elasticity of each brand. The lowest and highest fees of each brand are found out during the research period, and then estimated sales volume is yielded by applying the two fees into price response function of each brand.

A percentage of change in price between minimum and maximum price is used as a denominator and a percentage of change in estimated sales volumes in minimum price and maximum price is used as a numerator in order to calculate the price elasticity.

4 Findings and Future Study

4.1 Forms of Price Response Function for Brand

Four types of price response function model are applied to the online transaction data: linear, multiplicative, attraction, and Gutenburg models. Linear function displays the most reliable in 6 brands of 7 brands and multiplicative function is more reliable that other 3 functions in only one brand. The R2 of the price response function for 7 brands are showed as table 2.

Table 2. R^2 for each brand

Brand	Linear model	multiplicative model
DD	0.425	0.432
A	0.515	
B	0.389	
C	0.294	0.309
D	0.439	
E	0.551	
F	0.342	

4.2 Price Elasticities for Brand

The highest and lowest prices points for 7 brands are as table 3. These two price points are applied to price response function for each brand.

Table 3. Minimum and maximum price for each brand

brand	min relative ASP price	max relative ASP price
DD	0 925	1 114
A	1 057	1 357
B	1 030	1 355
C	0 915	1 031
D	0 931	1 150
E	0 447	0 653
F	0 971	1 139

Table 4. Price elasticity for each brand

brand	MS(%)	current price	relative ASP price level	price elasticities
DD	3,12	0,001182	1,0692	−1,810
A	3,12	0,001399	1,2658	−1,586
B	3,00	0,001377	1,2458	−1,505
D	2,96	0,001113	1,0066	−1,272
E	3,14	0,001246	1,1273	−1,611
F	3,68	0,000494	0,4472	−0,819
H	2,48	0,001270	1,1494	−1,191

Based on table 3, price elasticity is yield and the results are as follows. The lowest price elasticity among 7 brands is -0.819 and in case price decrease is carried out, there is a brand which can not be expected revenue increase, compared to absolute value of price decrease. On the contrary, the highest price elasticity is -1.810. Absolute values in 6 brands of 7 brands are greater than -1, which means that 6 brand managers can expect increase of sales volume by price decline. Especially, online trading system is featured not to make additional costs every transaction as a variable cost, so it is appeared that any brand which is its absolute value is larger than -1 does yield more profits by decreasing their price if response of competitors does not response at price decrease.

If price elasticity is displayed by comparing relevant market price, this is as figure 2. As seen at the figure, brands which are relatively higher price generally appear high price elasticity and brands which are comparatively low price appear low price.

In other words, it is appeared that brands having expensive fees can enjoy profits due to its revenue growth in spite of price decline. On the other hand, it is shown that brands having cheap fees as price obviously lose profits as its revenue does not elastically grow in spite of price decline.

4.3 Future Studies

This study is a descriptive report for on-line price elasticity which relatively has less performance than that of off-line. The subject is for price elasticity of Home Trading

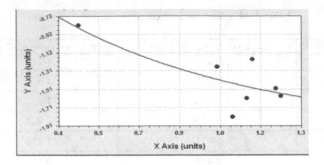

Where
x axis = relative ASP price
y axis = price elasticity

Fig. 2. Plot of price elasticities by brand

System in Korean securities market, which is one of online price. By utilizing DB of online securities trading system from Jan. 2007 to May 2008 price elasticities of 7 brands are measured by price response function.

As a result, price elasticity in 6 brands of 7 brands is greater -1, and so it is called "sensitive brands", yet one brand, getting the lowest fees appears the lowest price elasticity. The practical contribution of this study is to suggest objective price elasticity for brands to securities brand managers, that is, this can be specific materials that securities firms sometimes can refer to execute their functions as fees discount.

Simply, this study is for online stock trading of mature period on product life cycle. It is in need to be gauged price elasticity for option, futures, fund, and CMA, taking fees as ASP type. It is helpful to maintain profits of securities firms by periodically measuring price elasticity for various financial products.

References

1. Darin, J.C.: In-home shopping: Are There Consumer segment? Journal of Retailing (1987)
2. Kucher, E., Hilleke, K.: Value pricing through conjoint analysis: A practical approach. European Management Journal 11(3), 283–290 (1993)
3. Ku, Y., Kim, J.: Apparel purchasing behavior of cable TV home-shopping viewer. Journal of Korean Society Clothing Industry 1(3), 231–238 (1999)
4. Kwak, Y., Hong, J., Paik, J.: The Difference in the Latitude of Price Acceptance Depending on the Size of Consideration Set. Korean Marketing Journal 3(2), 25–45 (2001)
5. Simon, H.: Price Management. North-Holland, New York (1989)
6. Simon, H.: Hidden Champions of the Twenty-First Century; The Success Strategies of Unknown World Market Leaders. Springer, Heidelberg (2009)
7. Yoo, P.H.: Pricing Policy. Pakyoungsa, Seoul (1991)

The Development of Dynamic Brand Equity Chase Model and Its Application to Digital Industry Based on Scanner Data

Yongsik Nam[1] and Youngsik Kwak[2]

[1] OpenTide China, Beijing, China
[2] Jinju National University
Namys118@opentide.com.cn

Abstract. The purpose of this research is to develop a comprehensive modeling for measuring dynamics of brand power. We define brand power as brand specific coefficients to yield the sales volume for each period. The modeling consists of multinomal logit model for each product category, the brand-specific coefficients, mixture modeling and fuzzy clustering algorithm. We apply our modeling to TV scanner data in Tianjin China. The results show 5 brands have 12 to 23 times change on their brand power in a year. The lasting time of brand power spreads from 1 week to 12 weeks.

Keywords: Scanner Data, Brand Equity, China, Appliance.

1 Introduction

The research about brand equity is not a new subject. The subject for primary brand equity is mainly divided into three; study for definition of brand asset (Sung and Bong Woo, 2000; Jung 1999), study for constitution (Chung and Bak, 2007;Choi and Rhee, 2004), study for effect (Kim, 1996; Kim, 2008), and so on. If we analyze the previous studies for brand equity measurement, we regard it as the measurement from the view of stock concept. In other words, they are only divided into a big or low brand without specific period mentioned. As a result, we are likely to find out in a newspaper that that Coca-coloa has the biggest brand equity and Samsung has the biggest among Korean companies.

Have brand equity and brand power been changed when time goes by? If changed, what should a marketer do? If a marketer knows the period that brand power is more vulnerable and instead price sensitivity is high, price cut as a marketing tactic is likely to be employed instead of advertising. On the other hand, if there is a period that brand power is strong and price sensitivity is low, price cut is unnecessary. Accordingly, if a marketer can specifically measure a certain term that brand power is high or low, it can a guideline for him/her to practically implement effective marketing budgets.

This study is to gauge brand equity as flow concept rather than stock concept that previous researchers have carried out, that is, we would like to show dynamic forms with evidence that brand equity has been fluctuated during a certain period. As a

D. Ślęzak et al. (Eds.): UNESST 2009, CCIS 62, pp. 39–46, 2009.

consequence, this makes academic contribution by presenting concrete evidence that brand power has been dynamically changed. Besides, at practical fields marketing activities can be adjusted by capturing brand power is high or small during the period.

2 Modeling

This study takes following steps to measure lasting time of brand power. Firstly, related variables influencing on sales volume are extracted by using multinomial logit model. In this process it is proven that besides brand, other marketing variables influence revenue. Accordingly, the extent which brand influences revenue separate from other marketing variables is measured by calculating brand-specific coefficients which becomes brand power influencing revenue during a certain period. Additionally, this modeling reflects competitive condition by simultaneously considering both brand and price of competitors.

The second step is to adapt mixture regression modeling to measure brand power extracted from multinomial logit model time to time. In case of adapting the equation of multinomial logit model into mixture regression model, some sub-equations can be measured and it is expected the highest and lowest brand equities are extracted during a research period.

The third step is to calculate post hoc probability to classify dynamic changes in brand-specific coefficients of the second step. Through that brand equity is classified high and low according to seasons, at which time researchers utilize fuzzy clustering algorithm.

2.1 Step 1: Multinomial Logit Model

The multinomial logit model has been used primarily to examine customer choice behavior, although it has also been used to examine various market phenomena such as market share forecasting, store selection behavior, price cut effect on a market, market segmentation, choice set change, and brand switching (Bucklin, Gupta, & Han, 1995; Buckiln & Lattin, 1991; Hardie, Johnson, & Fader, 1993; Gupta, 1988). The majority of these studies have utilized non-durables based upon scanner data.

If individual i confronted with a choice from a set, Ci, of alternatives, utility can be expressed as follows, where alternative k is one of the alternatives Ci;

$$U_{ik} = V_{ik} + \varepsilon_{ik} \tag{1}$$

$$V_{ik} = u_{ik} + \beta X_{ik} \tag{2}$$

where V_{ik} = a deterministic component of i's utility

ε_{ik} = a random component of i's utility
u_{ik} = an intercept for brand k
   = brand specific coeffient for brand k
β = a vector of coefficients for variables X.

Both marketing variables and evaluative criteria are included in the X_{ik} vector. The ε_k are independently distributed random variables with a double exponential (Gumbel type II extreme value) distribution.

$$P(\varepsilon_k, \leq \varepsilon) = \exp[-\exp(-\varepsilon)]$$
$$-\infty < \varepsilon < \infty \tag{3}$$

We assume that individual i chooses the one with the highest utility among the alternatives.

$$p_{ik} = P\{ U_{ik} \geq U_{ij}, j \in Ci\} \tag{4}$$

Given assumptions (1)-(4), the conditional probability of choosing brand j can be expressed by the multinomial logit model (k=1, 2,..., m) as follows;

$$p_{ik} = \exp(V_{ik}) / \sum_{k=1}^{m} \exp(V_{im}) \tag{5}$$

where P_{ik} = the probability of choosing brand k.

This expression is known as the multinomial logit (Ben-Akiva & Lerman, 1993; Guadagni & Little, 1983).

Where, u_{ik} is an intercept for brand k or brand-specific coefficient for brand k. This is a brand power for brand k for a given time horizon as a stock approach.

2.2 Step 2: Mixture Regression Model

On Chusok (Korean Thanksgiving Day) and the Lunar New Year's Day, customers feel different about brands or promotion. So if we construct multinomial logit model that is based on the sales database of the year and make just one price response function or sales promotion response function on the basis of it, we are likely to neglect the different aspects of dull and active seasons, promotion and non-promotion seasons, normal and abnormal seasons, and high-demand and low demand seasons. Furthermore, we are likely to neglect the different brand power for a given time horizon.

To reflect differences in customers' responses to brand, price and promotion in these different seasons, we applied mixture modeling to the multinomial logit model. This process will generate the several brand-specific coefficients.

Mixture model is to unmix the sample, to identify the segments, and to estimate the parameters of the density function underlying the observed data within each segment. Therefore in the first stage of multinomial logit modeling, we find the most appropriate brand-specific coefficient for brand k for whole time horizon. Then in the second stage, we apply the mixture model within the multinomial logit model and divide it into several brand specific coefficients that explain differences by time to time. Therefore the brand specific coefficient of the first stage can be seen as an aggregated brand specific coefficient, and that of the second stage, as a disaggregated brand specific coefficient. The mixture regression model is as follows;

Data $y_n = (y_{nk})$ where k= no. of variables n= no of observations

S Classes with: $\sum_{s=1}^{S} \pi_s = 1$ where S= no of segment

Conditional density $f_s (y_n | \theta_s)$

Unconditional density $f(y_n | \phi) = \sum_{s=1}^{S} \pi_s f_s (y_n | \theta_s)$

Choice probabilities

Mixture model $p_{\scriptscriptstyle u} = \dfrac{\pi_. f_. (y_{\scriptscriptstyle u} | \theta_.)}{\sum_{s'=1}^{\scriptscriptstyle s} \pi_{s'} f_{s'} (y_{\scriptscriptstyle u} | \theta_{s'})}$

Mixture regression model $\eta_{nks} = \sum_{p=1}^{P} X_{nkp} \beta_{sp}$ where beta= estimated coefficients

2.3 Step 3: Post Hoc Probability

Some brand-specific coefficients separate from the second step just shows that brand equity the highest, lowest, or middle. Therefore, we adapt fuzzy clustering algorithm to capture seasons at which brand brand is the highest, lowest and middle. Then, we are capable of matching which brand specific coefficients of the second stage are related to a given time period.

3 Application to Digital Industry

3.1 Sample: Scanner Data

The weekly scanner data for 32-inch TVs from one of major retailers in China is used with the period from Jan. 2008 to Dec. 2008 in Tianjin, China. Major five brands' price and sales volume data has been used.

3.2 Our Model

The multinomial logit model will be employed to estimate beta coefficients for the model with dependent variables equal to weekly sales volume and independent variables of brand name and price.

$$V_{ik} = u_{ik} + \xi_{pik} price_k \qquad (6)$$

where V_{ik} = utility assigned to brand k by consumer i

   u_{ik} = the intrinsic utility/value of brand k for consumer i (brand-specific intercept)

      $price_k$ = the net available price of brand k for consumer i

   ξ_{pik} = the parameters to be estimated for consumer i

4 Findings and Future Study

In the first place, the results of multinomial logit model for whole observations of this study are shown as Table 1. For the study Brand 1 appears the highest brand power, and then Brand 3. Brand 5 has the lowest brand power.

Secondly, the results applied a mixture model are showed at Table 1 under condition that entire observations are kept on the form of multinomial logit model. Brand 3 in segment 1 has the highest brand power, Brand 1 in segment 2 has the highest, and again, Brand 3 in segment 3 shows the highest. We define brand power as brand specific coefficients to yield the sales volume for each period.

According to segments it is founded out that brand power is a different order. In segment 1 brand power is brand 3, brand 1, brand 2, brand 4, brand 5 in order, while in segment 2 brand power is brand 1, brand 3, brand 4, brand 2, brand 5 in order. Segment 3 has the same order of brand power as segment 1, however the extent of that is different.

In individual brands changes in brand power are appeared by segment. For instance, in case of Brand 1 it has the highest brand power in segmentation market 3, yet has the most poor brand power in segment market 1.

Thirdly, it is process through distribute to know which equitation among each multinomial logit model of the second stage is appropriate to which week. The following Table 2 shows some results of Brand 1 in the first half of the year 2008.

For example, in week 1 of 2008 brand 1 displays that revenue is calculated by equitation of segment 3. The equitation of segment 3 is no included in week 2 of 2008, but explains segment 2, which shows revenue should be calculated. In other words, brand power of Brand 1 in segment 3 has been just lasted 1 week, yet that of Brand 1 in the segment 2 has been just maintained 2 week later on.

If the process above is coupled with rest 4 brands, it is as Figure 2. At figure, periods brand power is high or low are different in each brand. Consequently, marketing tools marketers of each brand employ are totally different by time to time.

Table 1. Aggregate and disaggregate brand-specific coefficients

	the first stage	the second stage		
		seg1	seg2	seg3
Intercept	332.8	72.6	205.2	1702.0
brand1	39.8	7.2	26.3	132.9
brand2	11.3	4.6	−4.6	89.4
brand3	34.9	11.9	17.8	276.8
brand4	−27.1	−3.1	8.5	−221.5
brand5	−58.8	−20.7	−48.1	−277.5
price	−226.5	−32.8	−106.2	−1237.4
R^2		0.43	0.42	0.55
	0.11	0.88		

Table 2. Post hoc probabilities for Brand 1 for each week

wks	clu#1	clu#2	clu#3	clu#
801	0.0%	0.0%	100.0%	3
802	0.0%	99.9%	0.1%	2
803	0.0%	99.4%	0.6%	2
804	0.0%	0.0%	100.0%	3
805	0.0%	0.1%	99.9%	3
806	0.0%	99.5%	0.5%	2
807	0.0%	98.6%	1.4%	2
808	0.0%	99.8%	0.2%	2
809	0.0%	99.7%	0.3%	2
810	0.0%	99.9%	0.1%	2
811	0.0%	99.7%	0.3%	2
812	48.0%	51.9%	0.0%	2
813	57.6%	42.3%	0.1%	1
814	56.5%	43.5%	0.0%	1
815	98.3%	1.7%	0.0%	1
816	97.2%	2.8%	0.1%	1
817	96.8%	3.1%	0.1%	1
818	0.0%	0.0%	100.0%	3

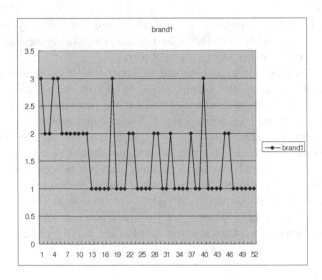

Fig. 1. Volatility of Brand 1 for a year

Technical difference about lasting time of brand power of each brand is existed. At Table 3 Brand 1 is more frequent than others in terms of long-standing brand power. On the other hand, it is rare to become the lowest brand power. In addition, with respect to changing frequency of brand power Brand 3 is large, while that of Brand 5 is small, especially Brand 5 often lasts low brand power.

The outcomes earned by designing this dynamic brand equity chaser model can be summarized as follows. First, different brand powers are derived by different aspects of high-demand and low-demand seasons and active and dull seasons. Marketers can trace the brand powers that appear differently in a low-demand season and in a certain period that all promotion concentrates.

Secondly, different brand powers are derived by regions in China. Therefore, brand power chaser model should be made for each region.

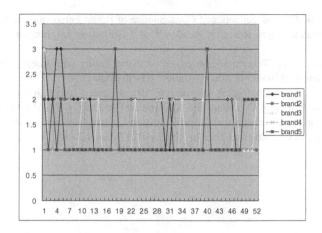

Fig. 2. Volatility for each brand

Table 3. The dynamics of brand equity or power

Level of Brand Power	brand 1	brand 2	brand 3	brand 4	brand 5
low	30	41	33	31	42
middle	17	8	15	19	8
high	5	3	4	2	2
no of change	18	13	23	20	12

Thirdly, different brand powers are derived by size and type even in the same group of product. For example, as for the sizes of TV like 32 inches or 40 inches, different degrees of brand loyalty and different price and promotion elasticities are derived in the same market. Therefore, brand power chaser model should be applied to product line as well as product category.

References

1. Bucklin, R.E., Gupta, S., Han, S.: A brand's eye view of response segmentation in consumer choice behavior. Journal of Marketing Research 32, 66–74 (1995)
2. Bucklin, R.E., Lattin, J.M.: A two-state model of purchase incidence and brand choice. Marketing Science 10, 24–40 (Winter 1991)
3. Hardie, B.G., Johnson, E.J., Fader, P.S.: Modeling loss aversion and reference dependence effects on brand choice. Marketing Science 12, 378–394 (Fall 1993)
4. Kim, H.: A study on the Effects of Brands on Proudcts Purchase and Choice. The Korean Society of Management Consulting, 155–177 (2008)
5. Jung, H.: Building Brand Equity Through Advertising and Evidence Utilization (Implications for Brand Extension Strategy). Industrial Relations Research, 158–171 (1999)

6. Chung, K., Bak, G.: Antecedents and Consequence of Brand Personality and Brand Equity on Private Brand. Korea Research Academy of Distribution Information, 97–120 (May 2007)
7. Kim, Y., Park, Y.: A Conjoint Measurement of Brand Equity with Internet Effect. Korean Academic Society of Business Administration, 61–96 (May 1996)
8. Sung, Y., Woo, S.: Psychological Approach to Brand Equity: Interaction of Consumer and Brand. Korean Journal of Consumer and Advertising Psychology, 39–61 (2000)
9. Choi, Y., Rhee, E.: Dimensions of Brand Equity of Luxury Fashion Brands. Journal of the Korean Society of Clothing and Textiles, 1007–1018 (March 2004)

Performance Analysis of RAID Implementations

Yun-Sik Kwak[1], Bongen Gu[1], Seung-Kook Cheong[2], Jung-Yeon Hwang[2],
and Young-Jae Choi[1]

[1] Dept. Of Computer Engineering, Chungju University, Chugju-si, 380-702, Korea
{yskwak, bggoo}@cjnu.ac.kr, choigoon312@hanmail.net
[2] Electronics and Telecommunications Research Institute, Daejeon, 305-700, Korea
{skjeong, jyhwang}@etri.re.kr

Abstract. There are many RAID configurations and two types of RAID implementations. To decide which configuration or implementation is suitable to an application, the performance information of RAID system are required. In this paper, we evaluate the performance of RAID system. For evaluating the performance, we use many parameters composed of two RAID configurations, two implementations, and two types of storage devices. Two configurations, which we use, are level 0 and 5. Two implementations are hardware and software RAID. As a result, if we want to construct the RAID level 0, it is good decision to use the software RAID. And the overhead of the software RAID level 5 is higher than that of hardware RAID.

Keywords: RAID, Performance Analysis.

1 Introduction

The high-speed internet infrastructure enables us to provide new types of services such as VOD, IPTV, searching engine, and etc. Such applications or services are required very high capacity of storage to store data and the seamless services to enhance the quality of services [1][2]. And some applications like the search engine require very high disk IO throughput to process many transactions. To cover all requirements, the high performance and high throughput disk system is required. But the improving of the performance of disk system reaches the limitation because the conventional magnetic disk system has many mechanical parts. Nevertheless, many approaches are proposed to enhance the performance of disk system. The RAID system is the most realistic approach to enhance the disk system [3][4][5].

The RAID means the redundant array of independent disks [3][4][5]. The features of RAID which are considered are the performance, the reliability, and the cost. There are many RAID configurations as what feature is mainly focused. To enhance the performance of RAID, we can use multiple disks to serve single disk IO request. This configuration is called as the RAID level 0, and maximizes the parallelism of disk operations. But if a disk in the RAID is fault, all disk IO services using RAID are stopped. To enhance the reliability or the availability, we can use the redundant information. Therefore, when some disks are fault, the RAID continuously provides the disk IO services using the redundant information. This configuration is called as

D. Ślęzak et al. (Eds.): UNESST 2009, CCIS 62, pp. 47–52, 2009.

the RAID level 1, and maximizes the redundancy of stored data in the disk. But in this configuration, the effective capacity of RAID is very small.

RAID level 5 has the features of level 0 and 1. In RAID level 5, the multiple disks are used to serve a disk IO request for enhancing the performance like the level 0. And the redundant information is used for enhancing the reliability like the RAID level 1. The redundant information in RAID level 5 is not the backup block of the original disk block. In RAID level 5, the redundant information is the parity information of the disk block group. This disk block group is called as the parity group. But in this configuration, the overhead for calculation of the parity information is very high when disk write operation is submitted.

Normally, there are two types of RAID implementations[6]. The hardware RAID implements RAID functions using the gate-level circuits such as ASIC, ROC(RAID-On-Chip from Adaptec Inc.). The hardware RAID has the acceleration circuit to calculate the parity block. Therefore this implementation gets the high performance of RAID functions. But the additional cost is required to construct the storage system. The software RAID implements RAID functions using the software at the application level or the kernel level. In this implementation, all RAID functions are provided by the software. Therefore the performance of RAID functions is relatively low. But the additional cost is not required.

In this paper, we evaluate the performance of RAID level 0 and 5 for each implementation. From the evaluation results, we describe which combination of RAID configuration and implementation is better. And we show the overhead of RAID level 5 from generating the redundant information to enhance the reliability and the availability. The result of this paper can contribute to decide what configuration and implementation of RAID is proper to the storage system. And the result of evaluation in this paper can be also used for development of the method to enhance the performance of RAID level 5.

2 RAID Evaluation

In this paper, we evaluate the performance of the RAID level 0 and 5 for two RAID implementations, software RAID and hardware RAID. In the software RAID, software modules provide all functions. Therefore, the performance of software RAID is dependent on the performance of the target system. In this RAID implementation, the additional cost for constructing the RAID system is not required. Another feature of this RAID implementation is that we can get higher performance of RAID when we use more powerful system. In this paper, we use the software RAID system provided by Linux. This is the kernel-level device driver, and is managed by the 'mdadm' utility[6].

The hardware RAID is the add-on board inserted into the system board. In the RAID board called as the RAID controller, the gate-level circuits implement all RAID functions. Therefore the performance of hardware RAID is relatively independent on that of the target system. In this RAID implementation, the additional cost for buying the RAID controller is required. Some high-end system board has the RAID functions by default. In this case, no additional cost is required.

Table 1. Specification of Target System

Item	Configuration
CPU	Intel Xeon E5420 2.5Ghz x 2
Memory	DDR2 2G x 8
RAID	3Ware 9650SE
RAID Disk	Seagate SATA-2 500GB x 4
Bus	PCI-e x4
OS	Ubuntu Server 9.04

Table 1 shows the target system used to evaluate the performance. All parts of the target system are not special, and all of them are commercially sold in the market. In our system board, the RAID functions are supported by default. But we don't use this system board's RAID because it is possible for the RAID function to interfere with the evaluation process. Therefore we use the add-on RAID controller provided by 3Ware. The 3Ware 9650SE RAID controller inserted in the PCI-express x4 slot supports the level 0, 1, 5, and other variations. In this paper, we use RAID level 0 and 5 to evaluate the performance. The RAID system is constructed with 4 HDDs, and the chunk size is 64KB, which is default size in the software and hardware RAID. The logical disk provided by RAID system is formatted with ext3 filesystem. And we use the separate OS disk to prevent the normal OS operations from the performance evaluating process.

To evaluate the performance of disk IO, we use the 'postmark' generally used for the disk IO benchmark. The postmark generates the read/write transfer rate per second and the number of the transaction per second by processing the transactions. The transaction in the postmark consists on the generation, read, appending, and deleting of files. Table 2 shows the parameters for postmark to evaluate the performance of the disk IO. For comparing the performance, we also evaluate the performance of the single HDD using the same parameters. We prepare the parameter for the postmark for each 8 buffer size in the five cases. The five cases are single HDD, the software RAID level 0, level 5, the hardware RAID level 0, and level 5. Therefore the parameter set consists of 40 parameter cases. For each parameter case, we execute the postmark five times, and average the performance results.

3 Evaluation Result

Table 3 shows the transfer rate of disk write. The single HDD column shows the performance when we use just one HDD. The hardware RAID column shows the performance when we use the hardware RAID add-on board for constructing the RAID system. And the software RAID shows the performance when we use Linux kernel-level device driver for construction the RAID system. The min row shows the minimum performance when we evaluate for all buffer size parameters. The max row shows the maximum performance when we evaluate for each buffer size parameters. For example, 238.4 MB/s in the hardware RAID level 0 column is the minimum transfer rate of the disk write operations evaluated for each buffer size from 1K to 128k.

Table 2. Parameter for Evaluation

Item	Parameter	
File Size	512~128K(randomly selected by postmark)	
Subdirectories	10	
Buffer Size(read/write)	1k, 2k, 4k, 8k, 16k, 32k, 64k, 128k	
Work Load	File	1,000
	Transaction	50,000

Table 3. Performance of Disk WRITE

		Single HDD	Hardware RAID		Software RAID	
			Level-0	Level-5	Level-0	Level-5
Min	MB/s	76	178.8	156	176	75.4
	Buffer	8k	1k	8k	1k, 8k	16k
Max	MB/s	104.3	238.5	212.2	206.8	84.7
	Buffer	16k	16k	64k	64k	64k

From the table 3, the minimum performance is showed at the small buffer size. But the maximum performance is showed at the large buffer size except the single HDD. We think the reason is the following. Assume that there is a 64k disk IO request. If the buffer size is 2k, the maximum 32 disk accesses are needed. But if the buffer size is 64k, just one disk access is needed. Because the chunk size of the RAID system is 64k. Therefore, when the buffer size is 64k, the RAID system shows the highest performance.

The software RAID level 0 shows the good performance without extra cost for RAID controller. At each case, the speed-up factor relative to the single HDD is 2.63(200.6/76.26) or 2.32(246.37/106.42). We think that the reason of this is the processing power of the target system. Because the processing power of our system is stronger than that of RAID controller, the RAID functions are efficiently provided in the software implementations. From this factor, we think that the software RAID has higher performance in the future because the more powerful CPU and system architecture are continuously developed. As a result, if we use the software RAID level 0, we can get the speed up of the disk write service.

Table 4 shows the transfer rate of disk write. Also, the minimum transfer rate is at the small buffer size, and the maximum transfer rate is at the large buffer size.

From previous performance result, if we focus on the performance of the storage system, the software RAID level 0 is the best solution for our needs. But RAID level 0 has very serious defect. If any disk in the RAID is fault, all disk services are stopped. That is, the RAID level 0 is not reliable.

If we focus on the reliability or the availability of the storage system, the RAID level 1 is good solution. In the level 1, all data blocks are redundantly stored in the multiple disks. This means that there are multiple copies for a block. Therefore, when any active disk is fault, the RAID system can continuously provide the disk IO services by using data block stored in other disks. The level 1 provides very high degree of the reliability. But the cost for constructing the RAID level 1 is very high, and the effective storage capacity is very low.

Table 4. Speedup Factor and Level5's Overhead

	Hardware RAID			Software RAID		
	Level-0	Level-5	Overhead	Level-0	Level-5	Overhead
Min(Speedup)	2.35	2.05	1.15	2.32	1.99	2.33
Max(Speedup)	2.29	2.03	1.12	1.98	0.81	2.44

The RAID level 5 provides the high performance and the high reliability. For the high performance, the level 5 uses multiple disks to serve the disk IO request. And for the high reliability, the level 5 uses the redundant information. If we focus on the performance and the reliability, the RAID level 5 is good solution. Table 3 shows the performance of the RAID level 5. From the tables, the performance of RAID level 5 is lower than that of single HDD in the case of the Software RAID. The reason of these results is that the overhead of generating the redundant information, especially parity strip, is very high in the RAID level 5.

Normally the hardware implementation of RAID has the acceleration circuit for generating the parity strip. Therefore the hardware RAID can efficiently generate the parity information.

We can't find the calculation method for the degree of the overhead. Therefore we compare the ratio of the performance of level 5 to level 0. Table 4 shows the speedup factors from table 3. The speedup factor in the hardware RAID level 0 is calculated by dividing the transfer rate of the hardware RAID level 0 by that of the single HDD. In this case, 178.8/76=2.35. This means that the hardware RAID level 0 is 2.35 times faster than the single HDD for serving the disk request using four HDDs.

If we use the n disks to construct the RAID, we expect the performance of RAID as the performance RAID level 0. But the performance of the RAID level 5 is lower than that of the RAID level 0 because of the overhead. Therefore we use the ratio of the expected speedup to the real speedup as the degree of the overhead. Table 4 shows the overhead of the level 4 under the 'Overhead' column. From table 4, the software RAID has more overhead than the hardware RAID.

4   Conclusion

New services such as VOD, IPTV, Cloud Computing, SAN, SaaS continuously is developed. All these services are based on the high speed internet infrastructure and the storage system. The features of the storage system for these services are the high performance and the high reliability. The high performance storage means that the storage system can server many disk IO request. The high reliability storage means that the storage system continuously provides the disk IO services in the case of fault in which some disk in the storage system don't operate, or are out of order.

For getting the high performance and the high reliability, the storage system is constructed by the RAID system. RAID system uses the multiple disks for the high performance, and the redundant information for the high reliability. In this paper, we evaluate the performance of the software RAID and the hardware RAID. As we describe in the previous section, the software RAID is good solution for constructing the RAID system. Because the performance of the system is continuously enhanced, the performance of the software RAID can be also enhanced. Additionally we calculate the degree of the level 5 overhead. When the degree of overhead proposed in this paper is used, the overhead of the software RAID level 5 is bigger than that of the hardware RAID more and less.

References

1. Gu, B., Kwak, Y., Cheong, S., Ko, D.: Performance Anaylsis between Implements of RAID System. In: 2009 summer conference, KIIT (June 2009)
2. Kang, Y., Yoo, J., Cheong, S.: Performance Evaluation of the SSD based on DRAM Storage System IOPS. Journal of KIIT 7, 265–272 (2009)
3. William, S.: Computer Organization and Architecture. Prentice Hall, Englewood Cliffs (2003)
4. Chen, P.M., Lee, E.K., Gibson, F.A., Katz, R.H., Patterson, D.A.: RAID: High-Performance, Reliable Secondary Storage. ACM Computing Surveys 26, 145–185 (1994)
5. Cao, P., Lim, S.B., Venkataraman, S., Wilkers, J.: The TickerTAIP Paralle RAID Architecture. ACM Tr. on Computer System 12(3), 23600269 (1994)
6. Vadala, D.: Managing RAID on LINUX. O'Reilly, Sebastopol (2003)

An Analysis of the Storage Management Initiative Specification Based on SMI 1.1.0

YoonSik Kwak[1], Boneun Goo[2], Donghee Park[3], Hyunsik Yun[4], Daesik Ko[5], Jeongjin Park[6], Donghui Kim[7], Ilnoh Oh[8], JungYeon Hwang[9], and Seungkook Cheong[10]

[1,2,3,4] Dept. of Computer Engineering, National University, Chungbuk, Korea
yskwak@cjnu.ac.kr
[5] Dept. of Electronic Engineering, Mookwon University, Chungnam, Korea
kds@mokwon.ac.kr
[6,7,8] Kubix
inoh@kubix.co.kr
[9,10] Principal Member of Engineering Staff, Network Research Group, Broadband Convergence Network Research Division, ETRI
skjeong@etri.re.kr

Abstract. This paper aims to suggest a Management Model of a storage system in distributed computing environment. Based on the Common Information Model and Web Based Enterprise Management, the SMI-S is a standard to manage a storage system. This specificction defines an interface for the management of a Storage Area Network that is a heterogeneous environment of management applications, storage devices and storage system from different venders. It consist of a Profile, Subprofile and Package. A Profile defines the base set of information and capabilities that allow a Client to manage a particular storage resource. A Subprofile represents additional functionality. Analyzing of the Profile, Subprofile and the Package, it is goal to find the method that we need to manage a storage system in this paper.

Keywords: SMI, SNIA.

1 Introduction

According to increase the complexity of computer, the cost and effort to manage the system are more bigger. To solve this problem, it has been studied a standard to manage a various computer resource. The CIM(Common Information Model) and WBEM(Web Based Enterprise Management) are showed as a result of research.[1][2][3] Also, the SMI-S(Storage Management Initiative-Specification) is proposed by the SNIA(Storage Networking Industry Association). [4][5][6]

This paper aims to suggest a Management Model of a storage system in distributed computing environment. Based on the Common Information Model and Web Based Enterprise Management, SMI-S is a standard to manage a storage system. This specificction defines an interface for the management of a storage Area Network that is a heterogeneous environment of management applications, storage devices and

D. Ślęzak et al. (Eds.): UNESST 2009, CCIS 62, pp. 53–59, 2009.

storage system from different vender. It consist of a Profiles, Subprofiles and Packages. A Profile defines the base set of information and capabilities that allows a Client to manage a particular storage resource. A Subprofile represents additional functionality. Analyzing of the Profile, the Subprofile and the Package, it is goal to find the method that we need to manage a storage system.

2 SMI-S

The SMI-S defines an interface for the management of a Storage Area Network that is a heterogeneous environment of management applications, storage devices and storage system from different venders. The interface uses standards based protocols and specifications(CIM/WBEM/SLP) to provide interoperability, security and extensibility.[1] It is composed of three elements so called the Profiles, the Subprofiles and the Packages.

2.1 Profiles

A Profile defines the base set of information and capabilities that allow a Client to manage a particular storage resource such as a disk array. It defines the classes that a Client will use to perform a particular management task in a SAN. The Profile defines the associations that will be used to traverse between classes. In addition to identifying the class used, a Profile defines the properties and extrinsic methods of each class that must be supported.

A Profile can defines Subprofiles which represents additional capability that a vender can choose to make available. Like Profile, it defines the classes, properties and extrinsic methods that must be implemented to support its functionality. Also, it can incorporate Packages. Likewise, a Package defines the classes, properties and extrinsic methods that must be implemented to support its functionality.

In SMI-S 1.1.0, the following groups of Profiles has been defined:

1. Storage: to manage different types of storage devices
2. Host: to manage components attached to host systems
3. Fabric: to manage the Fabric topology
4. Server: to manage the SMI Agent

Several Storage Profiles are defined for managing storage devices on a Storage Area Network. Each Profile is focused on a different aspect of storage device management. These devices are:

— Array: allows a Client to manage an external RAID array or disk storage system.
— Volume Management: allows a Client to manage physical disk as logical devices called volumes.
— NAS Head: allows a Client to manage a Network Attached Storage systems.
— Self-Contained NAS System: to manage a Client a Network Attached Storage systems.
— Storage Library: allows a Client to manage a storage system that has mechanism for retrieving data from different physical forms of storage media.

— Storage Virtualizer: allows a Client to manage a storage system that dose not directly include any local storage.

2.2 Subprofiles

A Subprofile can be referenced by a Profile to allow optional inclusion of additional capability. A Subprofile defines the classes that a Client will use to perform the additional management tasks provided by the Subprofile. Also it defines associations that will be used to traverse between classes. In addition to identifying the class used, a Subprofile defines the properties and extrinsic methods of each class that must be supported. However, a significant difference exists between a Profile and a Subprofile. A Profile represents a base set of classes and capabilities that all supporting implementations must make available. In contrast, a Subprofile represents an optional set of classes and capabilities that a vender may or may not choose to implement.

A Subprofile can contain the following components:
— The standards used
— The events that a Client can monitor
— The Packages that are incorporated into the Subprofile
— Etc

In SMI-S 1.1.0, the following groups of Subprofiles has been defined:

— Common: one that can apply to many different Profiles
— Common Initiator Port: one that can apply to Profiles that manage the generic SCSI capabilities and transport-specific aspects of target storage system.
— Common Target Port: one that can apply to Profiles that manage the generic SCSI capabilities and transport-specific aspects for hosts and storage systems to discover and make connections to connected storage.
— Profile-specific: one that applies to only one particular Profile.

The Storage Subprofile can reference the following storage specific Subprofiles as optional enhancements:

— File System Manipulation
— File Export Manipulation
— Block Service Resource Ownership
— Block Server Performance
— Copy Services
— Disk Driver Lite
— Disk Sparing
— Extent Composition
— Masking and Mapping
— Limited Access Ports

2.3 Packages

A Package can be referenced by Profile. It defines a set of CIM classes and the associations that will used to traverse between classes. In addition to defining the classes used, a Package defines the properties and extrinsic methods to be used. However, there exists a significant difference between a Subprofile and a Package. A Subprofile represents additional functionality that a vender can optionally choose to implement as a part of their Profile implementation. In contrast, when a Package is referenced by a Profile, all of the CIM elements in the Package are considered to be part of the Profile and hence, must be implemented.

A Package contains the following components as a Profile which are:

— The standards used
— The events that a Client can monitor
— The Subprofiles that can optionally be implemented
— Recipes for performing a particular management task using the Package
— The WBEM operations that the SMI Agent must support
— The CIM elements used by the Package
— Other Package

The Package defines the following four catalogues:

— Health: allows a Client to retrieve information about the status of the device managed by the referencing Profile.
— Physical Package: allows a Client to retrieve information about the physical characteristics of the device managed by the referencing Profile.
— Software: allows a Client to retrieve information about the software and firmware installed on the device or element managed by the referencing Profile.
— Block Services: allows a Client to manage storage pools and logical disks by the referencing storage Profile

3   Proposed SRM(Storage Resource Management)System

At this stage of implementation, A SRM System is defined as a set of functionality to manage a storage resource. The figure 1 is showed functionality of the SRM system to manage devices that are composed. The Menu of the Management System is composed of a Specification, a Status, a Fault, a Statistics, a Report Management.

The following five catalogues are implemented in the Manu:

— Specification(Setting) Management
       Storage Specification Management
       Service Information Management
— Status Management
       Status Information Management
       Status Monitoring
       Performance Measurement
— Fault Management
       Management of the Fault Information
       Fault Processing
— Configuration Management
       Information Configuration Management
       SRM Operation Management

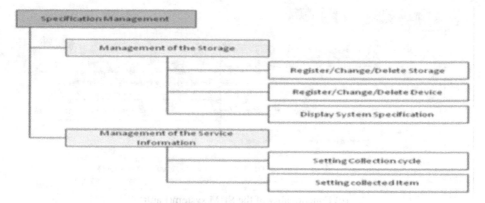

(a) Functionality of the SRM system(Specification)

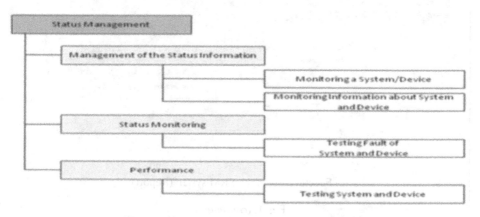

(b) Functionality of the SRM system(Status)

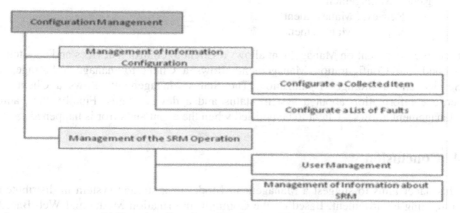

(c) Functionality of the SRM system(Configuration)

Fig. 1. Functionality of the SRM system

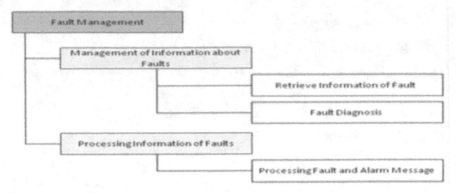

(d) Functionality of the SRM system(Fault)

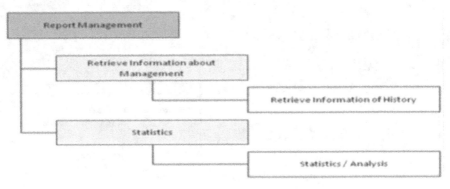

(e) Functionality of the SRM system(Report)

Fig. 1. (*continued*)

— Report Management
    Retrieval Management
    Statistics Management

First, the Specification Management allows a Client to control a devices and a system. Second, the Configuration Management allows a Client to manage a Storage, a Service and a Storage Organization. The Status Management allows a Client to retrieve information about a system status and a device status. Finally, the Fault Management allows a Client to be notified when the event and error is happened.

4   Conclusion

This paper aims to suggest a Management Model of a storage system in distributed computing environment. Based on the Common Information Model and Web Based Enterprise Management, the SMI-S is a standard to manage a storage system. This specificction defines an interface for the management of a storage Area Network that is a heterogeneous environment of management applications, storage devices and storage system from different vender. Like implemented SRM system, we design the functionality that a Client can control a device on a SAN.

References

1. DMTF, CIM System Model,
   http://dmtf.org.standards/cim/cim_schema_v28/
   CIM_System28-Final.pdf
2. DMTF, CIM Tutorial,
   http://wbemsolutions.com/tutorials/CIM/cim-model-app.html
3. DMTF, CIM Tutorial,
   http://wbemsolutions.com//tutorials/CIM/cim-model-dev.html
4. SNIA, SMI Technical Tutorial,
   http://www.wbemsolutions.com/tutorials/snia/SMI/Technical/
   index.html
5. SNIA, SMI-S 1.1.0 Functionality,
   http://www.wbemsolutions.com/tutorials/snia/SMI/Technical/
   smis-functionality.html
6. SNIA, CIM and WBEM Basics,
   http://www.wbemsolutions.com/tutorials/snia/SMI/Technical/
   cim-wbem.html

The Dual-Context Based Workflow Performance in Pervasive Environments

Xiping Liu[1], Wanchun Dou[2], and Jianxin Chen[1,3]

[1] Institute of Computer Technology, College of Computer, Nanjing University of Posts and Telecommunications, Nanjing, China, 210003
[2] Dept. of Computer Science and Technology, Nanjing University, Nanjing, China, 210093
[3] Gradiant ETSI Telecomunicación, Lagoas Marcosende s/n, Vigo Pontevedra, España, 36310
liuxp@njupt.edu.cn, douwc@nju.edu.cn, jianxinchen06@gmail.com

Abstract. The performing process of workflows consists of the performance of activities and transitions between activities. To perform workflows in pervasive environments needs to take account of the context information which affects both the performance way of activities and the transition control between activities. Accordingly, based on definitions of activity-context and transition-context, this paper proposes a dual-context based workflow performance framework applied in pervasive environments. Under such a framework, a context specifying method is presented for the workflow modeling, where activity-context and transition-context could be represented through simple and composite context. Moreover, the principles of performing a workflow definition with context specifications are provided for the process of context capture, mapping, and response.

Keywords: workflow performance, activity-context, transition-context, context mapping.

1 Introduction

Workflow technology, which was originally emerged for the automation of business processes, is usually deployed in desktop computing environments. Along with the fast development of varied computing devices, more and more activities in a process could be performed in pervasive ways [1-4]. Therefore, workflows need to migrate from traditional computing environments to pervasive environments.

One of key issues in the migration is to adapt to the change of performance ways. The change of performance ways includes two aspects. One is that a single activity could be performed at different places rather than comparatively fixed locations, or performed by different types of devices except for traditional desktop computers, etc. The other is that a transition between activities could be triggered by kinds of environment factors, i.e., transition conditions would consider certain environment factors except for traditional factors relevant to task logic. Sequentially, to perform workflow in pervasive environments should take two kinds of context into account, i.e. activity-context and transition-context, to adapt to the change of performance ways. The activity-context is used to determine the way in which an activity in a

D. Ślęzak et al. (Eds.): UNESST 2009, CCIS 62, pp. 60–67, 2009.
© Springer-Verlag Berlin Heidelberg 2009

workflow is performed. The transition-context is used to control whether transition conditions are satisfied and what the next activity should be.

More and more researchers have worked on the context-aware workflow performance. However, few existing researches put efforts on both kinds of context which affects the workflow performance in pervasive environments. Montagut et al. [2] propose an adaptive transactional protocol to support the execution of workflow in pervasive setting from the partial activity-context perspective. Joohyun Han et al. [3] propose a language uWDL to specify the context information on transition constraints to support the performance of adaptive service in workflows, which mainly handles the transition-context. Jinqiao Yu et al. [4] propose a generic framework EkSarva to support people's generic collaboration in heterogeneous computing environments, where little attention is paid to the context relevant to transitions between activities.

Differing from those researches, this paper proposes a dual-context based workflow performance framework applied in pervasive environments, which considers both activity-context and transition-context. The rest of this paper is organized as follows. Section 2 proposes a framework with two main parts, one is relevant to the modeling phase and the other is relevant to the performing phase. The details about the two parts are described respectively in section 3 and section 4. Finally, we conclude this paper at section 5.

2   The Dual-Context Based Workflow Performance Framework

Definition 1 (Activity-context). The activity-context means the context information used to determine the way in which an activity in the workflow is performed, i.e., how an activity performs, who or which device is relevant to the activity, where the activity performs, and etc.

Definition 2 (Transition-context). The transition- context means the context information used to control the progress of the workflow performance, i.e., what the next activity is and when it performs.

Both of activity-context and transition-context need to be considered for the workflow performance in pervasive environments. Fig. 1 shows our proposed dual-context based workflow performance framework. Firstly, both kinds of context relevant to the workflow performance should be specified at the workflow modeling phase, also with reaction rules corresponding to certain context, as showed in the context specification module of Fig. 1. Secondly, during the performance, the context capture module should proactively capture the actual context information relevant to the current activity or transition according to the specifications. Thirdly, the actual context generated during the performance should be compared with predefined context specifications through the context mapping module. Lastly, the context response module would make proper actions based on the matched context and corresponding rules. The more detailed discussion about each component will be presented at section 3 and section 4.

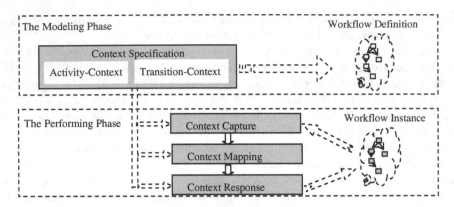

Fig. 1. The dual-context based workflow performing framework

3 The Dual-Context Specifying Method

To enable the automatic performance adapted to varied situations in pervasive environments, relevant context information must be pre-specified exactly and clearly. The presentation of the relevant context is concerned with the workflow definition model. There are lots of workflow definition methods, such as Petri Nets based ones [5], directed graph based ones [6-7], UML based ones [8], etc. As this paper does not focus on the modeling of workflow definition, we just choose one of those methods, i.e. directed graph, to represent workflows. Note that whatever the workflow definition method is, our dual-context specifications could be appended on the workflow definition without too much extra effort.

Context relevant to the workflow performance in pervasive environments usually includes kinds of information, such as location, time, device equipment, temperature, kinds of application-specified one, etc. Besides, context often concerns with certain entity such as a person. Therefore, we represent a simple context through a triple with three elements, i.e., the entity, the attribute, and the value. The simple context could be connected through logic operations, such as AND, OR, NOT, to compose more complicated context. Following definitions give more exact descriptions.

Definition 3 (Ontology library). It provides the information of basic elements in the simple context and is denoted as $\mathcal{O} = <\mathcal{E}, \mathcal{A}, \mathcal{V}>$, where $\mathcal{E} = \{e_i | e_i$ represents the certain entity about which certain information need to be sensed during the workflow performance$\}$, $\mathcal{A} = \{a_j | a_j$ represents the certain information type about certain $e_i\}$, $\mathcal{V} = \{v_k | v_k$ represents the certain value of certain $a_j\}$.

Definition 4 (Simple context). It represents a certain situation in pervasive environments through a single triple. The set of simple context relevant to a workflow is denoted as $\mathcal{SimC} = \{sim\_c_p = <e_i, a_j, v_k> | e_i \in \mathcal{E}, a_j \in \mathcal{A}, v_k \in \mathcal{V}\}$.

Definition 5 (Composite context). It represents a complex situation through a logic expression with one or more simple context triples. The set of composite context relevant to a workflow is denoted as $\mathcal{ComC} = \{com\_c_q ::= NOT <com\_c_q> | <com\_c_q> AND <com\_c_q> | <com\_c_q> OR <com\_c_q> | sim\_c_p$, where $sim\_c_p \in \mathcal{SimC}\}$. Note that a single sim_c_p is supposed to be simple context rather than composite context in the following sections.

Definition 6 (Activity-context Set and Transition-context Set). Action-context set represents the set of activity-context relevant to a workflow and is denoted as $ActC=\{act\_C_i \mid act\_C_i$ includes all activity-context relevant to the ith activity in a workflow and $act\_C_i \subseteq SimC \cup ComC\}$. Transition-context set represents the set of transition-context relevant to a workflow and is denoted as $TraC=\{tra\_C_i \mid tra\_C_i$ includes all transition-context relevant to the ith transition in a workflow and $tra\_C_i \subseteq SimC \cup ComC\}$.

To perform a workflow in pervasive environment, the workflow definition should be appended with specifications on the relevant context. Both activity-context and transition-context could be specified through the form of simple context or composite context. Each presented simple context is supposed to be reasonable in semantic logic. Besides identifying a certain situation through simple context or composite context, corresponding response actions should also be provided, which could be represented as reaction rules defined as follows.

Definition 7 (Reaction rule). It provides a context-based performance rule of a workflow in pervasive environments and the set of reaction rules is denoted as $R=\{<c_i, t_j, a_k \mid c_i \in ActC \cup TraC$ and represents certain context. t_j represents the type of action corresponding to certain context, and so on. a_k represents concrete action description.$\}$

Fig.2 illustrates the context specification for a workflow definition segment, where the number in the node means the ith activity in a workflow and the number besides the edge means the jth transition. Note that an activity or a transition might concerns with multiple rules. As rules with same type actions might be redundant or

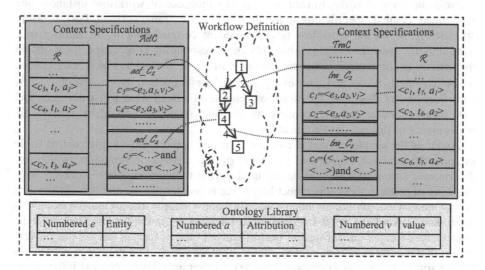

Fig. 2. The dual-context specification example of a workflow definition segment

inconsistent, it would be necessary to predefine a preference order of those rules. The ontology library presents detailed information about numbered entities, attributions, and values for references. The real content of the ontology library is application-specific and could be constructed based on lots of researches relevant to ontology technology.

4   The Dual-Context Based Performance Principles

With detailed dual-context specifications, the workflow engine could automatically control and manage the performance of workflows according to predefined workflow model and the real performance situation. After the workflow performance is commenced, the context capture module would check the activity-context specification on the first activity to determine what kind of context information should be captured proactively. The captured context would be transferred to the context mapping module to find out matched context specifications. Then the context response module would make proper actions according to reaction rules in which the matched context specifications locate. When the performance of an activity is finished, similar operations would happen to the transition-context appending on the edge adjacent to that activity. Such a dual-context based performance behavior would continue until the last activity of the workflow is completed. The more details are presented as follows.

4.1   Capture Relevant Context Based on Specifications

As both activity-context and transition-context could be simple context or composite context, we discuss the context capture mechanism without considering whether it is activity-context or transition-context.

To capture relevant context is a key step of the context based performance. Here, the relevant context is determined by both the progress of workflow instances and predefined context specifications, as showed in the framework in Fig. 1. More specifically, when the workflow is performed at certain point of an activity or a transition, the workflow engine would check corresponding context specifications on the activity or the transition, i.e. certain act_C_i or tra_C_s to decide which context need to be captured. Note that not every activity or transition has relevant context specifications, at this time, the workflow engine just does what it usually does and pay little attention on the context aware and response procedure during the performance of this activity or transition.

As far as the simple context is concerned, e_i and a_j in certain simple context triple provide the relevant object and the type of the context information, which are determinate and unnecessary to be captured during the performance. However, what this kind of context about this object looks like is indeterminate, and this is the value v_k that the context capture module should find out. As far as the composite context is concerned, it is a logic combination of multiple simple context triples. Therefore, the content to be captured during the performance is the values of all simple context triples in the composite context expression. In other words, to a context specification (either simple context or composite context), to capture relevant context information means to capture the value v_k in one or more simple context triples $<e_i, a_j, v_k>$. This process could be implemented with the assistances of wireless sensor network technology, mobile devices technology, and so on, while the details are not the emphasis of this paper.

4.2 Map Captured Context with Specifications

After the actual context information is captured from the performance scene, it would be sent to the context mapping module to search matched simple context or composite context specifications. The captured actual context information is associated with certain activity or transition, which limits the context specifications to be compared. Moreover, e_i and a_j in certain triple of actual context information is determinate. Therefore, the comparison operation mainly focuses on values in actual context information and ones in limitative specifications.

Algorithm: Context mapping.
  Input: a set of captured context triples relevant to the ith activity or transition, denoted as $\mathcal{T}$ $=\{t_1, ..., t_m\}$.
  Output: a set of matched context specifications in act_C_i or tra_C_i, denoted as MC
1 MAP(com_c_i)   //map $\mathcal{T}$ with com_c_i
2 **if** com_c_i is a single simple context triple
3   **then for** each t_j in $\mathcal{T}$ **do if** $com\_c_i=t_j$ **then return** TRUE
4   **return** FALSE
5 **else** represent com_c_i as a binary tree
6   **switch** the *root*
7   **case** '*NOT*': **return** not MAP(*left-subtree*);   //left subtree must be sim_c_i
8   **case** '*AND*': **return** MAP(*lef- subtree*) and MAP(*right-subtree*)
9   **case** '*OR*': **return** map(*left-subtree*)or MAP(*right-subtree*)
10 //find matched simple context
11 **for** each simple context triple sim_c_i in act_C_i or tra_C_i
12   **do for** each t_j in $\mathcal{T}$
13   **do if** $sim\_c_i=t_j$ **then** add sim_c_i in MC, **break**
14 //find matched composite context
15 **for** each composite context com_c_i in act_C_i or tra_C_i
16   **do** matched←FALSE, matched←MAP(com_c_i)
17   **if** matched=TRUE **then** add com_c_i in MC

Fig. 3. Context mapping algorithm description

As mentioned in section 4.1, the actual context information is represented as a single simple context triple or the conjunction of multiple triples. There might be multiple matched context specifications (either simple context or composite context) corresponding to the actual context information. All of these matched ones could be found out based on the algorithm described in Fig. 3. If the matched context specifications are found, they would be transferred to the context response module to make proper actions according to the corresponding predefined reaction rules. Otherwise, the context capture module would keep running until find the matched context.

4.3   Make Proper Actions According to Matched Context

As mentioned before, both activity-context and transition-context could be simple context or composite context, which makes the capture and mapping method similar. However, the response actions corresponding to activity-context and transition-context are different to some extent.

As far as activity-context is concerned, it affects the way in which an activity in a workflow is performed. Multiple reaction rules might be provided to specify different performance actions corresponding to different context situations. The context response module should arrange participants of a certain activity to perform the activity under the directions of those matched specifications. E.g., for the activity "hold the meeting", varied locations of all members could be represented by several simple context triples, which specify whether a member should attend the meeting in which meeting room or through the way of video conference. Then, actions corresponding to varied location context would be accordingly deployed based on reaction rules, such as, automatically open devices in certain meeting room or connect service provider of video conference.

As far as transition-context is concerned, it affects the progress of the workflow performance. After the performance of an activity is completed, the next activity could be started only if the matched transition-context satisfies certain specifications. Sometimes, there are transitions without special transition conditions. Such transitions would happen naturally without considerations on context capture and handling.

Sometimes, there might be more than one matched context specifications for an activity or a transition, which means that more than one reaction rule will be applied. At this time, if actions in those rules corresponding to matched context specifications are unrelated with each other, i.e. they are not the same type, then all of them could be carried out. For example the reaction rule which determines the person to perform certain activity and the reaction rule which determine the place to perform certain activity could be all applied. However, if those actions are same type, then they might be redundant or even conflict. At this time, the context response module could deal with the situation according to the preference order predefined at the modeling phase.

5   Conclusion and Future Work

To perform workflow in pervasive environments, context relevant to both activity and transition need to be taken into account seriously. However, most current related work only focuses on one kind of context and lacks a comparatively general consideration on the context relevant to workflows in pervasive environment [2-4].

Based on definitions of activity-context and transition-context, this paper proposes a dual-context based workflow performance framework applied in pervasive environments. At the modeling phase, context specifications appended on the workflow definition could be represented through our provided method. At the performing phase, the context capture module captures relevant actual context information according to predefined specifications. After that, the context mapping module compares the actual context with specifications to find matched ones through our proposed algorithm. Finally, the context response module takes proper actions based on matched specifications and reaction rules.

In the future, we are going to further research the validation and rationalization of reaction rules. Moreover, how to capture the value of certain attribution of certain entity is another research issue.

Acknowledgments. This paper is partly supported by the National Science Foundation of China under Grant No.60721002, No.60673017 and No.60736015, program for New Century Excellent Talents in University under Grant NCET-06-0440, National High Technology Research and Development Program of China under Grant No. 2009AA12Z219, Jiangsu Provincial NSF Project under Grant No. BK2007137, Foundation of Jiangsu Educational Committee under Grant No. 08KJD520024, and Foundation of NJUPT under Grant No. NY207138.

References

1. Chakraborty, D., Lei, H.: Pervasive Enablement of Business Processes. In: Proc. of 2nd IEEE Annual Conference on Pervasive Computing and Communications, pp. 87–97 (2004)
2. Montagut, F., Molva, R.: The Pervasive Workflow: A Decentralized Workflow System Supporting Long-Running Transactions. IEEE Transactions on Systems, Man, and Cybernetic-Part C: Applications and Reviews 38(3), 319–332 (2008)
3. Han, J., Cho, Y.Y., Kim, E.H., Choi, J.: A Ubiquitous Workflow Service Framework. In: Gavrilova, M.L., Gervasi, O., Kumar, V., Tan, C.J.K., Taniar, D., Laganá, A., Mun, Y., Choo, H. (eds.) ICCSA 2006. LNCS, vol. 3983, pp. 30–39. Springer, Heidelberg (2006)
4. Yu, J.Q., Reddy, Y.V.R., Bharadwaj, V., Reddy, S., Kankanahalli, S.: Workflow-Centric Distributed Collaboration in Heterogeneous Computing Environments. In: Shen, W.-m., Chao, K.-M., Lin, Z., Barthès, J.-P.A., James, A. (eds.) CSCWD 2005. LNCS, vol. 3865, pp. 504–515. Springer, Heidelberg (2006)
5. Van der Aalst, W.M.P.: The application of Petri Nets to workflow management. In. J. Circuits Syst. Comput. 8(1), 21–66 (1998)
6. Liu, X.P., Dou, W.C., Chen, J.J., Fan, S.K., Cheung, S.C., Cai, S.J.: On Design, Verification, and Dynamic Modification of the Problem-Based Scientific Workflow Model. Simulation Modelling Practice and Theory 15(9), 1068–1088 (2007)
7. Sadiq, S.W., Orlowska, M.E., Sadiq, W.: Specification and Validation of Process Constraints for Flexible Workflows. Information Systems 30(5), 349–378 (2005)
8. Bastos, R.M., Ruiz, D.D.A.: Extending UML activity diagram for workflow modeling in production systems. In: Proc. of the 35th Hawaii International Conference on System Sciences, pp. 3786–3795 (2002)

Ontology Evolution: A Survey and Future Challenges

Asad Masood Khattak[1], Khalid Latif[2], Songyoung Lee[1], and Young-Koo Lee[1]

[1] Department of Computer Engineering, Kyung Hee University, Korea
{asad.masood, sylee}@oslab.ac.kr, yklee@khu.ac.kr
[2] School of Electrical Engineering and Computer Science, NUST, Pakistan
khalid.latif@niit.edu.pk

Abstract. Ontology used in many Information Systems and Knowledge Sharing Systems to represent the domain knowledge. As use of ontology increased significantly in recent years that gives importance to proper maintenance of ontology. Ontology change management is a multifaceted and complex task incorporating research areas like; ontology engineering, evolution, versioning, merging, integration, and maintenance. Ontology evolves from one state to another state in response to the changes requested. Crucial task is how to accommodate the new changes while preserving its consistency. This paper provides state of the art analysis of existing approaches covering ontology evolution, and their critical analysis. Pending/Unsolved challenges that need to be address in order to get the process done automatically are also discussed.

Keywords: Ontology Evolution, Emerging Concepts, Change History Ontology, Change History Log.

1 Introduction

Ontologies are formal description of shared conceptualization of a domain of discourse. Ontology serves as back bone of many Information Systems and Knowledge Sharing Systems representing domain knowledge. Ontologies are complex and often large structured, their maintenance give rise to interesting research problems like; evolution, versioning, merging, and integration [FPA06]. The ontology based systems need to have complete and accurate information. So there is a need to keep the ontology up-to-date and should accommodate all the new changes which make the ontology to evolve. Ontology evolves as communities of practices concerned with knowledge develop better understanding of their perceived knowledge [SMM02]. The evolution process deals with the growth of ontology. More specifically, ontology evolution means *modifying or upgrading the ontology when there is a certain need for change or there comes a change in the domain knowledge.*

The process of evolution takes ontology from one consistent state to another [CFH06]. Ontology change management handles the evolution process which may involve different strategies like merging and integration (fundamentally different) [FPA06]. It has several subtasks (see Figure 1); 1) *Capture all the required change(s)* to be applied to ontology and is known as change request. 2) The required *changes are represented* using a common representation format. This representation may be using semantic structure/schema [KLK08a and KLL09] or simple text representation.

D. Ślęzak et al. (Eds.): UNESST 2009, CCIS 62, pp. 68–75, 2009.

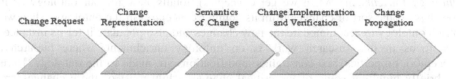

Fig. 1. Process of Ontology Evolution

3) The change effects are tested on the ontology for *consistency* and if required some *deduced changes* are also included in the change, which becomes part of the required changes. 4) The complete change request (modified) is executed by *implementing the changes* in ontology. *Change verification* subtask validates the subject ontology to confirm that the requested changes have been committed to the ontology [KLL09]. 5) Finally, the changes are propagated to dependent data, applications, and ontologies.

Different researchers have provided overlapping solution to the problem of ontology evolution. These approaches do have some pragmatic advantages, but also have several weaknesses, such as: manual specifications of new changes, manually resolving inconsistencies (selecting deduced changes from available alternatives), and also the absence of proper and complete undo and redo facilities in case we want to recover the ontology [KLL09]. To automate the process, these weaknesses need to be eliminated. The automation is also necessary because human intervention is time consuming and error prune. Goal of this research is to provide the survey of ontology evolution approaches. We highlight the main features of all the approaches with the limitations in those systems. After that we discuss some open problems that need to be addressed in order to completely automate the evolution process.

This paper is arranged as follows: Section 2 describes general terms related to ontology change management. Section 3 presents different ontology evolution approaches. In Section 4 we present the challenges still needs to be worked out for automation of evolution procedure. Finally we conclude our discussion in Section 5.

2 Ontology Change Management

Ontology change management activities are sometimes confused together while they are fundamentally different activities [FPA06]. 1) *Ontology Evolution:* is the process of *modifying the ontology when there is a certain need for change or a change in the domain knowledge.* 2) *Ontology Versioning:* is the process of modifying ontology while keeping the original version intact. Mostly used in CVS systems. It handles an evolving ontology by creating and managing different versions of it [FPA06]. 3) *Ontology Merging:* is composition of new ontology from two or more ontologies covering highly overlapping or identical domains, e.g. merging ontologies ACM hierarchy and MSC hierarchy. 4) *Ontology Integration:* is composition of a new ontology from two or more ontologies covering related domains, e.g. integration of health ontology and crime ontology for information of a person.

The evolution is mainly because of new changes and evolution can be of two types, i.e. 1) *Ontology Population:* When we get new instances of concept(s) already present in the ontology. Only the new instance(s) are added and the ontology is populated. 2)

Ontology Enrichment: When we get concept(s), totally new for our ontology or it does have some sort of changes from its counter concept(s) in the ontology. Then we enrich ontology to accommodate the new changes and also populate it for its instance. Our focus in this research work is on ontology enrichment, where hierarchy, concept(s), properties, and constraints modifications are made to the ontology. Here we briefly highlight some of the critical changes while most of these changes are discussed in [CFH06 and Kle04].

- *New Concept:* This is the most common change in any ontology. New concepts emerge and have to be accommodated in the concept hierarchy.
- *Concept Hierarchy:* In this case the concept in focus might have different hierarchical position to the existing one.
- *Concept with Changed Properties:* When the concept in focus is already present in the ontology but its properties are different from the existing one.
- *Concept with Changed Restrictions:* In this case, the concept in focus having restrictions that are dissimilar from those associated with existing concepts.
- *Simple vs. Aggregated Concept:* The concept in focus might be a combination of multiple existing concepts (or vice versa). The ontology evolution framework(s) shall properly detect and act accordingly to accommodate these types of changes.
- *Concept vs. Property:* The concept can either be a class in OWL or used as a property of some other existing class. For example, the concept *deliverable* could be a separate class or could be modeled as property of the concept *project*. In the first case it could have been implemented as a subclass of *document* and in the second case it could take the instances of *software* as its value.

Understanding of change types is necessary to correctly handle explicit and implicit change requirements, and these are the changes that introduce deduced changes in change request.

3   Ontology Evolution Approaches

Ontology over time needs to be updated to accommodate changes in domain, user requirements, and to incorporate incremental improvement in the system. In this section we discuss and critically analyze different ontology evolution approaches.

3.1   User Driven Evolution

L. Stojanovic et al. in [SMM02] proposed a four phase ontology evolution process which copes with ontology changes due to business requirements and dynamic environment. As ontologies are frequently used for information interchange among organizations, so changes in ontology also have ripple effects on the other side use of the same ontology. A process-oriented evolution procedure is presented that focus on the consistency of the ontology during evolution for complex changes. The main modules are; 1) Change representation, the business requirements for change (i.e. change request) is described in formal representational format. 2) Semantic of change, the requested changes are checked on ontology for consistency. It is checked for the actual effects on the dependent data (i.e. instances), applications, and the source ontology due to these changes. If it results in inconsistency, then the user introduce deduced changes to resolve the inconsistencies. 3) Implementation, the complete change request (included deduced changes) is applied to the source ontology and the ontology evolves to another state. The local instances of ontology as well as the instances of concepts in the ontology are all updated. 4) Propagation, propagation of these changes to dependent data, applications, and ontologies is very important. All the changes are propagated to remote instances as well as applications in a consistent and coherent manner. Change propagation for instances are done in a way that out-of-date instances are simply replaced with the up-to-date instances.

3.2 Evolution Framework for Distributed Ontologies

Change and Annotation Ontology presented in [KlN03] to represent ontology changes, while complete detail of number and types of changes are discussed in [Kle04]. They developed the idea on change ontology to drive various ontology evolution tasks [KlN03]. The idea of change representation is borrowed from [Kle04], but has made extensions like; identification of a changed resource, change author, timestamp, and link to annotations about change. A component based framework for distributed ontology evolution is presented using change representations that formally describe ontology changes required to perform in evolution of ontology.

In [NCL06], the authors on top of their previous work (discussed above) presented different scenarios for ontology maintenance and evolution in distributed and collaborated ontologies. Several features and high-level tasks that an editing environment must support for these scenarios are defined. For this, a unified set of tools for different scenarios and user navigation to different modes are provided.

3.3 Discovery Driven Evolution

In [CFH06], the authors presented an idea of evolution based on the changes recognized by the system after analyzing some domain artifacts. The new concept(s) discovery process proposed supports ontology enrichment activity for multimedia ontology. A multimedia object is first fragmented and then new resources are detected from the fragmented parts. Automatic discovery of change(s) using ontology matching techniques from multimedia objects with additional domain specific metadata is the main achievement. For discovery of new concepts from the fragmented objects, H-Match is used for finding the match for the new concept from the already existing concepts in the ontology. *WorldNet* thesaurus is used for additional metadata. For accuracy improvement, they have implemented four matching models namely; surface, shallow, deep, and intensive discussed in [CFH06].

3.4 Integrated Framework for Evolution Management

We proposed an integrated framework for ontology evolution management [KLL09] with four main modules that supports automatic evolution of ontology from one consistent state to another. 1) Change detection and description, the new changes are automatically detected. These changes are because of emerging concept(s) (single concept, group of concepts and concepts in a hierarchical structure). After detection, these changes are represented in a semantically sound structure (i.e. *Change History*

Ontology (CHO) [KLK08a]) to represent and log all the ontology changes. 2) Inconsistency detection, all possible syntactic and semantic inconsistencies due to change request are resolved here. For this resolution, deduce changes are introduced in the change request. For its implementation, we used the technique of KAON API [GSV04]. 3) Change implementation and verification, here complete change request is applied to the ontology. We focus on changes at atomic level and it completes in isolation. If after applying certain changes we get the ontology inconsistent then there is a loop back facility to inconsistency detection to make the ontology consistent by resolving inconsistencies. After implementation, all the changes are logged in *Change History Log (CHL)* [KLK08a] for undo/redo and recovery purpose. Verification is made to verify that all the requested changes are implemented properly by consulting the change request. 4) Change log, a repository that keeps track of all the changes applied. We have developed a semantic structure i.e. *Change History Ontology* [KLK08a] as a storage structure for ontology changes. It provides facilities like properly managing changes, undo/redo of changes, recovery, visual navigation of change effects on ontology, and visual navigation of ontology changes [KLK08b].

3.5 Critical Analysis

Most of the existing ontology evolution systems do not support automatic ontology evolution except the one proposed in [KLL09] for emerging concepts. In [PIT05 and SMM02], user manually creates requests for changes due to business requirements, while in [OVM04, PIT05, and SMM02], experts are required for conflict resolutions in case of inconsistencies. The system discussed in [CFH06] mostly focused on the discovery of the new change and afterwards the system needs expert to insert the concept at suitable place suggested by the system.

In [KLL09], work related to change detection, its implementation and conflict resolutions are all done automatically. The main concerns in this system are, still a best matching resource search problem for the newly detected change. The second problem is inconsistency resolution. This is the toughest problem that needs special attention. We have to train the system for different deduced changes but training a system for different changes is a tough job. After proper training the system results may not be according to user intentions, as for one conflict resolution there might be many alternative deduced changes. Secondly selecting a deduced change from alternative also needs some predefined criteria.

4 Open Challenges

In this section we will discuss some of the challenges that still need to be addressed to achieve the automated ontology evolution procedure.

4.1 New Change Detection

To detect new changes among the emerging concept(s) (single concept, group of concepts, and concepts in a hierarchical structure), different correspondence, difference, and matching [CFM06 andOVM04] techniques are applied. These techniques suggest the

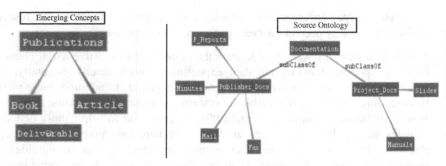

Fig. 2. Emerging concepts, the reason for change in *Documentation (*source) ontology

relevance of new emerging concepts to the source ontology. Then existence of new resources is checked, and if it does not then matching process starts to detect the most relevant concept(s) in the source ontology [CFH06 and KLL09] where the new concept should be inserted. Here we encounter two problems;

- *Relevance Detection:* best and mostly used difference, correspondence, and matching algorithms are defined in [CFM06, OVM04, and HuQ07]. But the results of these algorithms are still not matured for diverse domains, so using these algorithms are not completely reliable and user intervention is required.
- *Selection among Newly Detected Changes:* To understand this issue look at the Figure 2, where we have emerging concepts i.e. *Deliverable* and *Publications* with *Book* and *Article* as sub-concepts, and source ontology of *Documentation* to which the changes will be made. The *Publications* sub-tree is added as a sub-concept of *Documentation* concept. For concept *Deliverable,* we have three alternatives; 1) make *Deliverable* as sub-concept of *Documentation* concept, 2) make *Deliverable* as sub-concept of *Project_Docs* concept, 3) make *Deliverable* as a property of *Project_Docs.* An ontology expert knows that second alternative is more obvious, but the decision is to be made by the system. Proper heuristics should be implemented or system should be trained for such situations. But it is a tough task as ontology is very much different in its nature than any other information representation schemes [NoK04]. These issues are stilled unfolded.

4.2 Conflict Resolution

Introducing deduced changes in order to resolve conflicts and make ontology consistent is the most highlighted problem in ontology evolution literature without proper solution other then involving ontology expert [CFH06, KlN03, PIT05, SMM02, and StM02]. In KAON [GSV04], rules are specified prior to the start of evolution procedure. For example, if there are two alternatives for a concept change, 1) to become a *property* of some concept, and 2) to become a *sub-concept* of some concept in the source ontology (like *Deliverable* concept case in previous section), then the alternative of *sub-concept* should be selected. In [KLL09], we proposed that the system is trained for different types of deduced changes, and then accordingly select that alternative (deduce change) that have less impact on ontology. To resolve the conflicts in this way needs to address two very important issues.

- *System Training:* It is very hard to train the system for exhaustive list of changes (even of specific domain) and then expecting accurate results. Secondly, the results may also not be acceptable to ontology engineer. In addition, there might be cascading conflicts and in result the system will have weak response time.
- *Impact of Deduced Changes:* In [KLL09], we proposed to select those deduced changes having less impact on ontology. But here two points needs special attention. It is to be decided that impact on which aspect of ontology is considered for deduced changes. There are changes that have large change impact on the structure of ontology but have less impact on the semantics of resources in the ontology. For example (see Figure 2), adding the concept *Publications* as a sub-concept of *Documentation* have large structural impact but less semantic impact. The same way if we make *Publisher_Docs* (see Figure 2) disjoint with its sibling concepts, then this change have less structural impact but can have very large impact on semantic of the resources as its effects will also be reflected on the sub-concept(s) of all the disjoint concept(s).

Currently, these issues are still not resolved properly for automated ontology evolution from one consistent state to another.

5 Conclusions and Step Ahead

Ontology evolution is a collaborative process incorporating work from other related fields such as ontology matching, merging, integration, and reasoning. In this paper we talked about the change management activities and based on these changes the ontology evolves from one state to another state is discussed in detail. We discussed different approaches followed by the research community to handle the evolution process with their pros and cons. At the end we elaborated some open challenges still unhandled to fully automate the process of ontology evolution. Currently, we are working on solutions to these challenges and also on reconciliation of mapping in evolving ontologies.

Acknowledgement

This research was supported by the MKE (Ministry of Knowledge Economy), Korea, under the ITRC (Information Technology Research Center) support program supervised by the IITA (Institute of Information Technology Advancement)" (IITA-2009-(C1090-0902-0002)) and was supported by the IT R&D program of MKE/KEIT, [10032105, Development of Realistic Multiverse Game Engine Technology].

This work also was supported by the Brain Korea 21 projects and Korea Science & Engineering Foundation (KOSEF) grant funded by the Korea government(MOST) (No. 2008-1342).

References

[CFH06] Castano, S., Ferrara, A., Hess, G.: Discovery-Driven Ontology Evolution. In: The Semantic Web Applications and Perspectives (SWAP), 3rd Italian Semantic Web Workshop, PISA, Italy, December 18-20 (2006)

[CFM06] Castano, S., Ferrara, A., Montanelli, S.: Matching ontologies in open networked systems: Techniques and applications. In: Spaccapietra, S., Atzeni, P., Chu, W.W., Catarci, T., Sycara, K. (eds.) Journal on Data Semantics V. LNCS, vol. 3870, pp. 25–63. Springer, Heidelberg (2006)

[FPA06] Flouris, G., Plexousakis, D., Antoniou, G.: A Classification of Ontology Changes. In: The Poster Session of Semantic Web Applications and Perspectives (SWAP), 3rd Italian Semantic Web Workshop, PISA, Italy (2006)

[GSV04] Gabel, T., Sure, Y., Voelker, J.: KAON – ontology management infrastructure. D3.1.1.a, SEKT Project: Semantically Enabled Knowledge Technologies (March 2004)

[HuQ07] Hu, W., Qu, Y.: Falcon-AO: A Practical Ontology Matching System. Journal of Web Semantics (2007)

[KLK08a] Khattak, A.M., Latif, K., Khan, S., Ahmed, N.: Managing Change History in Web Ontologies. In: International Conference on Semantics, Knowledge and Grid, pp. 347–350 (2008); Fourth International Conference on Semantics, Knowledge and Grid (2008)

[KLK08b] Khattak, A.M., Latif, K., Khan, S., Ahmed, N.: Ontology Recovery and Visualization. In: 4th International Conference on Next Generation Web Services Practices, pp. 90–96 (2008)

[KLL09] Khattak, A.M., Latif, K., Lee, S.Y., Lee, Y.K., Rasheed, T.: Building an Integrated Framework for Ontology Evolution Management. In: 12th Conference on Creating Global Economies through Innovation and Knowledge Management (IBIMA), Malaysia (June 2009)

[KlN03] Klein, M., Noy, N.F.: A component-based framework for ontology evolution. In: Proceedings of the (IJCAI 2003) Workshop on Ontologies and Distributed Systems, CEUR-WS, vol. 71 (2003)

[Kle04] Klein, M.: Change Management for Distributed Ontologies. PhD Thesis, Department of Computer Science, Vrije University, Amsterdam (2004)

[NCL06] Noy, N.F., Chugh, A., Liu, W., Musen, M.A.: A Framework for Ontology Evolution in Collaborative Environments. In: Cruz, I., Decker, S., Allemang, D., Preist, C., Schwabe, D., Mika, P., Uschold, M., Aroyo, L.M. (eds.) ISWC 2006. LNCS, vol. 4273, pp. 544–558. Springer, Heidelberg (2006)

[NoK04] Noy, N.F., Klein, M.: Ontology evolution: Not the same as schema evolution. Knowledge and Information System 6(4), 428–440 (2004)

[OVM04] Oberle, D., Volz, R., Motik, B., Staab, S.: An extensible ontology software environment. In: Handbook on Ontologies. Series of International Handbooks on Information Systems, pp. 311–333. Springer, Heidelberg (2004)

[PIT05] Plessers, P., De Troyer, O.: Ontology change detection using a versioning log. In: Gil, Y., Motta, E., Benjamins, V.R., Musen, M.A. (eds.) ISWC 2005. LNCS, vol. 3729, pp. 578–592. Springer, Heidelberg (2005)

[SMM02] Stojanovic, L., Madche, A., Motik, B., Stojanovic, N.: User-driven ontology evolution management. In: Gómez-Pérez, A., Benjamins, V.R. (eds.) EKAW 2002. LNCS (LNAI), vol. 2473, pp. 285–300. Springer, Heidelberg (2002)

Improvement of u-Multiplex Services

Hyun Soo Kim[1], Hyung Rim Choi[1], Kangbae Lee[1], Jae Un Jung[2], Byung Ha Lee[3],
Jin Wook Lee[3], Ki Nam Choi[3], Jeong Soo Ha[3], and Chang Hyun Park[3]

Division of Management Information Systems
Bumin-dong, Seo-gu, Busan, Korea
[1]{hskim, hrchoi, kanglee}@dau.ac.kr, [2]share@donga.ac.kr,
[3]{leebh1443, jw6416, dreizehn, volt123, archehyun}@naver.com

Abstract. Movie theaters are a representative room to enjoy a cultural life. Recently, the type of theater gets changed into multiplex including the waiting space mixed with convenient and cultural facilities. To provide the continuous and successful improvement of the multiplex services, its economic evaluation is required in business point of view. However, existing studies for the substantial evaluation of multiplex services are insufficient. Therefore, this study aims to introduce models and plans to improve the services as evaluating multiplex services applied with ubiquitous technology(u-multiplex) by interview and simulation.

Keywords: u-Multiplex, Service, Evaluation.

1 Introduction

Movie theaters are changing their form from a small number of large showrooms to a small or medium sized multi-screens and evolving into a multiplex where the waiting space, various convenient and cultural facilities are complexly linked together aside from facilities to see movies. On the other hand, for continuous and successful service improvement, users' needs and preference of services, and other various cost-benefit analyses are necessary. Also in the business perspective, the analytic process of direct economic value from service provision as well as indirect service value is required. So this paper aimed to analyze value of the existing multiplex services based on u-Multiplex services to which information technology containing the ubiquitous concept as the newest service of multiplexes had been applied. It also aimed to present a service improvement model and plans to overcome problems found from the analysis. Results from literature review and case studies on the status of multiplex services are described in Chapter 2. On-site interviews with three staff members working in a domestic multiplex were conducted and 110 university students in their teens and twenties divided into three groups were interviewed in the form of workshop, whose results are described in Chapter 3. Also the computer simulation was conducted.

It summarized the paper published in Korean System Dynamics Review(2009. 07.) for presentation at the UNESST conference.

D. Ślęzak et al. (Eds.): UNESST 2009, CCIS 62, pp. 76–81, 2009.

2   Literature Reviews

2.1   Major Spaces and Service of a Multiplex

A multiplex is a complex containing 10 or more screens and subsidiary facilities like a large parking lot, restaurants, shopping areas, and various exhibition rooms in a building[1].

The space of a multiplex for seeing a movie consists of four areas of admission, waiting, seeing, and exit[2].

2.1.1   Reservation and Ticketing Service of the Ticket Office

A ticket office is for reservation and ticketing for a movie and information such as a movie title, time, and the status of reservation is made available in an electronic display, kiosks or bulletins to support decision making of cinema audiences[3].

2.1.2   Ticket Examination Service in a Space between the Waiting Space and Showroom

Audiences, after buying their tickets, will wait in a waiting space and come into the showroom when the ticket examination for a movie they have chosen begins.

2.1.3   Seat-Ushering Services at the Entrance of a Showroom

Audiences who have passed the ticket examination will come into the showroom for a movie chosen. He will check his own reserved seat through the seat guideboard at the entrance of a showroom.

2.1.4   Services Inside the Showroom and at the Exit Space

Audiences will sit on their reserved seats, see the movie inside the showroom, and leave the multiplex. Then they will receive a guiding service through the sign for the exit direction. However, this areas does not provide services using information technology. So discussion of spatial and service areas will be irrelevant at this point.

3   Improvement of u-Multiplex Services

3.1   Research Methods and Process

The research process to evaluate services of the existing multiplexes is as follows. First of all, for analysis of the service status of multiplexes, a visit has been made to a multiplex in Busan to interview employees on the site. Also cases of service use of audiences have been collected and the data necessary for a computer simulation has been processed. The workshop-typed interviews with 110 university students in their teens and 20s in Busan were conducted in three groups and a computer simulation was conducted to comparatively analyze the length of time spent by a movie-goer for each service. The problems and meaningful alternatives found in each research process were used to present new services or plans to improve services.

3.1.1 Evaluation of Service of the Existing Multiplex

3.1.2 Interview with Employees

On June 4, 2009, at 4 pm, the 30-minute-long interviews on overall multiplex services with 2 senior staffs (one for ticketing and the other for the multiplex operation and management) of CGV Seomyun were conducted. On the other hand, the unmanned automation system used to provide services like ticketing or ticket examination consists of kiosks and automatic ticket examiners and the services provided through a relevant system are as follows.

First, the kiosk has been introduced to reduce the number of employees in ticket offices by dividing the ticketing labor and to reduce the number of people waiting by improving the ticketing speed so that customers' convenience is improved through a relevant system. However, most of the audiences are using manned ticket offices. The main reason for the low level of use of kiosks was that kiosks were available only to

Table 1. Description and contents of the simulation subject

Division	Descriptive item		Length of time spent	Comment
Ticketing	Kiosk	Credit card settlement and ticketing	40 seconds~1 minute 30 seconds	A, C
		Ticketing reserved tickets	35 seconds~1 minute	
	Manned ticket office	Ticket reservation and ticketing	1~2 minutes	B
Ticket examination	Staff	Length of time spent for ticket examination and showroom guide	Around 10 seconds	B
	Bar code/RF card		2.4~4 seconds	A
Seeing a movie	Seat guideboard of a general showroom	Length of time spent to check the reserved seat	5~10 seconds	A
	Seat guideboard reading bar code/RF card		2~3 seconds	A New service

※ A: Error based on the level of the audience's skill to use the system
B: Error based on the level of the staff's skillfulness in work
C: Error based on whether there are pop-outs for ads (discount coupons)

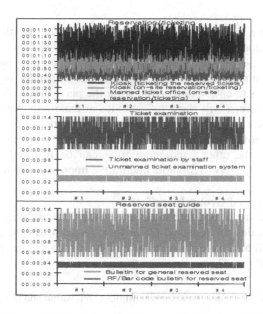

Fig. 1. The length of time spent for each service area and technology (In-Hour Minute Second)

credit card holders, according to the staffs. Second, the unmanned ticket examiner has been introduced to make the length of time spent by an audience to enter shorter than that spent for ticket examination by a staff at the examination point and ultimately to reduce personnel expenses (or to transfer ticket-examining staffs to other divisions) by automating the ticket examination system. However, it has been learned that the number of users came down from 10~20 per 100 at the beginning to 2~3 recently. So it has been found that the system is not in use as of June 4, 2009. Staffs thought that the reason for the failure in the unmanned ticket examination system related to insufficient promotion as they said that 'the customers do not seem to know the fact that the bar code or RF card is used in the process of ticketing and examining tickets.'

3.1.3 Computer Simulation
The computer simulation model was defined and a simulation was conducted for the relevant service to analyze which conveniences have been substantially provided to service providers and users through services of kiosks and unmanned ticket examiners that were introduced to provide improved services of multiplexes. Also it aimed to analyze why the level of use was so low as explained above.

The simulation contains the length of time (speed) for services of a kiosk and an unmanned ticket examiner and comparison of the length of time spent by staff in a ticket office and at the examination point. The descriptive content used for the simulation is as shown in Table 1.

Fig.1. is the result of creation of the data set on the length of time for each service and technology by using random numbers and seed values of Table 2. for a realistic simulation. The length of time was 1 minute and 16 seconds at minimum and 2 minutes and 25 seconds at maximum for ticketing by ticket office staff. Time spent in a kiosk was between 53 seconds and 1 minute and 57 seconds. The difference between the maximum value analyzed through the maximum length of time scenario and the minimum value analyzed through the minimum length of time scenario was about 1 minute and 30 seconds. This explains that more time can be invested to improve the operation rotation rate of showrooms and to manage internal facilities if the speed of audiences to enter is improved from the perspective of service providers of a multiplex. One screen will show 6~7 movies at maximum and if the audience's length of time to enter is cut by 5~10 minutes, 30~70 minutes can be of additional use. So one more movie with higher audience preference or shorter time can be considered while on the other hand more time can be invested to clean internal facilities and to inspect safety to promote qualitative improvement of the services.

3.1.4 Workshop –Typed Group Interview

20-minute-long workshop-typed free interviews with 110 university students in their teens and 20s (83 males, 27 females; 60 in their teens, 43 in their 20s) taking the cultural arts subject B at University A in Busan were conducted on June 8, 2009 at 10 am, 12 am, and 19:40 pm. The results from this are as follows.

Table 2. The status of use by type in ticket resrvation and ticketing

Division	Group 1	Group 2	Group 3	Total
On-site ticket office	26	41	27	94
On-site kiosk	0	0	1	1
Internet (PC)	4	5	3	12
Mobile	1	1	1	3
Total	31	47	32	110

To analyze the reasons for Table 2. as for ticket reservation and ticketing by type, the kiosk services are available only to the credit card (cheque card) holders while most in their teens or 20s belong to the age or income groups who cannot use credit cards. Also it was found that men were kinder than a system so the manned ticket office was preferred to a kiosk.

4 Conclusion

It was learned that the value of services provided by the unmanned automated system such as kiosks and unmanned ticket examiners using the ubiquitous concept, quite contrary to the intent of service providers, was providing inconveniences to users (audiences) or their awareness was low. While there may be diverse factors for the reasons, it can be analyzed that service providers have failed to clearly analyze use behaviors of service users. This means that efforts to collect examples of the customers' conveniences and opinions and to technologically improve them have been insufficient. This paper aimed to produce new services and plans to overcome the limits of the current services. It may be significant in that it analyzed effectiveness of multiplex services whose studies so far have been relatively insufficient.

As for the limits, any separate statistical verification techniques have not been used for interview results and there are items without concrete tests or verification in the process to present new services or plans to improve the existing services. So the future studies will include the process for concrete verification and tests of relevant factors.

References

1. http://www.encyber.com
2. Lee, H.: A study on the current architectural designs and space organization of multiplex cinema in Korea. Hanyang University (2000)
3. Woo, E.: A Study on the utilization of Waiting Areas in a Cinema – Focused on Multiplex Cinema in the Metropolitan Area-, Hong-Ik University (2001)

Assessment of IT Governance of COBIT Framework[*]

WoongChul Choi and DaeHun Yoo

Department of Computer Science, KwangWoon University
Seoul, Korea
{wchoi, yo2dh}@kw.ac.kr

Abstract. The IT governance has been drawn much attention, and the COBIT has been known as a framework for the IT governance. One of the key features of the IT governance is the alignment of business goals and IT goals. The COBIT framework basically provides the definitions of business, IT and processes' goals and the links among them. There has been much research on the assessment of the IT governance in terms of applying the COBIT framework to the IT governance of an organization. However, this paper studies the assessment of the IT governance of the COBIT framework itself. We develop an assessment method, apply it to the COBIT framework and derive several assessment results including the weights of the IT goals and the IT processes to the business goal. The results can also be applied to other IT governance areas such as the priority determination of the IT investment or IT audit.

Keywords: IT governance, COBIT framework, alignment, audit.

1 Introduction

IT governance has been recognized as a critical success factor in the achievement of corporate success by deploying information through application of technology [1]. Many organizations have started with the implementation of IT governance and a crucial element of IT governance is achieving a better link between business and IT, also referred to as strategic alignment [2]. The appropriate alignment between use of IT and the business goals of an organization is fundamental to efficient and effective IT governance.

To address the alignment challenges, it is important for an organization to have a clear and in-depth view regarding its business goals and how IT goals and IT processes support those goals. Each organization should own clear business goals and a related business strategy, communicated to and adopted by the entire organization. In order to help the definitions of business goals and IT goals, and to provide an organization ensure alignment between use of Information Technology (IT) and its business goals, the Control OBjectives for Information and related Technology (COBIT) has been introduced and known as an open standard [4] that is being used increasingly by a diverse range of organizations [5].

---

[*] The present research has been conducted by National Research Foundation of Korea and by the Research Grant of KwangWoon University in 2009.

D. Ślęzak et al. (Eds.): UNESST 2009, CCIS 62, pp. 82–89, 2009.

There has been much research on the IT governance [1][14], the alignment [2][6] and their related topics [4][11][16]. For the topic on the assessment, research has been done on the differences in priority of IT governance concerns among literature, practitioners, and COBIT [14]. In [3], the set of business and IT goals identified in the pilot study has been validated and prioritized. There are several research on the application of the maturity model to assess a COBIT and COBIT-related applications [16][17]. However, there has been little research on the COBIT framework itself in terms of assessing the IT governance. In this research, a system of linear equations are constructed by mapping the COBIT framework into a system of linear equations, and by solving it with constraints, several useful values can be derived such as the weights of the business goals, the IT goals and the IT processes, and the amount of the contribution of an IT goal to the business goal. These results can be applied to many IT governance areas such as the implementation of the COBIT for an organization and the IT governance audit.

The rest of this paper is organized as follows. In Section 2, the related works are presented. Then an assessment method of the IT governance of the COBIT framework is provided in Section 3. Finally, Section 4 concludes this paper.

2 Backgrounds

In this section, the COBIT framework in terms of the IT governance and the related research works are presented.

2.1 COBIT for IT Governance

The purpose of COBIT framework is to provide the management with an IT governance model that helps them control and manage the information and related technology [10][11][12]. The framework explains how IT processes deliver the information that the business needs to achieve its objectives. This delivery is controlled through 34 high-level control objectives, one for each IT process, contained in the four domains of PO(Planning and Organization), AI(Acquisition and Implementation), DS(Delivery and Support), and ME(Monitoring and Evaluation) as the building blocks of the COBIT framework[13].

When an organization wants to implement COBIT for governance purposes, it first has to make sure that there is a clear understanding of its business goals. These business goals need to be articulated and translated into IT goals that support the achievement of those business goals.

To guide an organization in defining those business goals, COBIT provides a list of 17 generic business goals, based on research in different industries. These business goals are categorized according to the four dimensions of a business balanced scorecard (financial perspective, customer perspective, internal perspective, and learning and growth perspective), and are also linked to the most relevant information criteria. In COBIT, these business goals are linked to 28 numbered IT goals, which are again linked to the information criteria. An organization can use these generic business and IT goals as input to identify its own specific business environment and IT environment and to make sure that business and IT goals are aligned.

When business goals and IT goals are defined and aligned, an organization can identify the most important COBIT processes that are essential enablers to achieve the identified IT goals. As guidance, all the 34 IT processes in COBIT are linked to one or more of the 28 generic IT goals defined previously. Again, an organization needs to customize this exercise for its own specific environment.

For each of these IT processes retained, the organization can then set specific IT process goals that are believed to support the achievement of the IT goals. In COBIT, examples of such IT process goals are provided for all 34 IT processes. To achieve the defined process goals, a number of activities within the process can be defined, with corresponding activity goals. Examples of such activity goals are also provided in COBIT.

2.2 Related Research on Assessment of IT Governance

In earlier research on aligning IT and business goals, it was shown that in practice, business strategy and goals are not always formally written out and if so, it is not always the case that people throughout the organization are aware of it [2][7]. In [20], authors present the ITOMAT(IT Organization Modeling and Assessment Tool) which has been created to overcome operationalization and subjectivity weaknesses in the COBIT framework. The authors of [21] present how ITOMAT's metamodel and its framework for assessment and prediction can be used to support decision making on IT organization change scenarios.

There has been research on topics related to prioritization among the goals. In [3], the existing list of 20 business goals and 28 IT goals were validated and prioritized by the group of experts. IT governance prioritization according to literature, practitioners and Cobit is presented [14].

Performance has been an important research topic. In [18], IT governance is assessed by BSC(Balanced Scorecard), and the research on its improvement has been done. In [19], authors analyze the IT Balanced Scorecard (IT BSC) as an important instrument in support of IT Governance processes. A systematic methodology is presented for IT governance assessment and design, specified through different phases, their activities and outcomes [22].

3 Assessment Method of IT Governance of COBIT Framework

In order to make an assessment, a system of linear equations is developed first by mapping Table 1 into the form of linear equations as follows.

$$b_1 * B\_goal_1 = i_{1,1} * IT\_goal_1 + i_{1,2} * IT\_goal_2 + \ldots + i_{1,28} * IT\_goal_{28}$$
$$b_2 * B\_goal_2 = i_{2,1} * IT\_goal_1 + i_{2,2} * IT\_goal_2 + \ldots + i_{2,28} * IT\_goal_{28}$$

$$\ldots\ldots\ldots$$

$$b_{17} * B\_goal_{17} = i_{17,1} * IT\_goal_1 + i_{17,2} * IT\_goal_2 + \ldots + i_{17,28} * IT\_goal_{28}$$

(1)

where B_goal_j and IT_goal_k are the percentage of the achievement of a business goal j $(1<=j<=17)$ and an IT goal k $(1<=k <= 28)$ and $0 <= B\_goal_j$, $IT\_goal_k <= 1$, respectively. It is also obvious that $IT\_goal_j = 0$ when there is no IT_goal_j in B_goal_k

Table 1. Linking business goals to IT goals (Part of [13], COBIT^{æ} 4.1)

		Business Goals	IT Goals							
Financial Perspective	1	Provide a good return on investment of IT-enabled business investments.	24							
	2	Manage IT-related business risk.	2	14	17	18	19	20	21	22
	3	Improve corporate governance and transparency.	2	18						
Customer Perspective	4	Improve customer orientation and service.	3	23						
	5	Offer competitive products and services.	5	24						
	6	Establish service continuity and availability.	10	16	22	23				
	7	Create agility in responding to changing business requirements.	1	5	25					
	8	Achieve cost optimisation of service delivery.	7	8	10	24				

(Table 1). b_j and $i_{j,k}$ are coefficients, and their meanings are presented in the following sections.

3.1 Calculation of the Weight Values of the IT Goals to the Business Goal

Given the system of linear equations in the above, map IT_goal_k *(for all k, 1 <=k <=28)* with the one in Table 1, which means that for each business goal, there are corresponding IT goals composing the business goal. For example, in Table 1, the business goal number 3 has 2 IT goals composing the goal. Therefore, for the business goal number 3, the equation becomes

$$b_3 * B\_goal_3 = i_{3,2} * IT\_goal_2 + i_{3,18} * IT\_goal_{18}$$

The rest of equations can be similarly derived. In order to solve the system of the linear equations, assume that all the business goals and the IT goals in the equations are 100% achieved, which means that B_goal_j *(1<=j<=17)* and IT_goal_k *(1<=k <= 28)* are set to 1. Then the system of linear equations reduces to the following.

$$b_1 = i_{1,24}$$
$$b_2 = i_{2,2} + i_{2,14} + i_{2,17} + i_{2,18} + i_{2,19} + i_{2,20} + i_{2,21} + i_{2,22}$$
$$\ldots\ldots$$
$$b_{17} = i_{17,9}$$

Since these equations are for calculating the weight, $\sum_{j=1}^{17} b_j = 1$. Assume further that all of the weights of the business goals, b_j *(1<=j<=17)*, are same, i.e. $b_1= b_2 = \ldots = b_{17}$ then the above equations become

$$1/17 = i_{1,24}$$
$$1/17 = i_{2,2} + i_{2,14} + i_{2,17} + i_{2,18} + i_{2,19} + i_{2,20} + i_{2,21} + i_{2,22}$$
$$\ldots\ldots$$
$$1/17 = i_{17,9}$$

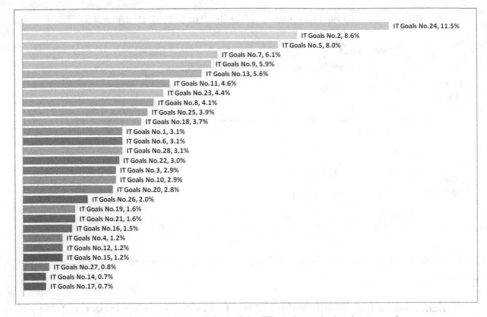

Fig. 1. The derived weights of the IT goals to the business goal

Table 2. Linking IT goals to IT processes (Part of [13], COBIT™ 4.1)

IT Goals		Processes									
1	Respond to business requirements in alignment with the business strategy.	PO1	PO2	PO4	PO10	AI1	AI6	AI7	DS1	DS3	ME1
2	Respond to governance requirements in line with board direction.	PO1	PO4	PO10	ME1	ME4					
3	Ensure satisfaction of end users with service offerings and service levels.	PO8	AI4	DS1	DS2	DS7	DS8	DS10	DS13		
4	Optimise the use of information.	PO2	DS11								
5	Create IT agility.	PO2	PO4	PO7	AI3						
6	Define how business functional and control requirements are translated in effective and efficient automated solutions.	AI1	AI2	AI6							
7	Acquire and maintain integrated and standardised application systems.	PO3	AI2	AI5							
8	Acquire and maintain an integrated and standardised IT infrastructure.	AI3	AI5								
		PO7	AI5								

For a given business goal $j (1 <= j <= 17)$, assume in a similar way that all of the weights of the IT goals, $i_{j,k}$ $(1 <= k <= 28)$, are same, i.e. $i_{j,1} = i_{j,2} = \ldots = i_{j,28} = i_j$ then the second equation in the above, for example, becomes

$$1/17 = 8\,i_2, \quad where\ i_2 = i_{2,2} = i_{2,14} = i_{2,17} = i_{2,18} = i_{2,19} = i_{2,20} = i_{2,21} = i_{2,22}$$

Therefore, the solution to the calculation of the weight value of an IT goal to the business goal is

$$the\ weight\ value\ of\ an\ kth\ IT\ goal\ to\ the\ business\ goal = \sum_{j=1}^{17} i_{j,k}$$

The following Fig. 1 shows the result in a graphical view of the weights of the IT goals to the business goal.

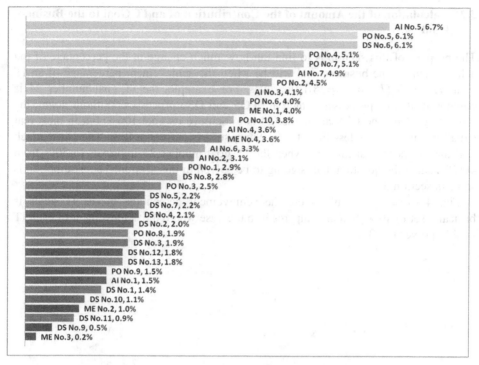

Fig. 2. The derived weights of the IT processes to the business goal

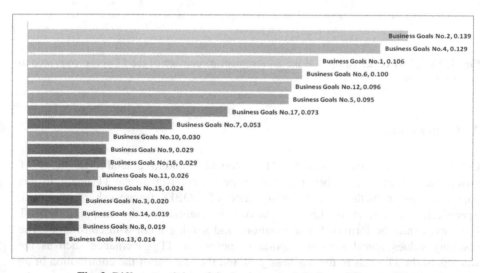

Fig. 3. Different weights of the business goals in financial sector [3]

The IT goals are also linked to the IT processes, as shown in Table 2. By applying the same procedure, we can calculate the weight values of the IT processes to the IT goals(Fig. 2).

3.2 Calculation of the Amount of the Contribution of an IT Goal to the Business Goal

The purpose of this section is to find out how much change in the percentage of the achievement to the business goal will be when the achievement percentage of an IT goal (IT_goal_k ($1 <=k <=28$)) improves. For example, the IT goal number 24 is composed of 2 IT processes, which are PO5 and DS6 processes. Without doubt, the ultimate goal for the IT goal number 24 is to achieve its goal 100%, but in most real situations, its value is less than 100%. Suppose it is currently 40%. Then how much will the business goal improve when the IT goal number 24 improves to 50% from 40%? That is the question that is going to be solved in this section. The assumption is same in section 3.1.

Fig. 4 shows the result where the achievement percentage of the IT goals is basically set to 40% [6] and compares it to the case where the achievement of each IT goal improves to 50 %.

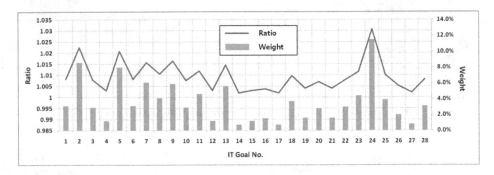

Fig. 4. The effect of the changes of the achievement percentage of the IT goals, compared to the result of Fig. 1

4 Conclusion

COBIT provides a framework for IT governance and a crucial element of IT governance is achieving a better alignment between business and IT goals. In this paper, an assess method for IT governance of COBIT framework is presented. Specifically, a system of linear equations is constructed by mapping COBIT framework into the form of linear equations and solving them with constraints. The resulting values reveal various important features of IT governance such as the weights of the IT goals to the business goal and the amount of the contribution of an IT goal to the business goal. These results can be good building blocks for many IT governance areas such as the implementation of the COBIT for an organization and the IT governance audit as well.

References

1. Hussain, S.J., Siddiqui, M.S.: Quantified Model of COBIT for Corporate IT Governance. In: First International Conference on Information and Communication Technologies, pp. 158–163. IEEE, Los Alamitos (2005)
2. Van Grembergen, W., De Haes, S., Moons, J.: Linking Business Goals to IT Goals and COBIT Processes. Information Systems Control Journal 4 (2005)
3. Van Grembergen, W., De Haes, S., Van Brempt, H.: Prioritising and Linking Business and IT Goals in the Financial Sector. In: 40th Annual Hawaii International Conference on System Sciences (HICSS 2007), p. 235a. IEEE, Los Alamitos (2007)
4. Pathak, J.: Internal Audit and E-Commerce Controls. Internal Auditing 18(2), 30–34 (2003)
5. Ridley, G., Young, J., Carol, P.: COBIT and its utilization: a framework from the literature. In: 37th Hawaii International Conference on System Sciences, p. 8. IEEE, Los Alamitos (2004)
6. De Haes, S., Van Grembergen, W.: Practices in IT Governance and Business/IT Alignment. Information Systems Control Journal-Value and Performance in IT 5 (2007)
7. Benson, R.J., Bugnitz, T.L., Walton, W.B.: From Business strategy tot IT Action: Right decisions for a better bottom line. Wiley & Sons, Chichester (2004)
8. ITGI(IT Governance Institute), http://www.itgi.org
9. Cram, A.: The IT Balanced Scorecard Revisited. Information Systems Control Journal-Value and Performance in IT 5 (2007)
10. Guldentops, E., De Haes, S.: COBIT 3rd Edition Usage Survey: Growing Acceptance of COBIT. Information Systems Control Journal 6, 25–31 (2002)
11. Guldentops, E., Van Grembergen, W., De Haes, S.: Control and Governance Maturity Survey: Establishing a Reference Benchmark and a Self-Assessment Tool. Information Systems Control Journal 6, 32–35 (2002)
12. IT Governance Institute: COBIT Executive Summary, 3rd edn. Released by COBIT Steering Committee, p. 3 (2000)
13. COBIT⊇E 4.1, ISACA, http://www.isaca.org
14. Simonsson, M., Johnson, P.: Assessment of IT Governance - A Prioritization of Cobit. In: Proceedings of the Conference on Systems Engineering Research (2006)
15. Krakar, Z., zgela, M., Rotim, S.T.: CobIT-Framework for IT Governance- Analysis and experience. In: 18th IIS Information anad Inteligent Systems, pp. 123–135 (2007)
16. Simonsson, M., Hultgren, E.: IT Governance Maturity in Electric Utilities - Cobit Assessments of Administrative Systems and Operation Support Systems (2005)
17. Simonsson, M., Johnson, P., Wijkstrom, H.: Model-Based it Governance Maturity Assessments with Cobit. In: European Conference on Information Systems (2007)
18. Van Grembergen, W., De Haes, S.: Measuring and Improving IT Governance Through the Balanced Scorecard. Information Systems Control Journal 2 (2005)
19. Kozina, M.: IT balanced scorecard as IT governance framework. In: DAAAM International Scientific Book (2006)
20. Simonsson, M., Johnson, P.: The IT organization modeling and assessment tool: Correlating IT governance maturity with the effect of IT. In: 41st Hawaii International Conference on System Sciences, p. 431. IEEE, Los Alamitos (2008)
21. Simonsson, M., Johnson, P., Ekstedt, M.: IT Governance Decision Support Using the IT Organization Modeling and Assessment Tool. In: Portland International Center for Management of Engineering and Technology, pp. 802–810. IEEE, Los Alamitos (2008)
22. Clementi, S., Cristina, T., Carvalho, M.B.: Methodology for IT Governance Assessment and Design 226, 189–202 (2008)

Design Middleware Platforms for Ubiquitous Smart Service on City Gas Environment in Korea*

Jeong Seok Oh, Jang Sik Park, and Jeong Rock Kwon

Institute of Gas Safety R&D, Korea Gas Safety Corporation,
Shighung-Shi, Gyoungg-Do, Korea
{dbstar, pjsik, jrkwon}@kgs.or.kr

Abstract. The information technology paradigm shifts to smart service environment, as ubiquitous technologies are used in the latest industry trend. The major features of ubiquitous smart service are high dynamism and heterogeneity of their environment and the need for context awareness. In order to resolve these features, it is necessary to develop middleware that meet various new requirements. This paper designed middleware on ubiquitous smart service for enhancing the safety and reliability to city gas environment in Korea. The object of this paper will support cornerstone in order to construct the framework of intelligent infrastructure and service for autonomic management.

Keywords: Ubiquitous, Smart service, Middleware.

1 Introduction

The information technology paradigm shifts to smart service environment, as ubiquitous technologies are used in the latest industry trend. Ubiquitous technologies are capable of innovating public services, increasing the quality of life, and enhancing business productivity as constructing intelligent network [8]. However, it is necessary to develop network infrastructures based on ubiquitous technologies on considering particularly industry characteristics and smart service platform which by analyzing the collected context-aware information in order to apply ubiquitous technologies [2, 3, 5]. Therefore, applying ubiquitous technologies to specific industry facilities must design the applicable infrastructure through analyzing characteristics of the surrounding environment, and require essentially smart service architecture for enhancing the safety and reliability.

Key features of smart service are the high the dynamism and heterogeneity of their environments and the need for context awareness. To cope with these features, ubiquitous smart services might rely on middleware platforms [1, 6, 9]. In general, middleware platforms manage interaction between application layer and distributed low-level layer. Besides the legacy middleware function, middleware platforms for

---

* This work was supported by MIKE (Ministry of Knowledge Economy) under the program of ETI (Energy Technology Innovation). This paper is a result of "Research Group of Energy Safety for Next Generation". (Project No 2007-M-CC23-P-03-1-000).

D. Ślęzak et al. (Eds.): UNESST 2009, CCIS 62, pp. 90–97, 2009.

ubiquitous must need various requirements such as access mechanism, control mechanism, abstraction to heterogeneous sub network, the high level modeling, and management of meta information and context awareness.

This paper is to design ubiquitous smart service platform for enhancing the safety and reliability to city gas facilities in Korea. To achieve our goals, we explain the outline of ubiquitous smart service to city gas environments, show two application layers of smart service. Furthermore, we define requirements for middleware platform to city gas facilities, and show there middleware layers for smart city gas management. The object of this paper will support cornerstone in order to construct the framework of intelligent infrastructure and service for autonomic managing related facilities in Korea.

2 Ubiquitous Smart Service to City-Gas Facilities in Korea

Fig.1 shows ubiquitous smart infrastructure and service. We select four target facilities in principal city gas facilities, which require preferentially ubiquitous technologies in Korea, and define stress/vibration in above pipeline, leakage gas/current/water level/pressure in gas valve boxes, and corrosion in the underground pipeline as parameters of context awareness in order to develop ubiquitous wireless infrastructures. Furthermore, our research aims to evolve smart visualized monitoring and control service. We are to provide autonomic process such as monitoring risk parameter, accumulating context-aware information, controlling target facility, and displaying visualized analysis result in these services.

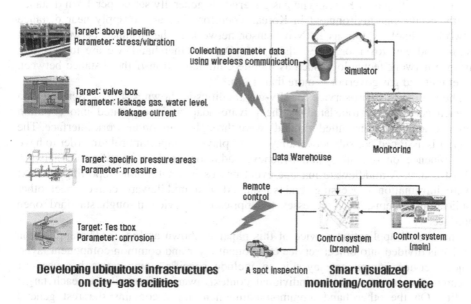

Fig. 1. Ubiquitous smart infrastructure system

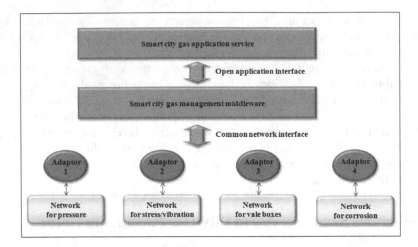

Fig. 2. The outline smart service for city gas environment

In order to send context aware information in city gas facilities, various methods may be used. Although the existing methods used wired communication such as PLC, wireless communication methods are introduced with a few benefits. Based on analysis results to measurable parameters and characteristics of city gas facilities, the facilities differ with the others on data domain characteristics, and should select the applicable wireless communication method by analyzing field status information. Actually, communication devices are already installed in specified places such as gas governor at city gas of Korea. The gas governor is generally set up per 1 km distance length in city gas environment in Korea. Therefore, we are to apply near distance network technology like as PAN or sensor network is the distance between target facility and gas governor is less than 1km. On the other hand, we are to use long distance network technology such as mobile communication if the distance between target unit and gas governor is more than 1 km.

The outline of smart service for city-gas facilities is shown as Fig. 2. Sensing data of each network are translated by the private adaptor, incorporated into common message, and then transmitted to middleware through common network interface. The adaptor is assigned per sub network layer, and plays an important role in order to have not influence on overall system whenever addition or drop specific sub network infrastructure. A middleware manage event processing, autonomic reporting, context aware information processing, and so on. Also, a middleware can connect other application systems, as it accesses to application service through standard open interface.

The overall application service of this paper is shown as Fig. 3. The application service is divided into object service component layer and common component layer. Object service component layer is to include specific components because our research aims to manage the individual context aware information in each target facility. On the other hand, common component layer contains the rest general components such as intelligent information, I/O, QoS, and visualization simulator. Intelligent information component can provide reporting and decision data by

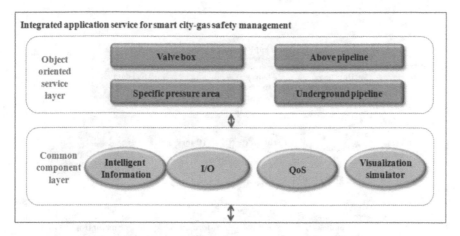

Fig. 3. Application service for smart city gas safety management

conducting analysis and prediction to the accumulated context aware and history information. QoS component is able to tune network and data quality related to intelligent service. Visualization simulator component imagines point of leakage gas on pipeline according to simulation suing cross correlation methodology. Besides the shown component, application services might include various kinds of component.

3 Design Middleware to City Gas Environment in Korea

Ubiquitous smart service to city gas environment might manage context aware information and can control their environment through heterogeneous network. To achieve the ubiquitous smart service, middleware is necessary for managing context aware information, controlling facilities, and providing applications and open API. Requirements on our middleware platform to city gas environment in Korea are followings.

- Access mechanism for diverse city gas context information: a middleware must offer access mechanisms according to the available network device and resource or application requirements such as data, condition, and location in heterogeneous environments.
- Management of meta information: a middleware might recognize totally meta information to the relevant network in order to operate satisfactorily application layer.
- Device control mechanism on sub network layer: the one of goals in ubiquitous smart service is control of the devices that are composed of sub heterogeneous network. Therefore, a middleware has technical mechanism to realize interactive controllable device.
- Abstraction to heterogeneous network: a middleware might provide system mechanism to simplify various network interfaces and hardware. Also, these mechanisms are able to support framework based on integrated information.

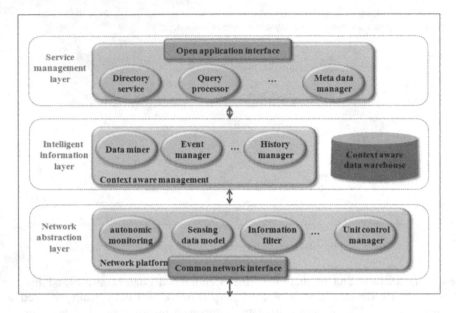

Fig. 4. Middleware for smart city gas environment

- The efficient management of context aware information: context aware information may create continuously in smart service to city gas environment. A middleware can provide the diverse view using very large information, such as the efficient store and access of information to protect excessive resource consumption problems, the definition of the ability and rule to create new information, knowledge service to merge dynamically the separated information, and easy incremental deployment to search the stored information.
- Architectural independence: One of the most elementary requirements for middleware systems is platform/hardware independence in heterogeneous environments. The network architecture modification in sub network level does not exert influence on middleware level.
- High level modeling in middleware layer: A platform must support the modeling of complex context aware information in order to generalize context information architecture. Furthermore, the modeling can be shown consistent and easy view to user according to hide the details in sub network.

Fig. 4 shows middleware for smart city gas management. The middleware is made up of network abstraction layer, intelligent information layer, and service management layer.

The network abstraction layer provides independency to various sub heterogeneous network by providing consistent common interface platform. The major components are shown table 1. The layer should be interacted each individual adaptor for heterogeneous sub network.

Table 1. The major components of network abstraction layer

Component	Description
Sensing data model	Each adaptor can support the standard message to common interface platform using pre-defined profile, as this component translates various message format data into the united message information
Autonomic monitoring	This component monitor heterogeneous network resource and device, detect change of resource and device, and inform changed information to intelligent information layer on real time
Unit control	If the control is needed by command of application service and autonomic monitoring, this component control sub network device and resource. In this case, adaptor can be able to translate message and command of the appropriate sub network

The intelligent information layer must store all related information to data warehouse, manage all information, and evolve intellectualization using data mining methodologies. Using data mining methodologies is able to display autonomic risk analysis and prediction. The key features of this layer are shown Table 2.

Table 2. The key components of intelligent information layer

Component	Description
Data warehouse	This component supports framework of information service that can preserve intact very large information. Also, this component provide context aware information model in order to associate among the related information.
Context information	This component conceptualize context aware data in sub network as the upper level information, and deliver the upper level context aware information to application service according to scenario and modeling
History and Event	This component processes, detects and analyzes complex events that might be created for many hours.
Data Mining	The first feature is detecting abnormal status and the second is prediction. The abnormal status can be detected by modifying classification, clustering and association algorithms using the stored information e data warehouse. These results are able to predict risk and life to resources in sub network.

The service management layer ought to deal with all interaction between middleware and service by means of supplying the standard application interface. The major functions of this layer are shown Table 3. Especially, because this layer plays a bridge role to requirements application service, it includes high-end components.

Table 3. The key components of intelligent information layer

Component	Description
Meta data	The management of meta data can register update and search meta data in sub network/middleware. The kinds of meta data are static and dynamic. The static data is sub network name, location, communication status, and so on, while the dynamic data is network resource, power, resource error status, and so on.
Query	This component process query of application service and deliver until network abstraction layer through intelligent information layer. Also, This returns the query result to application service.
Security	This component provides authentication and authorization for service security.
Directory	This component use related results of context-awareness, event, history information to user requirements

4 Conclusions

Applying ubiquitous technologies to specific industry facilities must design the applicable infrastructure through analyzing characteristics of the surrounding environment, and require essentially smart service architecture for enhancing the safety and reliability. Key features of smart service are the high the dynamism and heterogeneity of their environments and the need for context awareness. To cope with these features, ubiquitous smart services might rely on middleware platforms.

In general, middleware platforms manage interaction between application layer and distributed low-level layer. Besides the legacy middleware function, middleware platforms for ubiquitous must need various requirements such as access mechanism, control mechanism, abstraction to heterogeneous sub network, the high level modeling, and management of meta information and context awareness.

This paper designed ubiquitous smart service platform for enhancing the safety and reliability to city gas facilities in Korea. Firstly, we explained the outline of ubiquitous smart service on city gas environments. This service architecture is divided by four different sub network, adaptor, middleware, and application. Adaptor plays an important role in order to have not influence on overall system whenever addition or drop sub network. The middleware manages and incorporates all related messages.

Next, we proposed the roles of application service for city gas environment on two layers such as object service component and common component layer. The object service component layer manages the individual context aware information in each target facility. The common component layer contains general components.

Finally, we derived seven requirements for middleware platform to city gas facilities, and evolved middleware platform for smart city gas management. This middleware is made up of network abstraction layer, intelligent information layer, and service management layer. The network abstraction layer provides independency to various sub heterogeneous network by providing consistent common interface platform. The intelligent information layer manages all information and evolves intellectualization using data mining. The service management layer deals with interaction between middleware and service by means of supplying the open application interface.

The object of this paper will support cornerstone in order to construct the framework of intelligent infrastructure and service for autonomic managing related facilities in Korea.

References

1. Ricardo, A.R., Markus, E., Thiago, S.S.: Middleware for Ubiquitous Context-Awareness. In: Proceedings of the 6th International workshop on Middleware for Pervasive and ad-hoc Computing, Belgium, pp. 43–48 (2008)
2. Srisathapornphat, C., Jaikaeo, C., Shen, C.: Sensor Information Networking Architecture and Applications. IEEE Personal Communications 8(4), 52–59 (2001)
3. Culler, D.E., Hong, W.: Wireless Sensor Networks. Communications of the ACM 47(6), 30–33 (2004)
4. Llays, D.: Handbook of Sensor Networks: Concept Wireless and Wired Sensing System. CRC, Boca Raton (2005)
5. Akyidiz, F., Su, W., Sankara, Y.: A Survey on Sensor Network. IEEE Communication Magazine 40(8), 102–114 (2002)
6. Lopes, F., Delicato, F.C., Batista, T., Pires, P.F.: Context-based Heterogeneous Middleware Integration. In: Proceedings of the International workshop on Middleware for Ubiquitous and Pervasive Systems, Ireland, pp. 13–18 (2009)
7. Held, G.: Data over Wireless Networks Bluetooth, WAP, and Wireless LANS. McGraw-Hill, New York (2001)
8. Wang, H., Zhang, Y., Cao, J.: Ubiquitous Computing Environments and Its Usage Access Control. In: Proceedings of the First International Conference on Scalable Information System, Hong Kong, pp. 1–10 (2006)
9. Krco, S., Tsiatsis, V., Matusikova, K.: Mobile Network Supported Wireless Sensor Network Services. In: Proceedings of the IEEE International Conference on Mobile Adhoc and Sensor Systems, Italy, pp. 1–3 (2007)
10. Oh, J.S., Park, J.S., Kwon, J.R.: Selecting the Wireless Communication Methods for Establishing Ubiquitous City-Gas Facilities in Korea. In: Park, J.H., et al. (eds.) ISA 2009. LNCS, vol. 5576, pp. 823–828. Springer, Heidelberg (2009)

Website Evaluation of International Tourist Hotels in Taiwan

Yu-Shan Lin

Department of Information Science and Management System, National Taitung University,
Taiwan
YSL@nttu.edu.tw

Abstract. The policy of allowing Chinese tourists to visit Taiwan is estimated
to contribute twenty percent growth of occupancy rate. Therefore, hotel industry
is the beneficiary in this hot wave. How to seize the opportunity and promote
through the Internet becomes the most important issue of hotel industry in
Taiwan. The objective of this study is to analyze website contents of
international tourist hotels, that is to say, to figure out what information
websites offer to browsers. The research objects are 63 hotel websites. The
content analysis is used to analyze the website contents in terms of site design
(interactivity, navigation, and functionality) and site marketing characteristics
on the Internet. The findings provide a better modification direction for hotel
industry, and hope their websites can achieve the maximum marketing effect.

Keywords: Internet marketing, Website of international tourist hotels, Website
design, Website evaluation, Content analysis.

1 Introduction

The internet represents a significant change in the business and marketing model in
overall industries. At the same time users' habits are also changed. Users become
faithless because they can easily obtain similar products or services on the internet. A
high quality hotel website can provide detail information and users don't need to
contact the hotel through travel agencies or traditional methods, such as telephone,
fax, etc. Past research found that a significantly higher proportion of those who visited
the destination marketing organizations (DMO) Web sites actually went to the
destinations, and they also had a higher intention rate to return for future trips [1].
This shows that plentiful content websites have guiding function for users and help to
promote users' royalty because online browsers are often latent online purchasers [2].
When tourists get information more and more conveniently, the tailor-made website
can not only publicize hotel and set up the brand image but also let tourists easily
understand hotel facilities, reservation matters, nearby scenic spots information, and
etc. Hotels can promote the reputation and strengthen competition power by means of
tourists searching related travel messages. Even hotels can find the latent customers
out and acquire business benefits from the process. Building website is just the first
step to enter e-commerce. How to attract browser's attention let them stay in the
websites and become the actual hotel customers are the most important goals. In order

D. Ślęzak et al. (Eds.): UNESST 2009, CCIS 62, pp. 98–103, 2009.
© Springer-Verlag Berlin Heidelberg 2009

to understand the present situation of international tourist hotels, the main purpose of this study is to investigate the website content difference among hotels. It's the concerned point that the contents and functions of hotel websites could meet and satisfy customers' need or not.

2 Literature Review

Recently, some researchers study on related topics about hotel websites. Although variables, dimensions or research methods may have differences, it can be seen that the issue is highly valued.

Abdinnour-Helm and Chaparro used Balanced Usability Checklist (BUC) to evaluate the usability of ten Palestinian hotel websites. The BUC includes four dimensions, user friendliness, attractiveness, marketing effectiveness, and technical aspects of a website [3]. Hashim, Murphy, and Law proposed a framework for evaluating hotel websites. They found five dimensions of website quality — information and process, value added, relationships, trust, and design and usability — reflected by 74 websites features [4]. Baloglu and Pekcan analyzed the websites of a select group (4- and 5-star) of hotels in Turkey in terms of site design characteristics (interactivity, navigation, and functionality) and site marketing practices on the Internet [5]. Law and Hsu examined online browsers and online purchasers of international hotel Website on their perceived importance level of specific dimensions and attributes on hotel Websites. The dimensions included facilities information, reservations information, contact information, surrounding area information, website management [2]. Zafiropoulos and Vrana proposed six information dimensions to evaluate Greek hotel websites, facilities information, reservation/price information, guest contact information, surrounding area information, management of the website, and company profile [6]. Yeung and Law evaluated websites of all members of the Hong Kong Hotels Association (HKHA) through five dimensions, including language, layout and graphics, information architecture, user interface and navigation, and general [7]. Chung and Law presented an information quality evaluation model for measuring the performance of hotel websites. The model consists of five major hotel website dimensions, including facilities information, customer contact information, reservations information, surrounding area information, and management of websites [8]. Wan evaluated the web sites of international tourist hotels and tour wholesalers in Taiwan. The evaluation system consists of three user criteria: user interface, variety of information and online reservation [9].

Although there are lots of researches about hotel websites evaluation, no study proposes an integrated website information content framework with highly marketing effectiveness, especially for Taiwan local hotel websites. Therefore, the study hopes to make full exploration about this issue.

3 Methodology

Because the hotel star system is not put into practice, Taiwan tourism bureau classify hotels into four levels, international tourist hotels, tourist hotels, inns, and B & B. International tourist hotels are chosen as research objectives because their website building should be more complete than the other hotel levels. The research objectives are obtained from list of hotels on executive information system of tourism bureau ministry of transportation and communications. There are 63 international tourist hotels.

In this study, we use content analysis to evaluate 63 websites of international hotels in Taiwan objectively and systematically based on hotel owners' views. The evaluation criteria refer to the dimension addressed by Benckendorff and Black [10] and Baloglu and Pekcan [5]. The items include site design characteristic (interactivity, navigation, and functionality) and site marketing characteristic. To avoid bias from subjective evaluation, every website is evaluated by two graduate students majoring in Information Management. They evaluate independently first. When finishing the work, their results are compared. If there is any different evaluation, they must re-evaluate together to acquire a common consensus.

4 Findings

After analyzing the website content, we found that online communication with customers is apparently not enough. All websites list their phone number and address, but welcome page or each page which clearly list E-mail is less than 50%. Browsers need to click several pages and then get the E-mail of hotel. For online users, the use of E-mail is the same as telephone. Once browsers have problems about the accommodation or service anytime, they would choose E-mail or online information request form as communication tool first. Hotels which value customers' comments and offer online information request form are around 60%. The websites offering online information request form tend to not list E-mail. It is convenient to manage, but confine the browsers' choices. If the request form can't work, the communication channel will be obstructed and potential customers will be lost insidiously. Due to the need of management by dedicated person and immediately reply, there are three hotel websites offer the function of online guest book. It seems that hotels are still used to the traditional communication way by telephone, and inactive towards the online interaction. Nowadays the MSN and SKYPE are in widespread use, and there are five hotel websites provide the online customer service system (Skype or web call). As to

Table 1. Site design characteristics-Interactivity

Site design characteristics-Interactivity	Number	Percentage (%)
Phone number clearly listed	63	100
Address clearly listed	63	100
E-mail clearly listed(homepage or each page)	29	46
E-mail hyperlink	32	50.8
Online information request form	38	60.3
Calendar (special holidays)	0	0
Updated exchange rate	2	3.2
Online survey	2	3.2
Online comment form	36	57.1
Online guest book	3	4.8

Table 2. Site design characteristics-Navigation

Site design characteristics-Navigation	Number	Percentage (%)
Links to other sites (travel information, etc.)	22	34.9
Links to other departments (restaurant, bar, etc.)	62	98.4
Consistent navigation	60	95.2
Ease of navigation	63	100
www links (hyperlinks)	38	60.3
Index page	62	98.4
Search capabilities	6	9.5

Table 3. Site design characteristics-Functionality

Site design characteristics-Functionality	Number	Percentage (%)
Clear corporate identity	63	100
Clear background color	61	96.8
Light background Image	62	98.4
Video	11	17.5
Audio (speech sound or music)	16	25.4
Date last updated or news not overdue	58	92.1
Banner advertisement	6	9.5
Not have to scroll down on first page	29	46
Download facilities	24	38.1
Ease of download	19	30.2
Hot news	58	92.1
Variety of information	26	41.3
Detailed information	27	42.9
Multilanguage	56	88.9
Flash animation	57	90.5
Ease of access to website (loading time of first page <10s)	57	90.5

the online survey, websites of some chain hotels are too complicated to search for browsers and there are just three hotels provide the survey function. No websites offer the calendar for special festivals, and most of them show the sale messages in latest news. Only two websites have exchange rate information through links to bank website.

Then, we discuss about the navigation. Most websites don't provide search function; even though offering consistent navigation and index page for browsers to enter pages what he/she wants, browsers still can't quickly find webpage they need. There are 34.9% websites offering links to other sites. Most websites don't want browsers leave their websites, so they just supply related travel information to introduce nearby scenic spots and choose not to link websites with detail travel information.

Following is functionality. As to the language interface, about 90% of international tourist hotels provide English webpages. Secondly 78% have Japanese webpages. Hotels offering simplified Chinese increase gradually in response to opening up mainland Chinese tourists to Taiwan. Seven hotels only provide traditional Chinese

Table 4. Site marketing characteristics

Site marketing characteristics	Number	Percentage (%)
Hotel Picture	62	98.4
Room Picture	63	100
Good quality of pictures	60	95.2
Good quality of text	60	95.2
Promotion information	62	98.4
Description of product and services	49	77.8
Location map of the hotel	59	93.7
Online payment	49	77.8
Online Reservation	55	87.3
Reservation by E-mail	31	49.2
Links of travel information	42	66.7
Transparent price information	57	90.5

interface, and their internationalization aren't enough. Because of the high quality and high download speed of flash animation, homepages of most websites show in flash technique. The average download time of six websites is over suggested 10 seconds [11]. Furthermore, if the show time of flash animation is too long, browsers would lose their patience and leave websites. 41.3% websites provide various information, such as transportaion, travel maps, weather conditions, and etc. Although 42.9% websites are not varied, the information they offered is exhaustive, for example, cuisine, facilities, fees, description of other departments, etc.

Following is the site marketing characteristics. All websites provide hotel and guest room pictures. 77.8% have detailed description of product and services, such as facilities, accommodations and etc. Even eight websites have virtual reality. High quality content is one of the most important reasons for customer revisit [12]. The fly in the ointment is the fact that three websites can't be viewed normally because of neglecting maintenance. Online reservation is the main buying behavior of hotel websites. There are 55 websites (87.3%) offer the service, and 49 websites (77.8%) can let customers reserve rooms by online payment. However, it costs very much for the online payment system, and the profitability is unproportionate. Therefore, chain hotels which have self-building system seize a higher rate. About half websites use shared online reservation system to save cost, but they should take the risk of customer's go away and reserve other hotel rooms. To avoid losing customers and save cost, seven websites use packaged system, that is, the same interface but no homepage of shared system appeared. It avoids the risk of customer's transferring to other hotels. Besides online reservation, parts of hotels also offer online shopping for other merchandise, such as spare parts, dining reservation and etc. Some hotels proceed to make strategic alliance with other industry, tour packages of nearby scenic spots for example. The way may open business chance through attracting different customers as compared with travel agencies.

5 Conclusion and Future Research

Generally speaking, international tourist hotels get great performance on site marketing characteristics. Obviously they build up websites for marketing purpose.

However, on the aspect of site design characteristics, hotels should put more effort and strengthen some important parts.

Website must be customer-orientation. What information is browsers want to understand and acquire? If the information can be displayed in a more attractive way and evoke the interest of browsers, then the browsers is very likely to become lodgers. So, in the future we will set the research objects as general browsers. Their perceptions about the site design and site marketing characteristics will be investigated. At the same time, their experiences and satisfaction of browsing international tourist hotel websites will be examined. At last, compare results of two stages together, namely, compare website contents offered by tourist hotels and important information required by consumers. The objective is to analyze the difference between them. The findings will be expected to provide a better modification direction for hotel industry, and hope their websites will achieve the maximum marketing effect.

Acknowledgments. The author would like to thank the National Science Council of the Republic of China, Taiwan for financially supporting this research under Contract No. NSC 97-2410-H-143-015-.

References

[1] So, S., Morrison, A.: Destination Marketing Organizations' Web Site Users and Nonusers: A Comparison of Actual Visits and Revisit Intentions. Information Technology & Tourism 6(3), 129–139 (2003)

[2] Law, R., Hsu, C.: Importance of Hotel Website Dimensions and Attributes: Perceptions of Online Browsers and Online Purchasers. Journal of Hospitality & Tourism Research 30(3), 295–312 (2006)

[3] Abdinnour-Helm, S., Chaparro, B.S.: A Balanced Usability Checklist Approach to Evaluate Palestinian Hotel Websites. The Electronic Journal on Information Systems in Developing Countries 31(2), 1–12 (2007)

[4] Hashim, N.H., Murphy, J., Law, R.: A Review of Hospitality Website Design Frameworks. In: Proceedings of the International Conference in Ljubljana, Slovenia (2007)

[5] Baloglu, S., Pekcan, Y.: The Website Design and Internet Site Marketing Practices of Upscale and Luxury Hotels in Turkey. Tourism Management 27(1), 171–176 (2006)

[6] Zafiropoulos, C., Vrana, V.: A Framework for the Evaluation of Hotel Websites: The Case of Greece. Information Technology & Tourism 8, 239–254 (2006)

[7] Yeung, T.A., Law, R.: Evaluation of Usability: A Study of Hotel Web Sites in Hong Kong. Journal of Hospitality & Tourism Research 30(4), 452–473 (2006)

[8] Chung, T., Law, R.: Developing a Performance Indicator for Hotel Websites. International Journal of Hospitality Management 22(1), 119–125 (2003)

[9] Wan, C.S.: The Web Sites of International Tourist Hotels and Tour Wholesalers in Taiwan. Tourism Management 23, 155–160 (2002)

[10] Benckendorff, P., Black, N.: Destination Marketing on the Internet: A Case Study of Australian Regional Tourism Authorities. Journal of Tourism Studies 11(1), 11–21 (2000)

[11] Nielsen, J.: The Need for Speed [Web document]. Retrieved from the World Wide Web (1997), http://www.useit.com/alertbox/9703a.html

[12] Rosen, D.E., Purinton, E., Lloyd, S.J.: Web Site Design: Building a Cognitive Framework. Journal of Electronic Commerce in Organizations 2(1), 15–28 (2004)

Design of U-Healthcare Service System Based on Personalized Model in Smart Home

Jong-Hun Kim[1], Kyung-Yong Chung[2], Kee-Wook Rim[3], Jung-Hyun Lee[1],
Un-Gu Kang[4], and Young-Ho Lee[4]

[1] Dept. of Computer Science Engineering, Inha University, [2] School of Computer
Information Engineering, Sangji University, [3] Dept. of Computer and Information Science,
Sunmoon University, [4] Dept. of Information Technology, Gachon University of Medicine and
Science, Korea
ddcome@korea.com, dragonhci@hanmail.net, rim@sunmoon.ac.kr,
jhlee@inha.ac.kr, {ugkang, leeyh}@gachon.ac.kr

Abstract. U-Healthcare provides healthcare and medical services, such as prevention, diagnosis, treatment, and follow-up services whenever and wherever it is needed, and its ultimate goal is to improve quality of life. This study defines the figure of U-Healthcare personalized services for providing U-Healthcare personalized services and proposes a disease-based personalized model. Also, this study performs a design for an upper level architecture in pilot services under smart home environments. This system is designed to mutually operate it with various environments and sensors/devices through exchanging Soap and XML.

Keywords: Personalization, U-Healthcare, Ubiquitous, Smart Home.

1 Introduction

In recent years, interests in health have been increased according to changes in life styles and environments including aging. Also, interests in U-Healthcare [1], which monitor one's health condition and provide specialized healthcare services whenever and wherever it is needed, have been increased. The U-Healthcare stands for Ubiquitous [2] Healthcare and that provides healthcare services using remote medical technologies without any limitations in time and space. However, the conventional U-Healthcare systems shows a lack in extensibility and device dependency and some troubles in the support of customized information based on personal context information.

Thus this study designs a customized U-Healthcare service system. Also, this study defines a personalized U-Healthcare service for providing personalized services and proposes an environment and disease-based personalized model.

The U-Healthcare personalized service system was designed as an Agent-based system by considering various environments and distributed processing systems. In addition, it is possible to analyze personal and context information through a data analysis module and operate it with various devices through establishing a Home Server using Open Service Gateway Initiative (OSGi) middleware.

D. Ślęzak et al. (Eds.): UNESST 2009, CCIS 62, pp. 104–111, 2009.

2 Related Work

2.1 U-Healthcare System

U-Healthcare means a system that can monitor bio-information in real-time using certain devices and mobile equipments in a home network and provide medical examination and treatment whenever and wherever it is needed through linking it to hospitals and doctors automatically.

U-Healthcare can be classified as sensing, monitoring, analyzing, and alert according to the role in a system. The sensing plays a role in the sense of the physical and chemical changes in patients. The monitoring is a step that first processes the measured bio-information and plays a role in the verification of patients' information in real-time. The analyzing is a step that obtains some information from the collected data and plays a role in the figuration of the state of patients. The alert plays a role in the notification of related information to users based on the obtained information.

The characteristics of the U-Healthcare can be summarized as fast medical services, disease prevention, central processing of bio-data management, distribution of diagnosis, and management of aged, handicapped, and isolated persons. Fast medical services actively deal with bad conditions in patients by monitoring the state of patients.

2.2 Open Service Gateway Initiative (OSGi)

OSGi is an organization that establishes standards on the transmission of multi-services that independently home networks and information domestic appliances through access networks by defining network technology and common open architecture structures. OSGi was founded on March 1999, consisted of 15 businesses, and was expanded to include more than 50 software, hardware, and service provider companies.

OSGi is a nonprofit organization that not only defines the API between middlewares and application programs but also plays a role in the separation between specified application programs and middlewares. Standards established by OSGi provide dynamic services for devices with small capacity memories using the platform independence of Java and network mobility of execution codes. In particular, it is an open architecture network technology that can support various network techniques, such as Bluetooth, Home Audio/Video Interoperability (HAVi), Home Phoneline Networking Alliance (PNA), Home Radio Frequency (RF), Universal Serial Bus (USB), Video Electronics Standards Association (VESA), and other networks. It also provides management and connection functions for most products. These include set-top boxes, cable modems, routers, warning systems, power management systems, domestic appliances, and PCs, in which the Java based gateway consists of Java environments, service frameworks, device access management functions, and log services that include the connection technology for these elements when access and new services are required. The OSGi service platform displayed in Fig. 1 consists of the OSGi framework and standard services.

Three major entities of the OSGi are Service, Bundle, and Framework. Service includes Java interfaces that perform specific functions, actually implements objects,

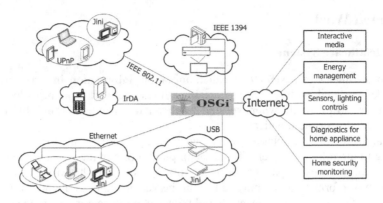

Fig. 1. The Overview of OSGi

and is a component that is accessed through a predefined service interface. A single application can be configured through the cooperation of several services and is able to request services during run-time. Bundle is a functional distribution unit that provides services. Framework is an execution environment that manages the life cycle of the Bundle. Bundle is a service set and a component unit that uses the service registered in service registries. The implementation of Service can be performed physically, distributed, and sent to the Framework through the Bundle in logical units. Bundle exists as JAR files. A JAR file includes more than one service implementation object, resource files, and manifest files. The manifest file represents the service provided by each Bundle and other services that are used to implement Bundle. Finally, Bundle can be implemented or terminated using the Start and Stop function in the Framework.

3   Personalized Model for U-Healthcare Service

3.1   U-Healthcare Personalized Service

U-Healthcare services provide medical and healthcare services continuously and generally for the "healthy life" of customers through active participation and cooperation in all members employed in industries based on wire and wireless IT technologies through merging it to other advanced technologies. In addition, personalization is a service that provides static and dynamic information from the customers who are similar to users themselves according to the personality in order to satisfy the requirements of customers.

Therefore, the U-Healthcare personalized service can be defined as a service that provides the U-Healthcare service adapted to users by analyzing and learning current situation, behavior, tendency, preference, and bio-information in a ubiquitous service environment.

3.2   Disease Model

For managing diabetes it is necessary to recommend proper foods and its amount and control it for avoiding foods, which include lots of sugars, and maintaining a normal

Table 1. Blood Pressure Stages

BP Stages	Systolic (mmHg)	Diastolic (mmHg)
Normal	<120	<80
High Normal	120-139	80-89
Stage 1	140-159	90-99
Stage 2 & 3	≥160	≥100

glucose level and body weight of patients in order to prevent and delay of complications. Also, because excessive exercises cause low glucose shock for patients, it is necessary to control the proper type of exercise and its strength through advise with a doctor about the exercise. The management of low blood sugar is that the glucose level represents lower than 70mg/dl due to the insufficient sugar, overdose of insulin, excessive taking oral blood pressure depressants, and excessive exercises. If the blood sugar is not to be increased as soon as possible in this case, some treatments that include applying some sugar water, sugar, or other foods are to be applied to patients unless patients will show stupor or coma.

It is important to control diet in high blood pressure. A recommendation for the diet excludes some foods with much salt and prohibits instant foods in order to reduce sodium, which is the major factor to increase such blood pressure. It is necessary to always remind the important of reducing sodium. Also, excessive exercises affect the high blood pressure negatively, and it is necessary to select proper types of exercises through advise with a doctor and control the strength of exercises in the case of certain complications, such as heart diseases. In addition, it should be considered to properly select medicines and dose it by following the prescription of a doctor because types of medicines are varied according to complications in the high blood pressure.

It is important to follow some controls on body weight, diet, and exercise to manage and prevent obesity. For achieving these controls, patients should check their standard body weight and configure a loss level in body weight. Also, in the diet control, a proper amount of foods is to be taken excluding calories in order to complement insufficient calories through decomposition of fat mass. Thus, it is necessary to take foods with high diet fiber in order to reduce energy density and digestibility rate and provide satiation. Aerobic exercises are helpful to continuously simulate heart-lung relations as exercise therapies while it uses global muscle.

3.3 Environment Model

This study represents environmental models by grouping them through some factors, such as Location, User info., Environmental, User's health, and Material, related to environment and personalization. In the factors in these groups, sex, age, smoking, diet tendency, number of dosing in medicines, evaluation of appropriateness in exercises, and environmental information are selected as the important factors for

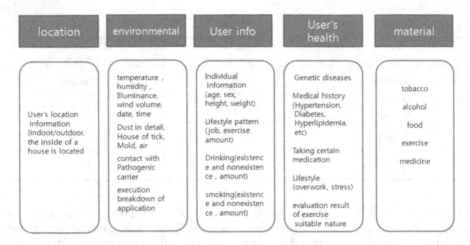

Fig. 2. Grouping of Factors related to Environment and Personalization

providing customized services for patients. Among these factors the environmental information, such as temperature, humidity, luminance, wind flow, date and time, location, and content of applications, is configured as a factor that affects the context of users.

4   System Architecture for U-Healthcare Personalized Service

A U-Healthcare personalized service transmits the bio-signal and environmental information produced from a home to a server and provides some functions, such as diet control, excise control, and well-being index, in order to improve the health of customers using the information analyzed and reasoned by personal, bio-, and environmental information in various Agents.

As illustrated in Fig. 3, the data obtained from several bio- and environmental sensors is transmitted to a server through the Vital Data Management Module and Context Factor Management Module and is to be stored in database. These two modules perform the work that changes the measured bio-signals to a standardized format before transmitting the bio-signals to the server. Such cumulated data draws well-being indexes of users through the analysis and inference of the data and will be used as basic materials for preparing customized diet and prescribing exercises to users as it is required. In addition, the results of such prescription it is to be transmitted to corresponding applications through a result transferring process by changing it to a proper format for the applications.

Regarding each module, the sensor hardware collects the bio- and environmental information of subjects periodically and provides it to the grouping of subjects, analyzing of health information/preference, and inference of environmental information/behavior as basic materials. The sensor employed in the initial stage measures bio-signals using manual ways under the recognition of subjects and transmits the results to the Vital Data Management Module through wire/wireless

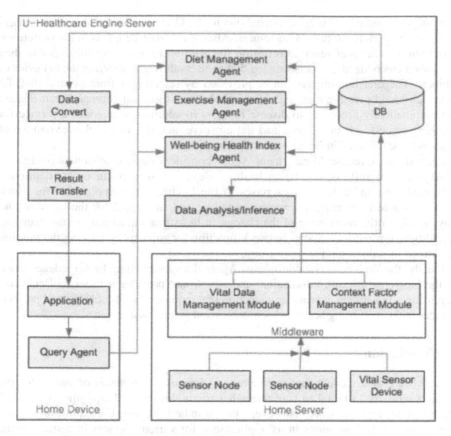

Fig. 3. System Architecture for U-Healthcare Personalized Service

means in which the environmental information is transmitted to the Context Factor Management Module by measuring it using specific periods and events automatically.

The Vital Data Management Module stores the bio-signals of subjects obtained from sensors and provides data for analyzing and grouping subjects including the inquiry of consequences in bio-signals. In addition, the Context Factor Management Module stores the environmental data measured from sensors by normalizing it and provides data for analyzing and inference the high dimensional environmental information and behavior of subjects.

Data Analysis/Inference Modules analyze the current status of subjects based on subjects' personal information and family history and produce a group using them. In the case of the early system that shows insufficient measured data, estimation can be performed using already known estimation models and that draws and applies a more precise estimation model through cumulated data. Also, this model is used to classify the environmental data as a type of high dimensional environmental information using the estimation model for customers and that leads to estimate the behavior of customers.

This system is also able to support the management of some diseases in customers through Agents. First, the Diet Management Agent considers disease models according to bio-signals and provides an optimized diet to the U-Healthcare Application for users based on the preference data of customers. Also, it can replace a loss in the preference information to the preference information for a group by grouping subjects and then provides a customized and personalized diet to users through modeling the behavior of subjects. The diet for subjects can be provided by selecting it from general diet, fat diet, high blood pressure diet, high blood cholesterol diet, and coronary heart disease diet automatically according to disease models. In addition, it provides a service for changing some foods in the diet, and the nutritive lack due to the change/remove of foods is to be reflected in the next prescription of diet.

Second, the Exercise Management Agent considers disease models according to bio-signals and reflects well-being health indexes of subjects in order to provide optimized type and amount of exercises to the U-Healthcare Application for users. Also, it is able to manage an exercise schedule and set a goal for the exercise and plays a role in the monitoring of the change in bio-signals according to the exercise. In addition, it provides a Social Network function for subjects by ranking the mission performed by subjects in the same group.

Finally, the Well-being Health Indexes Agent draws well-being health indexes based on the bio-signals, health information, and SF-36 and provides it to the U-Healthcare Application. In addition, it provides a function that inquiries data by subjects and presents changes in the well-being health index to tables and graphs on a screen.

5 Conclusion

U-Healthcare is a method that maintains and improves the status of health for the subjects who are to be taken care through various devices and equipments installed around their environments. However, the standard of the U-Healthcare service represents certain limitations in its applications for various devices in a smart home due to the lack of a standard service platform. Also, it is not easy to get some specific personalized and customized services because the healthcare services have been conducted based on clinical manners.

This study defines the U-Healthcare personalized service and draws a personalized model that is configured by disease and environmental models. The service system consists of Home Server, U-Healthcare engine server, and Home Device. The Home Server supports various sensors using OSGi middleware, and applications in the Home Device requires information to the engine server through the Query Agent and make outputs by receiving information from it. The U-Healthcare engine server is a core part of the U-Healthcare service and plays a role in analyzing data and transmitting various health information to applications based on various formats.

In future studies, this study will achieve the sections of data analysis and inference for an advanced level and investigate a service method of U-Healthcare personalized services.

Acknowledgement

"This research was supported by the MKE(Ministry of Knowledge Economy), Korea, under the ITRC(Information Technology Research Center) Support program supervised by the IITA(Institute of Information Technology Advancement)" (IITA-2009-C1090-0902-0020).

References

1. Lee, H.S.: IBM U-Healthcare. In: Tutorial of Database Technology for U-Healthcare Bio Medical Industry, Proc. KISS Spring Tutorial, pp. 49–62 (2006)
2. Weiser, M.: The Computer for the Twenty-first Century. Scientific American 265(3), 94–104 (1991)
3. Rodriuez, M., Favela, J.: A Framework for Supporting Autonomous Agents in Ubiquitous Computing Environments. In: CICESE, Ensenada, Mexico (2002)
4. Gu, T., Pung, H.K., Zhang, D.Q.: A service-oriented Middleware for Building Context-aware Services. Journal of Network and Computer Applications, 1–18 (2005)
5. Gong, L.: A Software Architecture for Open Service Gateways. IEEE Internet Computing 5(1), 64–70 (2001)
6. Bellavista, P., Corradi, A., Stefanelli, C.: Mobile Agent Middleware for Mobile Computing. IEEE Computer 34(3) (March 2001)
7. Liu, T., Martonosi, M.: Impala: A Middleware System for Managing Autonomic, Parallel Sensor Systems. In: ACM SIGPLAN Symp. Principles and Practice of Parallel Programming (June 2003)
8. Moreno, A., Garbay, C.: Software agents in healthcare. Artificial Intelligence in Medicine 27, 229–232 (2003)
9. Mikkelsen, G., Aasly, J.: Concordance of information in parallel electronic and paper based patient records. International Journal of Medical Informatics 63, 123–131 (2001)
10. Weiss, G.: Multi-agent systems. A modern approach to Distributed Artificial Intelligence (1999)
11. http://www.goliving.co.kr/prevention
12. http://www.hidoc.co.kr/HealthPedia
13. http://neps.welltizen.com/home/index.asp

Business-Oriented SOA Test Framework Based on Event-Simulating Proxy*

Youngkon Lee

e-Business Department, Korea Polytechnic University,
2121 Jeongwangdong, Siheung city, Korea
yklee777@kpu.ac.kr

Abstract. This paper presents an implementation case study for business-centric SOA test framework. The reference architecture of SOA system is usually layered: business process layer, service layer, and computing resource layer. In the architecture, there are so many subsystems to affect system performance, moreover they relate with each other. As a result, in the respect of overall performance, it is usually meaningless to measure each subsystem's performance separately. In SOA system, the performance of the business process layer with which users keep in contact depends on the summation of the performance of the other lower layers. Therefore, measuring performance of the business layer includes indirect measurement of the other SOA system layers. We devised a business-centric SOA test framework in which activities and control primitives in business process managers are simulated to invoke commands or services in a test scenario. That is, in the test framework, a real business process scenario can be replaced to a mimicked business process test scenario, which is executed in a test proxy based on event mechanism. In this paper, we present the concept of BPA (Business Process Activity) simulation, 2-layered test suites model, and reference architecture.

Keywords: SOA, BPA, test suites, event-driven.

1 Introduction

Service Oriented Architecture (SOA) is generally defined as a business-centric IT architectural approach that supports integrating businesses as linked, repeatable business tasks, or services [1]. SOA enables to solve integration complexity problem and facilitates broad-scale interoperability and unlimited collaboration across the enterprise. It also provides flexibility and agility to address changing business requirements in lower cost and time to market via reuse.

SOA has a lot of promises of interoperability, however, at the cost of: lack of enterprise scale QoS, complex standards which are still forming, lack of tools and framework to support standards, and perform penalty. Recently, as SOA has been

---

* This test framework has been implemented in an e-Government project sponsored by KIEC(Korea Institute of Electronic Commerce).

D. Ślęzak et al. (Eds.): UNESST 2009, CCIS 62, pp. 112–122, 2009.

widely adopted in business system framework, performance issues in SOA are raised continuously from users and developers.

SOA system is generally composed of various subsystems, each of which relates intimately with others. Therefore, if performance issues are raised, it's very difficult to find out clearly what's the reason. For example, if a business process in SOA system has longer response time than before, there could be various reasons: cache overflow in a business processor, wrapping overhead in service interface, or exceptions in computing resources, etc. One thing clear is that the performance of business process layer depends on the lower layer and measuring the performance of business layer includes indirect measuring the performance of all the lower layers. But, most test frameworks developed until now focus on measuring SOA messaging performance, as we present in section 2. They almost adopt batch-style testing where all the test cases are executed in a sequence.

OMG published a standard SOA reference model, MDA (Model Driven Architecture) [2]. It is widely adopted in real world because it presents normative architecture and enables SOA system to be implemented in a business-centric approach. In the MDA, a business process is designed firstly in a way for satisfying business requirements and later services are bounded to the activities in the business process. Business processes are described in a standardized language (e.g. WSBPEL) and they are executed generally on a business process management (BPM) system.

For testing SOA systems implemented according to the MDA reference model in business-centric way, test harness should have business process simulation functionality so that it may behave as BPM and at the same time test overall performance. This means that the test harness can execute business process, perform tests, and gather metric values.

We devised a new SOA test harness, **BOSET**[1], focusing on business process layer. It adopts a proxy mechanism, in which business processes and activities are simulated and executed to invoke events. The events initiate the service invocation so that the test system can gather the metric of the service performance. For the business-centric test execution, we also designed **test suite**, which is a document including structured and standardized test script. The test suite enables test harness to change its configuration flexibly according to the change of test target.

In section 2, we present some related works. Section 3 provides the principle requirement for test suite. In section 4, we describe the principle of test suite design. Section 5 presents briefly event-driven execution model and section 6 shows reference architecture for SOA test framework. Conclusions are presented in last section.

2 Related Works

There are various test frameworks and script languages developed or proposed for testing Web services systems, business processes, or business applications. This section briefs representative test systems and scripts.

---

[1] BOSET: Business Oriented SOA Execution Test Framework.

2.1 Web Services Quality Management System

This system has been developed by NIA(National Information Agency in Korea) in order to measure Web services quality on the criteria of WSQM (Web Services Quality Model) quality factors [3]: interoperability, security, manageability, performance, business processing capability, and business process quality. This system contributes to consolidate the quality factors of SOA. However, it requires expanding its architecture to apply SOA system, because it targets to only Web services system.

2.2 ebXML Test Framework

This framework has been implemented by NIST and KorBIT for testing ebXML system according to OASIS IIC Specification [4]. It could test packaging, security, reliability, and transport protocol of ebXML messaging system implemented by ebMS specification [5]. The main purpose of it is to test conformance and interoperability of ebXML messaging system, so it is not proper to test service oriented systems. Besides, it cannot test ad hoc status resulting from various events, because it is not event-driven but batch-style test framework.

2.3 JXUnit and JXU

JXUnit [6] and JXU [7] is a general scripting system (XML based) for defining test suites and test cases aimed at general e-business application testing. Test steps are written as Java classes. There is neither built-in support for business process test nor support for the event-driven features. However, as a general test scripting platform that relies on a common programming language, this system could be used as an implementation platform for general e-business test.

2.4 ATML (Automatic Test Mark-Up Language)

In its requirements, this specification provides XML Schemata and support information that allows the exchange of diagnostic information between conforming software components applications [8]. The overall goal is to support loosely coupled open architectures that permit the use of advanced diagnostic reasoning and analytical applications. The objective of ATML is focusing on the representation and transfer of test artifacts: diagnostics, test configuration, test description, instruments, etc.

2.5 Test Choreography Languages

These are standards for specifying the orchestration of business processes and/or transactional collaborations between partners. Although a markup like XPDL [9] is very complete from a process definition and control viewpoint, it is lacking the event-centric design and event correlation / querying capability required by testing and monitoring exchanges. Also, a design choice has been here to use a very restricted set of control primitives, easy to implement and validate, sufficient for test cases of modest size. Other languages or mark-ups define somehow choreographies of messages and properties: ebBP[10], WS-BPEL[11], WS-Choreography[12]. The general focus of these dialects is either the operational aspect of driving business process or business transactions, and/or the contractual aspect, but not monitoring and validation. Although they may express detailed conformance requirements, they fall short of covering the various aspects of an exhaustive conformance check e.g. the generation of intentional errors or simulation of uncommon behaviors. In addition, the focus of these languages is mainly on one layer of the choreography – they for instance ignore lower-level message exchanges entailed by quality of service concerns such as reliability, or binding patterns with the transport layer.

3   Requirements for Test Suite

Because SOA system is very complex and variable and has a number of heterogeneous subsystems, test suites including test logic and test cases should satisfy following requirements.

Event-Driven and Time-Independent Execution Model: The test script must be executable either for real-time verification or as off-line (deferred) validation over a log of the interaction. Test cases also must be able to react to all sorts of events, and correlate past events. For these reasons, all input must be captured in the form of events and wrapped into a standard event (XML) envelope. The coordination of test-case executions within a test suite is also event-driven. The state of the test case workflow is also represented as events so that no additional persistence mechanism is required by a recoverable test engine.

Protocol-Agnostic and Platform-Ubiquitous: Test script logic and control are abstracted from SOA protocols; it is versatile for messaging, business process, and business content testing regardless of technologies. Hence it can be used with either ebXML AS2 or Web Services message profiles. Of course a test case script that verifies business headers in ebXML may not apply to Web service messages, but a change in event-adapter should be the only modification needed to adapt a test script focused on verifying business transaction and payloads, from one message protocol to the other.

Adaptable Interface: In our approach, the SOA test framework should have proxy which is delegated to replace temporarily BPM system. As a result, test framework has facilities to interface seamlessly services, functions, and components. For example, we implemented a service adapter, which transforms service appearance for adapting services. There could be plug-in systems which enable module or components to be easily connected and service wrappers which encompass functions in legacy systems into service types.

Extensible Coverage of BPA Simulated: BPA set simulated in test framework should be extensible to cope with the change of BPM systems which could be test target. Each BPA simulated should follow a standardized interface for connecting services.

116   Y. Lee

4 Test Suite Design

Test suite means a document which describes the test target and test procedures. Test target is usually extracted from SOA standard specification. Test procedure could be used to control test flows. For making it easy, we designed 2-layered model for test suites: abstract test suites (**ATS**) and executable test suites (**ETS**) as shown in Figure 1. ATS describes test metadata of target expressed in test assertions and procedure and ETS describes executable test steps in the format of test execution language.

A test assertion is a testable or measurable expression for evaluating the adherence of part of an implementation to a normative statement in a specification. There is always a need to make explicit the relationship between a test assertion and the precise part of the specification to which it applies.

Test procedure describes test flow composed of a series of test activities which are simulated to business process activities. It is used in a test proxy, which is delegated as a process controller for test on replace of a BPM system. Test environment is a configuration description of a test harness.

ETS is a script for presenting each test step (in the other words, test case). It is independent from the SOA standard specification and domain environment but depends on the test execution model. For supporting machine and human readability, its format follows predefined XML schema and it has basic operation sets to initiate, control, and process events. Table 1 shows the basic operation sets in ETS.

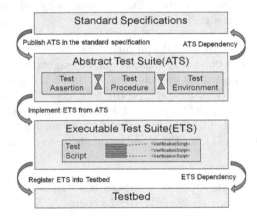

Fig. 1. BOSET Test Suit Structure

Table 1. Basic Operations in ETS

Operation type	Operation name	Description
Event operation	*post*	generate an event
	find	select event(s) from EventBoard
	mask	mask or unmask some past events to a monitor instance
Monitor flow Control	*start*	start a new instance of a monitor

Table 1. (*continued*)

	set	assign a value or an XML infoset
	sleep	suspend an instance of a monitor
	cad	check-and-do operation.
	jump	pursue the execution thread at another (labelled) test step in the monitor
External resources	call	invoke either an event-adapter or an evaluation-adapter
Test case control	actr	dynamically activate a trigger
	exit	terminate the current test case

5   Event-Driven Execution Model(EDEM)

For invoking services, we adopted event-triggering mechanism according to business process activity. The event-triggering mechanism includes following concepts:

- **Event Invocation by Simulated BP.** This means an event invocation by a business activity which is mimicked for execution in test proxy.
- **Workflow Control Based on a Thread Model.** This is embedded in the notion of Monitor, which is the basic execution unit for test cases.
- **Event-Driven Scripts.** The general control of test case execution within a test suite and of the test suite itself is represented by Triggers which define under which conditions and events an execution takes place.
- **Event Logging and Correlation.** Event management, central to BOSET, is supported by an entity called Event Board. The Event Board normally suffices for mediating all inputs to a test case, as well as outputs.
- **Messaging Gateways.** Message traffic expected in all e-Business applications, is mapped to and from events. Event-Adapters perform these mappings, allowing for abstracting test cases from communication protocol aspects.
- **Semantic Test Plug-Ins.** Agile verifications on business documents, ranging from schema validation to semantic rules over business content, are delegated to Evaluation-Adapters.

While these features may themselves be potentially complex, it has been possible in BOSET to identify a minimal set of controls sufficient for SOA testing. For example, workflow control only makes use of the simplest control primitives that have proved sufficient for test cases, not pretending to replicate the full range of workflow operators. Event correlation and querying rely on simple selection expressions based on XPath.

Based on the main concepts, the test execution model requires following components (Figure 3):

Monitor: This represents the logic of a test case. A test case may use several monitors in its definition, and a test case instance may engage the concurrent or sequential execution of several monitor instances. A monitor is a script that specifies the steps and workflow of the test case. A monitor instance is always created as the result of a start operation executed either by another monitor or by a trigger. The first monitor started for a test case (i.e. Started by a Trigger) is called root monitor for the test case. There is always a trigger at the origin of monitor(s) execution (directly or indirectly). A monitor instance can start another monitor instance concurrently to its own execution, and can activate another trigger. The outcome of a test case (pass / fail / undetermined) is determined by the final outcome of the monitor(s) implementing this test case. The execution of a monitor produces a trace that can be posted as an event.

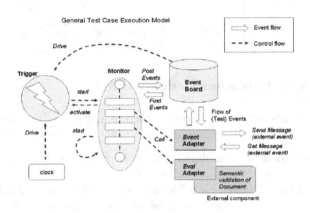

Fig. 2. Event-Driven Execution Model

Trigger: The trigger is a script that defines the event or condition that initiates the execution of the test case, i.e. the execution of a monitor. A trigger can be set to react to an event (event-watching) or to a date (clock-watching), and is associated with one or more monitors. Because a trigger initiates the execution of a test case, it is usually not considered as part of the test case itself, but part of the test suite that coordinates the execution of several test cases. A trigger is active when ready to react to events for which it has been set, and ready to trigger its associated monitors. When a trigger starts a test case, a case execution space (CES) is allocated, within which the created monitor instance as well as all subsequent dependent instances will execute. The CES defines a single scope of access to events and to other objects referred to by variables. When activated, a trigger is given to a context object, which will be part of the CES of the monitor(s) the trigger will start.

Test Suite: A test suite is a set of test cases, the execution of which is coordinated in some way. This coordination may be represented by a monitor, that will either directly start the monitors that represent individual test cases, or that will instead activate triggers that control these monitors. For example, a test suite may serialize the execution of test cases TC1 and TC2 by setting a trigger for TC2 that reacts to the event posted by TC1 at the end of its execution. Or, the test suite may set a trigger that will initiate the concurrent execution of several test cases. The following figure illustrates the structure of a test suite:

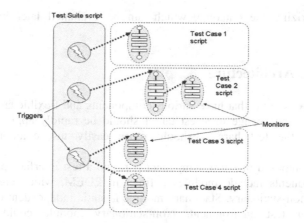

Fig. 3. Test Case Triggering

Event (or Test Event): An event is a time-stamped object that is managed by the Event Board. Events are used to coordinate the execution of a test case, and to communicate with external entities. For example an event may serve as a triggering mechanism (in event-driven triggers) for test cases, as a synchronization mechanism (e.g. a test step waiting for an event) or as a proxy for business messages, in which case the mapping between the event representation and the business message is done by an event adapter. Some events are temporary, which means they are only visible to monitors from the same test case execution (CES) and are automatically removed from the event board at the end of the CES they are associated with.

Event Board (EB): The event board provides event management functions. Events can be posted to the board, or searched. An event board can be seen as an event log that supports additional management functions. The event board is the main component with which a monitor interacts during its execution.

Event Adapter: An event adapter is a mediator between the external world and the event board. It maps external events such as message sending/receiving, to test events and vice versa. For example, an event adapter will interface with an SOA gateway so that it will convert received business messages into a test event and post it on the event board. Conversely, some events posted on the event board by a monitor can be automatically converted by the adapter into business messages submitted for sending. An event adapter can also be directly invoked by a monitor. Whether the adapter is designed to react to the posting of an event on the board or is directly invoked by the monitor, is an implementation choice. In both cases, it would convert a test event into an external action.

Evaluation Adapter: An evaluation adapter is implementing – or interfacing with an implementation of - a test predicate that requires specific processing of provided inputs that is not supported by the script language. Typically, it supports a validation check, e.g. semantic validation of a business document. An evaluation adapter is always invoked by a monitor. On invocation, an evaluation adapter returns an XML infoset summarizing the outcome, which can be evaluated later in the monitor workflow.

6 Reference Architecture

For testing SOA systems that have various components and flexible architecture, test requirement and the change in a test target should be rapidly applicable on a test harness. Thus, the test harness should reuse easily test components and be reconfigurable.

BOSET is composed of a test component part and a test interface part (Figure 4). The test components include modules defined in EDEM, which are classified as stationary and non-stationary. Stationary module is static independent of any specific standard and/or test environment. Non-stationary module could be changed dynamically according to standards or test suite designs.

Stationary test components is composed of **TMC**(Test Main Component, Test Driver) and **TCE**(Test Configuration Engine). TMC orchestrates other test components and interfaces, and consequently drives the execution of test. TCE dynamically sets up test components in accordance with a configuration profile. **TSE**(Test Sequence Engine) interprets and drives executable test steps and interacts with test other components and interfaces.

Non-stationary test components include a test service module and an interpreter. Test Service stimulates target **SUT**(System Under Test) with pre-defined actions, which include instructions at the test state. The actions could be modified or created for the test specifics. Interpreter reads the test case and then parses it into test procedure, test assertions, and configuration information. Interpreter could be modified according to test suite design.

For interaction with SUTs, test drivers, and test users, BOSET has following interfaces:

- **MEI** (Messaging Engine Interface): delivers messages to/from SUTs based on the message protocol used. i.e., ebMS engine, SOAP engine, etc.

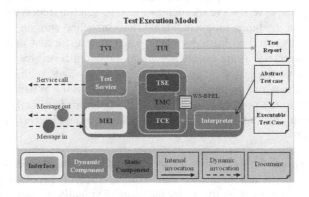

Fig. 4. Reference Architecture for EDEM

Table 2. Abstract Definition of Test Interfaces

Interface	Operation Name	Input	Output
Test Validation Interface(TVI)	Validation	Validation script and target messages	Validation result
Message Engine Interface(MEI)	Sending	Message	Message Log
	Query (Receiving)	Query Script	Message Log
Test User Interface(TUI)	Reporting	Results	Report Document

- **TVI** (Test Validation Engine): validates messages according to verification script. i.e, Xpath, Schematron, Xquery, JESS, OWL, etc.
- **TUI** (Test User Interface): provides user-interface using web or intranet. i.e, IIC web UI, WS-I UI, etc.

For interface model for Service Description, we adopted WSDL (Web Service Description Language), a standard specification. TCE discoveries and dynamically deploys interface modules in the Universal Test Module Repository. Configuration document could be registered in a registry implemented according to UDDI (Universal Description, Discovery and Integration) specification. TSE orchestrates deployed test component and interface modules. For dynamic invocation, WS-BPEL (Web Service Business Process Execution Language) primitives could be used.

7 Conclusion

We presented a SOA test framework, which has been implemented in Korea government side for testing public SOA systems. The framework facilitates to test SOA systems by introducing the concept of business activity simulated event proxy. For the framework, we also devised 2-layered test suites: abstract test suite and executable test suite. The abstract test suite describes test workflow based on a business process. The executable test suite represents test operations in detail for test case execution. This model decouples test procedure and test cases; as a result it enhances the reusability of test components. We also provide reference architecture for SOA test framework, which will be a guideline to later implementation of business-centric test framework.

References

1. Nickul, D.: Service Oriented Architecture (SOA) and Specialized Messaging Patterns. Adobe technical paper (December 2007)
2. Miller, J., Mukerji, J.: MDA Guide Version 1.0. OMG (June 2003), http://www.omg.org/docs/omg/03-06-01.pdf
3. Lee, Y., et al.: Web Services Quality Model 1.1. OASIS WSQM TC (October 2008)

4. Durand, J., et al.: ebXML Test Framework v1.0. OASIS IIC TC (October 2004)
5. Wenzel, P., et al.: ebXML Messaging Services 3.0. OASIS ebMS TC (July 2007)
6. Java XML Unit (JXUnit), http://jxunit.sourceforge.net
7. JUnit, Java for Unit Test, http://junit.sourceforge.net
8. ATML, Standard for Automatic Test Markup Language (ATML) for Exchanging Automatic Test Equipment and Test Information via XML. IEEE (December 2006)
9. XPDL: XML Process Definition Language (Workflow Management Coalition) Document Number WFMC-TC-1025: Version 1.14 (October 3, 2005)
10. OASIS, Business Process Specification Schema 1.0.1, May 2001 and ebBP, v2.0.4 (October 2006)
11. OASIS, Web Services Business Process Execution Language 2.0 (committee draft in review phase) (August 2006)
12. Web Services Choreography Description Language (WSCDL), Version 1.0 (candidate recommendation) (November 2005)

Fuzzy Identity-Based Identification Scheme

Syh-Yuan Tan[1], Swee-Huay Heng[1], Bok-Min Goi[2], and SangJae Moon[3]

[1] Faculty of Information Science and Technology, Multimedia University
Melaka, Malaysia
{sytan,shheng}@mmu.edu.my
[2] Faculty of Engineering and Science, Tunku Abdul Rahman University
Kuala Lumpur, Malaysia
goibm@utar.edu.my
[3] Mobile Network Security Technology Research Center, Kyungpook National University
Daegu, Korea
sjmoon@ee.knu.ac.kr

Abstract. We present a new type of Identity-Based Identification (IBI), namely Fuzzy Identity-Based Identification (FIBI). FIBI is an extension of traditional IBI where the identity (ID) is viewed as a set of values. In FIBI, identification is considered successful if and only if the ID set presented by the prover overlaps the verifier's ID set for certain distance metric d. The proposed scheme is secure against impersonation under passive attack based on the discrete logarithm assumption, and is secure against concurrent attack based on the one-more discrete logarithm assumption. We provide the security proof in the fuzzy selective-ID security model.

Keywords: fuzzy, identity-based, attribute-based, identification.

1 Introduction

An identification scheme assures one party (through acquisition of corroborative evidence) of both the identity of a second party involved, and that the second party was active at the time the evidence was created or acquired. Informally speaking, an identification protocol is an interactive process that enables a prover holding a secret key to identify himself to a verifier holding the corresponding public key.

The concept of identity-based (ID-based) cryptography was introduced by Shamir in 1984 [27] where the public key is the user's public identity string (e.g. email, name, ID number, etc.). A trusted third party called private key generator (PKG) is required to generate private key for every user based on their public identity. Numerous ID-based schemes have been proposed since then, such as ID-based encryption (IBE) schemes [6,4,5], ID-based signatures (IBS) schemes [21,12,7], and ID-based identification (IBI) schemes [14,1,15,16,9]. Some IBI schemes were published but there was no rigorous definition as well as security proof until the work of Kurosawa and Heng [14] and Bellare et al. [1]. Kurosawa and Heng proposed transforming any standard digital signature scheme having 3-move honest verifier zero-knowledge proof of knowledge protocol to an IBI scheme, while Bellare et al. concerned about transforming standard identification schemes to IBI.

D. Ślęzak et al. (Eds.): UNESST 2009, CCIS 62, pp. 123–130, 2009.
© Springer-Verlag Berlin Heidelberg 2009

In year 2005, Sahai and Waters introduced a new type of IBE scheme, namely Fuzzy-IBE (FIBE) [24]. In FIBE, identity is viewed as a set of descriptive attributes. FIBE allows a private key corresponding to an identity set ω to decrypt ciphertext encrypted with a public identity set ω', if and only if the identity sets ω and ω' are at least overlapped by some distance metric d. FIBE was created to serve biometric identity-based encryption which is having advantage on the uniqueness of the biometric identity. The biometric identities of every human being are distinctive and no key revocation is needed since these identities last forever [24]. However, only a few FIBE schemes appeared in the literature and it lost focus when attribute-based encryption (ABE) was introduced [23,11,3,8,29]. Sahai and Waters claimed that their FIBE is an ABE but it can only be considered as a general framework of ABE. ABE inherits the main concept of FIBE whereby the identity set is considered as an attribute set. Anyway, the application scenario is different for FIBE and ABE during encryption and decryption: FIBE uses two identity sets which belong to the same user while ABE uses two identity sets which belong to the encrypter and the decrypter respectively [11].

To the best of our knowledge, there is still no fuzzy IBI (FIBI) scheme appeared in the literature. In this paper, we combine the idea of fuzzy cryptography with identification scheme and proposed the initial idea for FIBI schemes. We provide the formal definition and security model for FIBI schemes and then proceed to propose a concrete FIBI scheme which is secure against impersonation under passive attack based on the discrete logarithm assumption, and is secure against concurrent attack based on the one-more discrete logarithm assumption. The FIBI scheme uses Schnorr identification scheme [25] as the building block and adopts the "fuzzy" technique of Sahai and Waters FIBE [24]. We view FIBI as an extension to IBI where ID in traditional IBI is now a set of ID. Therefore, traditional IBI is actually a special case of FIBI where there is only one value in the ID set.

Organization. The rest of the paper is organized as follows. We provide some preliminary background information and definitions in Section 2. In Section 3, we provide the formal model and security definition for FIBI. We present the construction of the FIBI scheme in Section 4 followed by its security proof in Section 5. Finally, we draw the conclusion in Section 6.

2   Preliminaries

2.1   Discrete Logarithm Problem

Definition 1. *Let $\mathbb{G}$ be a cyclic group with prime order q. The discrete logarithm problem is the problem of finding a given (g, g^a) with choices of $a \xleftarrow{R} \mathbb{Z}_q^*$ and $g \xleftarrow{R} \mathbb{G}$. The discrete logarithm assumption states that there is no polynomial time algorithm M with non-negligible advantage in solving the discrete logarithm problem.*

2.2   One-More Discrete Logarithm Problem (OMDLOG)

Definition 2. *Let $\mathbb{G}$ be a cyclic group with prime order q. The one-more discrete logarithm problem is described by the following game. Given (g, g^a) with choices of*

$a \xleftarrow{R} \mathbb{Z}_q^*$, $g \xleftarrow{R} \mathbb{G}$ *and has access to two oracles, namely a discrete logarithm oracle DLOG that given g^a returns a, and a challenge oracle CHALL that each time it is invoked, returns a challenge value $W \xleftarrow{R} \mathbb{G}$. Let $W_1, \ldots, W_n$ denote the challenges returned by CHALL. The one-more discrete logarithm assumption states that there is no polynomial time algorithm M with non-negligible advantage in solving the discrete logarithm problem of every values W returned by CHALL, with the restriction that the number of queries made by M to its DLOG oracle is strictly less than n.*

2.3 Lagrange Coefficient

Let $q(\cdot)$ be a random $(d-1)$-degree polynomial and $q(i) = s_i$, the polynomial $q(\cdot)$ can be reconstructed by having the knowledge of d-pair values of (i_η, s_{i_η}):

$$q(\cdot) = \sum_{\eta=0}^{d-1} s_{i_\eta} \triangle_{i_\eta, S}(\cdot)$$

where $S = \{i_0, i_1, \ldots, i_{d-1}\}$.

Definition 3. *The Lagrange coefficient $\triangle_{i,S}$ is defined as:*

$$\triangle_{i,S}(x) = \prod_{j \in S, j \neq i} \frac{x - j}{i - j}$$

where i and j are elements in the set S.

3   Fuzzy Identity-Based Identification (FIBI) Scheme

In this section, we provide the definition of FIBI scheme as well as the fuzzy selective-ID security model.

3.1   Definition

Definition 4. *A FIBI scheme $\mathcal{FIBI} = (\mathcal{S}, \mathcal{E}, \mathcal{P}, \mathcal{V})$ consists of four probabilistic polynomial time algorithms, namely, setup, extract, proving and verification (identification protocol).*

1. *Setup ($\mathcal{S}$). $\mathcal{S}$ takes as input the security parameter 1^k. It generates the master public key mpk and the master secret key msk. The master public key will be publicly known while the master secret key will be known to the PKG only.*
2. *Extract ($\mathcal{E}$). PKG takes as input mpk, msk and a public identity set ID. It runs $\mathcal{E}$ to extract a user private key upk.*
3. *Identification Protocol ($\mathcal{P}$ and $\mathcal{V}$). $\mathcal{P}$ receives as input (mpk, upk, ID) and $\mathcal{V}$ receives as input (mpk, ID'), where $|ID \cap ID'| \geq d$ and upk is the private key corresponding to the public identity set ID. $\mathcal{P}$ and $\mathcal{V}$ will run an interactive protocol which consists of the following steps:*
4. *Commitment: $\mathcal{P}$ sends a commitment CMT to $\mathcal{V}$.*

5. **Challenge:** $\mathcal{V}$ sends a challenge CH to $\mathcal{P}$
6. **Response:** $\mathcal{P}$ sends a response RSP to $\mathcal{V}$

Finally, $\mathcal{V}$ outputs a boolean decision 1 (accept) or 0 (reject) based on RSP. A legitimate $\mathcal{P}$ should always be accepted.

3.2 Security Model

In this section, we define the fuzzy selective-ID security model for FIBI. The fuzzy selective-ID security game allows the impersonator I to query user private keys for identity sets which have less than d-overlap with the target identity set.

1. **Init.** I declares the identity set ω', that it wishes to be challenged upon. Therefore, one identity set ω_i such that $|\omega_i \cap \omega'| \geq d$ will be under attack in the Phase 2 of the game.
2. **Setup.** The challenger takes as input 1^k and runs the setup algorithm $\mathcal{S}$. It gives I the resulting master public key mpk and keeps the master secret key msk to itself.
3. **Phase 1**
   (a) I issues some extract queries on $\omega_1, \omega_2, \ldots$. The challenger responds by running the extract algorithm $\mathcal{E}$ to generate the private key upk_i corresponding to the public identity set ω_i. It returns upk_i to I.
   (b) I issues some transcript queries for passive attack or some identification queries for concurrent attack on ω_i such that $|\omega_i \cap \omega'| \geq d$.
   (c) The queries in step (a) and step (b) above can be interleaved and asked adaptively. Without loss of generality, we may assume that I will not query the same ω_i that has been issued in the extract queries, through the transcript queries or identification queries again.
4. **Phase 2**
   (a) I plays the role as a cheating prover (impersonation attempt on the prover holding a challenged identity set ω_i such that $|\omega_i \cap \omega'| \geq d$), trying to convince the verifier that it knows the upk of ω_i.
   (b) I can still issue some extract queries as well as transcript queries or identification queries as in Phase 1.
   (c) I wins the game if it is successful in convincing the verifier.

Definition 5. A $\mathcal{FIBI}$ is (t, q_I, ϵ)-secure under passive (concurrent) attack if for any passive (concurrent) impersonator I who runs in time t,

$$\Pr[I \ can \ impersonate] < \epsilon$$

where I can make at most q_I extract queries.

4   Construction

Recall that we view identity as an identity set and we let d represent the error-tolerance parameter in terms of minimum overlapped set. Let k be the security paremeter and $l(\cdot) : \mathbb{N} \to \mathbb{N}$ be the super-logarithmic challenge length, the source of identities will be sets of n elements of $\mathbb{Z}_{2^{l(k)}}$. In fact, we can describe an identity set as an assortment of n strings of arbitrary length where the strings can be hashed into members of $\mathbb{Z}_{2^{l(k)}}$ using a collision-resistant hash function.

On the input of a user biometric identity set ID, PKG computes the corresponding user private key upk by binding a random $(d-1)$-degree polynomial, $q(\cdot)$ with $q(0) = t$ to the upk, where t is a component of user private key which is known to the PKG only. PKG then returns the upk (which is normally stored in a smart card) to the user.

When the user approaches a verifier for the execution of an identification, the verifier's biometric identity reader will read the user biometric identity set ID'. Take as input ID' where $|ID \cap ID'| \geq d$, the verifier will output 1 (accept) or 0 (reject) at the end of identification protocol based on the user's response RSP.

4.1 Scheme Construction

We now describe our construction in detail as follows.

Setup. On input 1^k, generate two large primes p and q of size k such that $q|(p-1)$ and an element $g \xleftarrow{R} \mathbb{Z}_p$ of order q, where g is a generator of $\mathbb{G}$, a subgroup of $\mathbb{Z}_p^*$ of order q. Choose the distance metric d and a cryptographic hash function H : $\{0,1\}^* \times \mathbb{G} \times \mathbb{G} \rightarrow \{0,1\}^{l(k)}$ for $2^{l(k)} < q$ where $l(\cdot) : \mathbb{N} \rightarrow \mathbb{N}$ is the super-logarithmic challenge length. Choose $s \xleftarrow{R} \mathbb{Z}_q$ and compute $v = g^{-s}$. Let the master public key be $mpk = (p, q, g, v, d, H)$ and the master secret key be $msk = s$ which is known to the PKG only.

Extract. Let ID be the set of n identities for some fixed n and d represent the distance metric of two identity sets. Randomly select a $(d-1)$-degree polynomial $q(\cdot)$ such that $q(0) = t \xleftarrow{R} \mathbb{Z}_q$. Compute the set $\{Y_i\} = \{q(i) + s\alpha_i\}_{i \in ID}$ and the set $\{\alpha_i\} = \{H(i, X, v)\}_{i \in ID}$ where $X = g^t$. Return the user private key as $upk = (\{\alpha_i\}, \{Y_i\})$.

Identification Protocol

1. $\mathcal{P}$ first computes $\{X_i\} = \{g^{Y_i} v^{\alpha_i}\}_{i \in ID}$. $\mathcal{P}$ next chooses $\{r_i\}_{i \in ID} \xleftarrow{R} \mathbb{Z}_q$, computes $\{x_i\} = \{g^{r_i}\}_{i \in ID}$ and sends $(\{X_i\}, \{x_i\})$ to $\mathcal{V}$.
2. $\mathcal{V}$ chooses $c \xleftarrow{R} \mathbb{Z}_{2^{l(k)}}$ and sends c to $\mathcal{P}$.
3. $\mathcal{P}$ computes $\{y_i\} = \{r_i + cY_i\}_{i \in ID}$ and sends $\{y_i\}$ to $\mathcal{V}$.
4. $\mathcal{V}$ randomly chooses $S = \{ID \cap ID'\}$ where $|S| = d$ and for every $i \in S$, $\mathcal{V}$ checks if $g^{y_i} = x_i (X_i / v^{\alpha_i})^c$ where $\{\alpha_i\} = \{H(i, X, v)\}_{i \in S}$ and $X = \prod_S X_i^{\Delta_{i,S}(0)}$.

Correctness:

$$\begin{aligned}
x_i(X_i/v^{\alpha_i})^c &= g^{r_i}(g^{Y_i} g^{-s\alpha_i}/g^{-s\alpha_i})^c \\
&= g^{r_i}(g^{Y_i})^c \\
&= g^{r_i + cY_i} \\
&= g^{y_i}
\end{aligned}$$

If the equality holds, output **1 (accept)**, else output **0 (reject)**.

5   Security Analysis

5.1   Security against Impersonation under Passive Attack

Theorem 1. *If the discrete logarithm problem is hard, then the above FIBI scheme is secure against impersonation under passive attack (imp-pa) in the random oracle model where:*

$$Adv_{FIBI}^{imp\text{-}pa} \leq \sqrt{\left(\sum_{i=0}^{d-1} \binom{n}{i} \frac{(1-q^{-1})^{n-i}}{q^i}\right)^{-q_e} \left(\sum_{i=d}^{n} \binom{n}{i} \frac{(1-q^{-1})^{n-i}}{q^i}\right)^{-1} \cdot Adv_M^{dlog}} + 2^{l(k)}$$

The proof will be given in the full version of the paper.

5.2   Security against Impersonation under Concurrent Attack

Theorem 2. *If the one-more discrete logarithm problem is hard, then the above FIBI scheme is secure against impersonation under concurrent attack (imp-ca) in the random oracle model where:*

$$Adv_{FIBI}^{imp\text{-}ca} \leq \sqrt{\left(\sum_{i=0}^{d-1} \binom{n}{i} \frac{(1-q^{-1})^{n-i}}{q^i}\right)^{-q_e} \left(\sum_{i=d}^{n} \binom{n}{i} \frac{(1-q^{-1})^{n-i}}{q^i}\right)^{-1} \cdot Adv_M^{1mdlog}} + 2^{l(k)}$$

The proof will be given in the full version of the paper.

6   Conclusion

We presented the the formal definition and security model for FIBI schemes. We also constructed a concrete and provably secure FIBI scheme in the random oracle model. The proposed scheme is secure against impersonation under passive attack based on the discrete logarithm assumption, and is secure against concurrent attack based on the one-more discrete logarithm assumption in the fuzzy selective-ID security model.

It still remains an open problem to be able to construct a FIBI that is provably secure in full security model. Besides, we observe that it is possible to develop a key-policy attribute-based identification scheme, and a verifier-policy attribute-based identification scheme from our FIBI scheme, by extending the identity set to an access structure.

Acknowledgement. This research was supported by the Ministry of Knowledge Economy (MKE) of Korea, under the ITRC support program supervised by the IITA (IITA-2008-C1090-0801-0016).

References

1. Bellare, M., Namprempre, C., Neven, G.: Security proofs for identity-based identification and signature schemes. In: Cachin, C., Camenisch, J.L. (eds.) EUROCRYPT 2004. LNCS, vol. 3027, pp. 268–286. Springer, Heidelberg (2004)

2. Bellare, M., Palacio, A.: GQ and Schnorr identification schemes: proofs of security against impersonation under active and concurrent attacks. In: Yung, M. (ed.) CRYPTO 2002. LNCS, vol. 2442, pp. 162–177. Springer, Heidelberg (2002)
3. Bethencourt, J., Sahai, A., Waters, B.: Ciphertext-policy attribute-based encryption. In: IEEE Symposium on Security and Privacy, pp. 321–334 (2007)
4. Boneh, D., Boyen, X.: Efficient selective-ID secure identity based encryption without random oracles. In: Cachin, C., Camenisch, J.L. (eds.) EUROCRYPT 2004. LNCS, vol. 3027, pp. 223–238. Springer, Heidelberg (2004)
5. Boneh, D., Boyen, X.: Secure identity based encryption without random oracles. In: Franklin, M. (ed.) CRYPTO 2004. LNCS, vol. 3152, pp. 443–459. Springer, Heidelberg (2004)
6. Boneh, D., Franklin, M.: Identity-based encryption from the Weil pairing. In: Kilian, J. (ed.) CRYPTO 2001. LNCS, vol. 2139, p. 213. Springer, Heidelberg (2001)
7. Cha, J.C., Cheon, J.H.: An identity-based signature from gap Diffie-Hellman groups. In: Desmedt, Y.G. (ed.) PKC 2003. LNCS, vol. 2567, pp. 18–30. Springer, Heidelberg (2002)
8. Cheung, L., Newport, C.: Provably secure ciphertext policy ABE. In: ACM — CCS 2007, pp. 456–465 (2007)
9. Chin, J.-J., Heng, S.-H., Goi, B.-M.: An efficient and provable secure identity-based identification scheme in the standard model. In: Mjølsnes, S.F., Mauw, S., Katsikas, S.K. (eds.) EuroPKI 2008. LNCS, vol. 5057, pp. 60–73. Springer, Heidelberg (2008)
10. Fiat, A., Shamir, A.: How to prove yourself: practical solutions to identification and signature problems. In: Odlyzko, A.M. (ed.) CRYPTO 1986. LNCS, vol. 263, pp. 186–194. Springer, Heidelberg (1987)
11. Goyal, V., Pandey, O., Sahai, A., Waters, B.: Attribute-based encryption for fine-grained access control of encrypted data. In: ACM — CCS 2006, pp. 89–98 (2006)
12. Hess, F.: Efficient identity based signature schemes based on pairings. In: Nyberg, K., Heys, H.M. (eds.) SAC 2002. LNCS, vol. 2595, pp. 310–324. Springer, Heidelberg (2003)
13. Khader, D.: Attribute based group signature with revocation, http://eprint.iacr.org/2007/241.pdf
14. Kurosawa, K., Heng, S.-H.: From digital signature to ID-based identification/signature. In: Bao, F., Deng, R., Zhou, J. (eds.) PKC 2004. LNCS, vol. 2947, pp. 248–261. Springer, Heidelberg (2004)
15. Kurosawa, K., Heng, S.-H.: Identity-based identification without random oracles. In: Gervasi, O., Gavrilova, M.L., Kumar, V., Laganá, A., Lee, H.P., Mun, Y., Taniar, D., Tan, C.J.K. (eds.) ICCSA 2005. LNCS, vol. 3481, pp. 603–613. Springer, Heidelberg (2005)
16. Kurosawa, K., Heng, S.-H.: The power of identification schemes. In: Yung, M., Dodis, Y., Kiayias, A., Malkin, T.G. (eds.) PKC 2006. LNCS, vol. 3958, pp. 364–377. Springer, Heidelberg (2006)
17. Li, J., Kim, K.: Attribute-based ring signatures, http://eprint.iacr.org/2008/394.pdf
18. Maji, H., Prabhakaran, M., Rosulek, M.: Attribute-based signatures: achieving attribute-privacy and collusion-resistance, http://eprint.iacr.org/2008/328.pdf
19. Menezes, A.J., van Oorschot, P.C., Vanstone, S.A.: Handbook of Applied Cryptography. CRC Press, Boca Raton (1997)
20. Nishide, T., Yoneyama, K., Ohta, K.: Attribute-based encryption with partially hidden encryptor-specified access structures. In: Bellovin, S.M., Gennaro, R., Keromytis, A.D., Yung, M. (eds.) ACNS 2008. LNCS, vol. 5037, pp. 111–129. Springer, Heidelberg (2008)
21. Paterson, K.G.: ID-based signatures from pairings on elliptic curves. Electronic Letters 38(18), 1025–1026 (2002)
22. Paterson, K.G., Schuldt, J.C.N.: Efficient identity-based signatures secure in the standard model. In: Batten, L.M., Safavi-Naini, R. (eds.) ACISP 2006. LNCS, vol. 4058, pp. 207–222. Springer, Heidelberg (2006)

23. Pirretti, M., Traynor, P., McDaniel, P., Waters, B.: Secure attribute-based systems. In: ACM — CCS 2006 (2006)
24. Sahai, A., Waters, B.: Fuzzy identity-based encryption. In: Cramer, R. (ed.) EUROCRYPT 2005. LNCS, vol. 3494, pp. 457–473. Springer, Heidelberg (2005)
25. Schnorr, C.P.: Efficient identification and signatures for smart cards. In: Brassard, G. (ed.) CRYPTO 1989. LNCS, vol. 435, pp. 239–252. Springer, Heidelberg (1990)
26. Shahandashti, S.F., Safavi-Naini, R.: Threshold attribute-based signatures and their application to anonymous credential systems. In: Preneel, B. (ed.) AFRICACRYPT 2009. LNCS, vol. 5580, pp. 198–216. Springer, Heidelberg (2009)
27. Shamir, A.: Identity-based cryptosystems and signature schemes. In: Blakely, G.R., Chaum, D. (eds.) CRYPTO 1984. LNCS, vol. 196, pp. 47–53. Springer, Heidelberg (1985)
28. Waters, B.: Efficient identity-based encryption without random oracles. In: Cramer, R. (ed.) EUROCRYPT 2005. LNCS, vol. 3494, pp. 114–127. Springer, Heidelberg (2005)
29. Waters, B.: Ciphertext-policy attribute-based ecnryption: an expressive, efficient, and provably secure realization, http://eprint.iacr.org/2008/290.pdf
30. Yang, P., Cao, Z., Dong, X.: Fuzzy identity based signature, http://eprint.iacr.org/2008/002.pdf
31. Yang, G., Chen, J., Wong, D.S., Deng, X., Wang, D.: A new framework for the design and analysis of identity-based identification schemes. In: Theoretical Computer Science, vol. 407, pp. 370–388. Elsevier, Amsterdam (2008)

DCNL: Disclosure Control of Natural Language Information to Enable Secure and Enjoyable E-Communications

Haruno Kataoka[1], Natsuki Watanabe[2], Keiko Mizutani[2], and Hiroshi Yoshiura[2]

[1] NTT Information Sharing Platform Laboratories, NTT Corporation,
3-9-11, Midori-cho Musashino-Shi, Tokyo 180-8585 Japan
[2] Graduate school of Electro-Communications, University of Electro-Communications,
1-5-1 Chofugaoka, Chofu, Tokyo, 182-8585 Japan
yoshiura@hc.uec.ac.jp

Abstract. Natural language communications using social networking and blogging services can result in the undesired revelation of private information. Existing disclosure control is tedious and error-prone because the user must set the disclosure level manually and must reconsider the level every time a new text is to be uploaded. This can lead to the revelation of private information or reduced enjoyment of the communication due to either disclosing too much text or hiding text that is meant to be shared. To solve these problems, we are developing a new disclosure control mechanism called DCNL or disclosure control of natural language information. DCNL automatically checks texts uploaded to social networking services or blog pages, detects words that might reveal private information, and warns the user about them. The granularity of DCNL is not the text but the words in the text. Consequently, it is not tiresome for the user and balances the protection of privacy with the enjoyment of communications. DCNL checks not only words that directly represent private information but also those that indirectly suggest it. Combinations of words are also checked. Analysis of the co-occurrence between words and reachability analysis with a search engine are used to infer what words imply what information.

Keywords: SNS, social networking service, privacy, disclosure control.

1 Introduction

E-communications such as through social networking services (SNSs) and blogs are becoming more and more popular. Large SNSs have more than 100 million users and the numbers of users are still increasing. While these e-communication media have been penetrating more and more into society, even newer types of e-communication media have appeared. For example, micro blogging services are successfully attracting young users.

Although e-communication media make communications more effective and enjoyable, they can also lead to the revelation of private and confidential information

D. Ślęzak et al. (Eds.): UNESST 2009, CCIS 62, pp. 131–140, 2009.

[1, 2, 3, 4, 5], the abuse of users, the posting of pornographic and violent content, crimes [6], and suicides [7].

Among these problems, the revelation of private information has been analyzed in several studies [1, 2, 3, 4, 5], which have shown that the revelation can occur in various parts of SNS pages such as the user profile, text in the blog part, photos, and videos. Revelation from the user profile can be prevented by setting the disclosure levels properly because the types of private information in the user profile are limited and relatively static [3]. In contrast, revelation from the other parts is much more difficult to prevent because, in these parts, new information is regularly uploaded, and it is difficult to predict what information will be uploaded in the future. The user should therefore not use the default disclosure settings but should consider the settings every time something new is uploaded. However, this is a tiresome and error-prone task. Moreover, existing disclosure control is typically all-or-nothing; i.e., the whole text is disclosed or hidden, leading to either possibly revealing private information or impairing the enjoyment of SNS communication.

In this paper we describe a new disclosure control mechanism called DCNL or disclosure control for natural language information, which we are implementing. DCNL analyzes the texts in the blog part of a given SNS page and automatically detects words that might reveal private information about the page owner. Its disclosure control is not all-or-nothing but word-by-word, thus balancing the protection of privacy with the enjoyment of communication. It detects not only direct mention of private information but also its indirect suggestion and suggestion by combinations of words.

The difficulty of this detection is that semantic analysis for natural language sentences is not yet established, so problematic words must be detected without being able to analyze their meanings reliably. DCNL uses analysis of word co-occurrence and reachability analysis using a search engine to infer what words imply what information and uses the results to complement the incompleteness of semantic analysis.

Section 2 of this paper presents the analysis of example sentences to clarify the requirements for DCNL. Section 3 describes the DCNL system design and algorithms. Section 4 reports the simulation of DCNL operations, and Section 5 concludes with a summary of the key points and a mention of future work.

2 Example Analysis and Requirements

As mentioned above, existing disclosure control requires a user to predefine disclosure control rules for the texts expected to be uploaded or to manually set the disclosure level for each text. We illustrate the problems with these methods and clarify the requirements for our DCNL by using example sentences taken from an SNS pages.

2.1 Unsafe Expressions

Consider the three diaries in Figure 1[1], which were actually entered onto an SNS page by a female student at our university (UEC).

---

[1] The sentences were actually written in Japanese; they were translated into English for this paper.

Diary 1

> Picture taking for graduate album. First floor of
> Lissajous Hall, 10 through 19, on 14 and 15 October.

Diary 2

> Yesterday, I met Satoko at Chofu Station. She looked
> tired from doing graduate research, like I have.

Diary 3

> Kyosuke and I enjoyed "Enchanted" in Odaiba.
> It was very funny and lovely because....

Fig. 1. Examples of unsafe expressions

Although the phrase "Lissajous Hall" in the first diary seems harmless enough, it actually is harmful. A Google search (in Japanese) on this phrase found five mentions of her school in the first ten retrievals. She thus unintentionally revealed her affiliation, which she wanted to hide due to the risk of stalking victimization. She could have avoided this inadvertent disclosure by predefining a disclosure control rule, but it is difficult to anticipate all (or most) of the words that might reveal private information. She also could have manually set the disclosure level of this text so that only her friends could read it, but she might overlook the danger of the phrase "Lissajous Hall" because this phrase does not directly represent her affiliation. Both predefining many rules for the various possible cases and setting disclosure levels manually for each text would likely be troublesome enough to cause a user to stop using the service, even if doing either were possible.

The combination of "Chofu Station" and "graduate research" in the second diary also reveals her affiliation because "graduate research" implies she is a university student, and the only university around "Chofu Station" is UEC. Moreover, it reveals that she is a graduate student. Thus, even though each phrase alone is relatively harmless, their combination is not. Writing rules or setting disclosure levels for all such combinations would be even more troublesome.

The use of "Odaiba," the name of an entertainment area, in the third diary implies she has a boyfriend because Odaiba is a popular place for couples. This illustrates that the attributes of objects represented by a phrase need to be considered.

In addition, this diary reveals the name of her boyfriend. This example as well illustrates the difficulty of preparing rules or setting levels for disclosure control.

In addition to these problems, disclosure control is typically all-or-nothing, i.e., whether all the sentences in the target text are disclosed or hidden. It thus leads to either unsafe disclosure or no communication.

2.2 Desirable Transformation

The sentences above reveal private information but could be disclosed after being transformed as shown in Figure 2.

The transformation of the first diary is straightforward omission of the problematic phrase, which is not difficult once it has been identified. The transformation of the

Diary 1': for those who are neither self nor friend

> Picture taking for graduate album. First floor of
> the University Hall, 10 through 19, on 14 and 15 October.

Diary 2': for those who are neither self nor friend

> Yesterday, I met Satoko at the station. She looked
> tired from doing graduate research, like I have.

Diary 3': for friend

> I enjoyed "Enchanted" in Odaiba with my friend.
> It was very funny and lovely because....

Diary 3'': for those who are neither self nor friend

> I enjoyed "Enchanted" in the Bay area with my friend.
> It was very funny and lovely because....

Fig. 2. Desired transformations

second is trickier: the two problematic phrases must first be identified, and then the best one to eliminate must be determined. In the third diary, her boyfriend's name should be omitted, even for friends, because revealing it could damage their friendship. "Odaiba" should be omitted for those other than self and friend because she wants to hide not only the name but also the existence of her boyfriend from them. However, simply omitting it would make the sentence dull and unlively. Its replacement with the ambiguous "the Bay area" results in a sentence that is less revealing but still lively.

As shown in these analyses, the original or the transformed sentence should be disclosed depending on whether the reader is herself or not. Furthermore, different transformations are desired depending on the reader class. One possible solution to this problem is to write different sentences for each class of reader. This, however, would be tiresome and would reduce the enjoyment of the SNS.

2.3 Requirements for DCNL

From these examples, we can derive requirements for a method that would enable safe e-communication.

- Before sentences in the communications are disclosed, they should be checked automatically.
- The granularity of disclosure control should not be the whole text but the words in the text. Thus, any word that could reveal private information should be detected.
- In the detection, not only direct mentions of private information but also indirect mentions should be taken into account. Not only each word but also their various combinations should be taken into account.
- The detected phrases should be either shown to the user so that he/she can modify them or transformed so that they are no longer revealing.
- The burden imposed on the user should not be large. For example, the user should not have to define many detection rules or to modify many sentences.

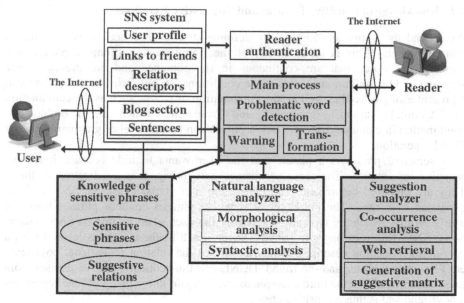

Fig. 3. System structure of DCNL

3 DCNL Design

3.1 System Structure

The system structure is shown in Figure 3. DCNL comprises the four shaded components. When the user uploads text to the blog section of the SNS, the main process reads and sends it to a natural language analyzer, which recognizes the words in the sentences. The recognized words are sent to a suggestion analyzer, which estimates whether the recognized words or their combinations imply private information represented by sensitive phrases. The suggestion analysis is based on a suggestion matrix generated by using word co-occurrence analysis and reachability analysis with a search engine. When it receives the result from the suggestion analyzer, the main process judges whether the words or their combinations directly represent, indirectly suggest, or do not suggest sensitive information. The result of suggestion analysis is stored in knowledge of sensitive phrases for future use. The words that are judged to reveal sensitive information are shown to the user so that he/she can modify them, or they are automatically transformed. When a reader accesses the text, he/she is authenticated, and his/her class is identified. On the basis of the reader's class, DCNL sends the modified sentences instead of the original ones. The current implementation does not include the automatic transformation of detected phrases; they are simply shown to the user as a warning. The knowledge of sensitive phrases consists of sensitive phrases and suggestive relations between phrases.

3.2 Knowledge of Sensitive Phrases and Suggestive Relations

We extend the notion of "phrase" by defining it as a sequence of words with an arbitrary length. This is an extension of the linguistic definition: "a phrase is a sequence of words that are continuous in the sentence and are grammatically structured." Our definition ignores these conditions. In our definition, a phrase can represent a single word as well as any combination of words, such as the combination of "'Chofu," "station," "graduate," and "research," which are a problematic combination in example diary 2. Thus, a phrase can be the level of granularity of any DCNL operation.

A sensitive phrase is a phrase that the user wants to hide because it reveals sensitive information. The sensitive phrases part in Fig. 3 is a collection of them. They are prepared beforehand, i.e., before the user starts to use the SNS, and are expanded over time. The initial set of sensitive phrases contains phrases from the user's profile, which are typically entered by the user when joining an SNS system. Some SNSs link user pages to friends' pages. Each of these links is labeled with a user-defined relation descriptor, which describes the relation (classmate, boyfriend, etc.) between the user and the friend. DCNL can thus collect sensitive phrases from these descriptors. For the third example diary, it would know that Kyosuke represents a boyfriend and is thus a sensitive phrase.

A suggestive relation shows which phrase suggests a sensitive phrase and how strongly it suggests it. The suggestive relations part in Fig. 3 is a collection of them. Because of our extended notion of a phrase, a suggestion by a combination of multiple words is naturally represented as a suggestive relation between a phrase and a sensitive phrase. The strength of the suggestive relations is normalized in the range 0.0–1.0. The strength of a suggestive relation between the same phrases is 1.0. The direct mention of a sensitive phrase is thus naturally represented. The suggestive relations are calculated for each phrase in the given text. Once calculated, they are recorded in the knowledge of sensitive phrases and used for the same phrases in other texts.

Suggestive relations are calculated by generating a suggestion matrix using the results of phrase co-occurrence analysis and reachability analysis with a search engine. In the second example diary, "Chofu" suggests the sensitive phrase "University of Electro-Communications (UEC)" because these two phrases have a strong co-occurrence relationship. The strength of the suggestion is the degree of the co-occurrence. In the first example diary, "Lissajous Hall" is recognized as suggesting "UEC" because five mentions of UEC were found in the first ten retrievals using Google API with the keywords "Lissajous Hall." In this case, the strength of the suggestion is the degree of reachability, which is calculated using the Web retrieval result.

3.3 Suggestion Matrix and Generation Algorithm

Suggestion Matrix. The suggestive relations are represented by a suggestion matrix. As shown in Figure 4, each row of the matrix corresponds to a phrase and each column corresponds to a sensitive phrase. The number of rows is N!, where N is the number of words in the target text because we consider every phrase (i.e., every

Phrases \ Sensitive phrases	1	2	...	j	...	M
1	S(1, 1)	S(1, 2)		S(1, j)		S(1, M)
2	S(2, 1)	S(2, 2)		S(2, j)		S(2, M)
⋮						
i	S(i, 1)	S(i, 2)		S(i, j)		S(i, M)
⋮						
N!	S(N!, 1)	S(N!, 2)		S(N!, j)		S(N!, M)

Fig. 4. Structure of suggestion matrix

sequence of words) in the text. The number of columns is M, where M is the number of phrases sensitive for the user. Elements $S(i, j)$ represent the strength with which the i-th phrase suggests the j-th sensitive phrase.

Generation Algorithm. The algorithm for generating the suggestion matrix uses co-occurrence and reachability analyses. Co-occurrence analysis is used to obtain the (normalized) degree of co-occurrence between the i-th phrase and the j-th sensitive phrase, $C(i, j)$, for $1 \leq i \leq N!$ and $1 \leq j \leq M$. Reachability analysis is used to obtain the normalized degree of reachability from the i-th phrase to the j-th sensitive phrase, $R(i, j)$. Element $S(i, j)$ is the larger of $C(i, j)$ and $R(i, j)$.

Calculating Co-Occurrence and Reachability Degrees. The degree of co-occurrence between words A and B is defined by the following equations, where the numbers of pages are those in the corpus [8].

$$C(A, B) = \frac{\text{Number of pages in the corpus that include } A \text{ and } B}{\text{Number of pages in the corpus that include } A \text{ or } B}. \tag{1}$$

The corpus used here is the complete collection of Web pages retrieved by a search engine. Thus, the numerator in equation (1) is the number of Web pages retrieved by the search engine under the condition that words A and B are included. The denominator is similarly calculated. The co-occurrence degree between Chofu and UEC and that between Cambridge and UEC are

$$C(Chohu, UEC) = \frac{14000}{1960000} = 7.14\text{E}^{-3}, \tag{2}$$

$$C(Chofu, Cambridge) = \frac{19200}{111000000} = 1.73\text{E}^{-4}. \tag{3}$$

These degrees show that "Chofu," the location of UEC, implies UEC much more strongly than "Cambridge," which is not. The degree of reachability is calculated using the Web retrieval results for the target phrase as the search expression, that is, on the basis of the number of retrievals containing the sensitive phrase and their position in the search results.

3.4 Detection of Problematic Words and Warning

The algorithm for detecting words that reveal private information is run when the user uploads text. The algorithm first generates suggestion matrix S for the text. Each row of S corresponds to the suggestive relations between a phrase in the text and sensitive phrases (which are or are not included in the text). If DCNL has encountered the same phrase in a previous text and thus has stored the suggestive relation for the phrase, it simply retrieves the stored relation. If not, it calculates the suggestive relation from scratch. Figure 6 shows the suggestion matrix for the first example diary.

If $S(i,j) \leq T$ for $1 \leq i \leq N!$ and $1 \leq j \leq M$, where T is the decision threshold, then do nothing. Else omit words in the text so that $S'(i,j) \leq T$ for $1 \leq i \leq N'$ and $1 \leq j \leq M$, where S' is a submatrix of S made by the omission and N' is the number of rows of S'. Note that if word W is omitted, all the phrases that contain W and the corresponding rows are deleted from the suggestion matrix. The strategy for omission is as follows.

- If $S(k, l) > T$ and the k-th phrase consists of only one word, omit this word.
- The larger the $S(k, l)$, the more preferred the omission of the k-th phrase. This means that one of the words contained in the k-th phrase is preferably omitted.
- The greater the number of matrix elements that are larger than T and that would be deleted by the omission of a word, the more preferable the omission of this word.

The set of words that have been omitted are the problematic words, and they are shown to the user.

4 Simulation

The operation of DCNL was simulated using the example diaries in Figures 1 and 2. For the first sentence in Figure 1, the suggestion matrix shown in Fig. 5 was generated. Detection threshold T was set to, for example, 1.0E-01. The algorithm for detecting problematic words found that {Lissajous, Hall} suggests a sensitive phrase {UEC} with a degree greater than T. Because {Lissajous} suggests {UEC} more strongly than {Hall} does, the algorithm omits "Lissajous" from the text and shows this phrase to the user. The user repairs the diary, changing it, for example, to Diary 1' in Figure 2.

For Diary 2, the algorithm works the same as for the first example. Because of the extended notion of a phrase, all combinations of words are listed in the rows of the suggestion matrix, and the combinatorial suggestion of "Chofu," "station," "graduate," and "research" is naturally identified. For Diary 3, the system uses two different values for threshold T. The value used for Diary 3' is larger than that used for Diary 3''; i.e., more disclosure is allowed for a friend.

Phrases \ Sensitive phrases	UEC	Kyosuke	...
picture	4.93E-04	3.17E-03	
taking	4.78E-04	3.09E-04	
for	3.40E-03	8.41E-04	
graduate	2.18E-03	3.35E-04	
album	1.83E-04	6.09E-05	
...			
Lissajous	3.02E-03	2.69E-04	
Hall	1.44E-03	1.70E-04	
...			
picture taking	5.52E-04	9.48E-04	
graduate album	6.10E-04	3.42E-04	
Lissajous Hall	1.29E-02	2.03E-03	
...			
for graduate album	1.03E-04	1.32E-03	
...			
Picture taking for graduate album. First floor of Lissajous Hall, 10 through 19, on 14 and 15 October.	0	0	

Fig. 5. Suggestion matrix for example diary 1

5   Conclusion and Future Work

Private information can be revealed by natural language text entered into social networking services or onto blog pages that are written by page owners and their friends. Existing techniques for disclosure control are not effective because consideration of the disclosure level for each text to be uploaded is tedious and error-prone, and the all-or-nothing approach to disclosure impairs the enjoyment of communications. Our proposed disclosure control of natural language information automatically checks texts on SNS and blog pages and detects words that might reveal private information. Its disclosure control is not all-or-nothing but for each word. Thus, DCNL is not tiresome for users and balances the protection of privacy with the enjoyment of communication.

DCNL detects not only direct mentions of private information but also indirect suggestions and suggestions by combinations of words. This broad detection is made possible by the generation of a suggestion matrix for each text to be uploaded. Each element in the matrix represents the strength with which a word combination in the text suggests private information. The matrix is automatically calculated using word co-occurrence analysis and reachability analysis using a search engine. DCNL enables different levels of disclosure in accordance with user class. This is made possible by evaluating suggestion matrix elements with different thresholds.

References

1. Gross, R., Acquisti, A.: Information Revelation and Privacy in Online Social Networks. In: Proceedings of the 2005 ACM Workshop on Privacy in the Electronic Society (WPES), New York, pp. 71–80 (2005)
2. Lam, I., Chen, K., Chen, L.: Involuntary Information Leakage in Social Network Services. In: Proceedings of 2008 International Workshop on Security, Kanagawa, Japan, pp. 167–183 (2008)
3. Lewis, K., Kaufman, J., Christakis, N.: The Taste for Privacy: An Analysis of College Student Privacy Settings in an Online Social Network. Journal of Computer-Mediated Communication 14(1), 79–100 (2008)
4. Data Protection Working Party: Opinion 5/2009 on online social networking, http://epic.org/privacy/socialnet/Opinion_SNS_090316_Adopted.pdf
5. Viegas, F.: Bloggers' Expectations of Privacy and Accountability: An Initial Survey. Journal of Computer-Mediated Communication 10(3) (2005)
6. Calvo-Armengol, A., Zenou, Y.: Social Networks and Crime Decisions: The Role Of Social Structure in Facilitating Delinquent Behavior. International Economic Review 45(3), 939–958 (2004)
7. ABC news: Florida Teen Live-Streams His Suicide Online, http://abcnews.go.com/Technology/MindMoodNews/story?id=6306126&page=1
8. Weeds, J., Weir, D.: Co-occurrence retrieval: A Flexible Framework for Lexical Distributional Similarity. Computational Linguistics 31(4), 439–475 (2005)

Software Infrastructure
for e-Government – e-Appointment Service

Vincent Douwe[1], Elsa Estevez[1,2], Adegboyega Ojo[1], and Tomasz Janowski[1]

[1] P.O. Box 3058, Macao SAR, China
[2] On leave of absence from National University of the South, Argentina
{vincent, elsa, ao, tj}@iist.unu.edu

Abstract. E-Appointment services could be considered as simple solutions providing significant benefits for improving the accessibility and efficiency for delivering public services requiring face-to-face interactions. Given the high number of services requiring appointment scheduling across government, a government-wide approach which provides e-appointment service as part of a software infrastructure for e-Government is clearly appealing over agency-specific solutions. The paper presents a case study of a one-stop e-Appointment service proposed as part of software infrastructure for e-Government. Relying on appointment-related information maintained by individual agencies, the service enables applicants to seamlessly arrange appointments to visit government agencies or centers providing public services through the one-stop government portal. We define a generic business process underpinning the delivery of one-stop e-Appointment service, propose an approach for implementing each of the business process steps, and present a concrete software solution to support the process. In addition, the paper discusses how the proposed solution addresses some of the challenges identified for delivering the service as part of software infrastructure for e-Government.

Keywords: Software Infrastructure, e-Government, e-Appointment Service.

1 Introduction

The delivery of some public services requires applicants to visit a government agency or center providing these services. For example, a business owner may need to visit a government agency for signing the establishment of a new company while a patient needs to visit a hospital for receiving medical assistance. For enhancing the accessibility and efficiency for such services, some kind of agreement is required for scheduling the visits – an appointment. E-Appointment is an electronic or Internet mediated agreement between a service consumer and the service provider for interacting at a certain future time and place (i.e. service location - physical or virtual) for a specific purpose. The agreement is achieved through a series of ICT-supported interactions. Several solutions exist for managing appointments for delivering public services, from services provided by private organizations to custom-made applications deployed by government agencies. In this paper, five case studies are presented - two solutions offered as services and three e-appointment services offered

D. Ślęzak et al. (Eds.): UNESST 2009, CCIS 62, pp. 141–152, 2009.

by government agencies in Greece and Singapore. A common feature of solutions provided by governments is the lack of support for managing appointments with various service providers; therefore, the limitation for offering them through the one-stop portal. However, the provision of a one-stop e-Appointment service presents a set of challenges. Based on the challenges presented by Klichevski [1], we identify the following: 1) the need for clear understanding of the business process; 2) the need to provide a technical infrastructure supporting secure communications between the one-stop government portal and service providers; 3) addressing organizational issues and 4) addressing regulatory issues.

After analyzing existing solutions and the challenges for addressing their limitations, the paper presents a one-stop e-Appointment service proposed as part of software infrastructure for e-Government. First, organizational features of the solution are presented, including a generic business process underpinning the delivery of a one-stop e-Appointment service and implementation approaches for each of the business process steps. Second, technological features of the solution are introduced, including functional and non-functional requirements, domain concepts, software architecture and the tools and technologies used for its implementation. Finally, the paper discusses how our solution addresses the identified challenges for providing a one-stop e-Appointment service. The contribution of the paper is two-fold. First, it provides a concrete solution for delivering one-stop e-Appointment service, as part of software infrastructure for e-Government. Second, it contributes to literature on e-appointment in terms of the exploration of the domain as there are very limited scholarly materials in this area.

The rest of the paper is organized as follows. Section 2 introduces the concept of one stop e-Appointment service and explains why such service is needed. Section 3 presents existing solutions. Section 4 explains challenges for providing a one-stop e-Appointment service. Sections 5 and 6 introduce organizational and technological features of the solution. Section 7 assesses the solution. Finally, Section 8 draws some conclusions.

2   One-Stop e-Appointment Service

E-Appointment is an appointment scheduling service offered through an electronic channel such as the Internet or electronic kiosk. Klischewski [1] defines e-appointment as an internet-based mediated agreement between two or more parties as social subjects (persons or institutions) to interact at a certain time and place for a certain purpose. Essentially, appointment making involves matching openings in the calendars of involved parties subject to a set of constraints and updating the status of these calendars as required.

Typically, two basic roles are involved in appointment making – the Service Consumer and Service Provider. The service consumer is the party seeking a convenient time and location to receive a service and the service provider is the party offering the desired service. While in general service provider or service consumer could propose an appointment time, experience from practice shows that service providers present available options (time slots and locations) to the service consumer with room for negotiation in some cases.

Appointment making is a fundamental aspect of public service delivery. A good number of public services either require an appointment for requesting them (e.g. appointment for service on establishing a new business) or are implemented by processes subsuming appointment making as one of steps (e.g. appointment for inspecting school premise during a school registration process).

An appointment services in government may be distributed or managed by individual government agencies and departments or centralized for a group of related services or for the whole service portfolio of government. Therefore, e-appointment services could also be provided as standalone e-services or as a one-stop service.

One-stop e-appointment services enable citizens to book appointments for services offered by government from a single point regardless of the agency offering such services. There are a number of scenarios for implementing a one-stop e-appointment service in government. Two examples of possible implementation modes are:

1) *Routing service* - the service simply forwards appointment requests to appropriate agency (service provider) and returns responses from agency to appointment seeker or service customer. The service continues to route the information between the service consumer and the agency until an agreement is reached between the two parties.

2) *Mediator service* - the service receives request; obtains additional appointment-related information from service consumer account (subject to privacy constraints); forwards the consolidated request to the appropriate agency; receives the response from the agency and replies the service consumer. The service continues to intelligently mediate between the two parties until an agreement is reached.

The routing model is obviously simpler to implement than the mediation mode and avoids legal and regulatory constraints (e.g. privacy) that needs to be considered in the second model. However the mediator model provides advanced features which could greatly reduce time for reaching agreement.

In a theoretical sense, appointment booking is a scheduling problem, similar to resource booking [1] and subject to constraints of different kinds including prioritization. Thus, appointment booking could be an arbitrarily complex problem with a range of possibilities in terms complexity and solutions. In practice, appointment booking is often conceived as a simple problem involving matching of time of parties and handling negotiations as exceptions.

The case reported in this paper follows the routing model with an architectural feature which embeds the e-appointment service as part of software infrastructure for e-government. As shown in Figure 1, the one-stop e-appointment service enables the citizen to request for a service and later select appropriate location, date and time for the service based on the information received from the agency through the government portal. The one-stop appointment service relies on another lower level e-appointment service provided as part of the software infrastructure.

The next section examines existing e-appointment solutions both in the public and private sector and comments on the strength and shortcomings of these solutions.

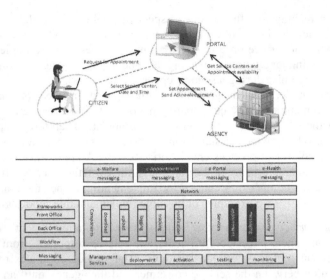

Fig. 1. Schematic View of the One-stop e-Appointment Service

3 Existing Solutions

This section presents five existing solutions for managing appointments: two services provided by private organizations – Appointment-Plus and YouBookIn, and three e-Appointment services provided by government in Greece and Singapore.

Appointment-Plus [2] is a web-based online scheduling system allowing customers of an organization to book appointments. The system offers a customizable solution enabling management of single or multiple appointments per time slot; notifying customers and the service provider about appointment-related events - like setting, modifying or cancelling an appointment; producing flexible reports; exporting appointments to Excel or Outlook calendars; and configuring the system - for instance, the time in advance customers can book appointments and how close to the appointment time customers can cancel appointments. A main limitation of using such a solution in government is that it is a proprietary solution offered as a service.

YouBookIn [3] is an online appointment scheduling manager deployed as service. In addition to managing automated appointment reminders and credit card deposits, it presents similar features and limitations as the solution described above.

The selected example from Greece is the e-Appointment service provided by the Validation of Applications and Marketing Authorization Division (DDYEP) from the National Organization for Medicines (EOF) [4]. The service enables pharmaceutical companies to arrange scheduled appointments with DDYEP [5]. Observations after the system deployment include: (1) increased transparency for scheduling visits; (2) improved efficiency in managing the workload based on analysis of visit statistics; and (3) better services delivered to customers by making informed staffing decisions [5]. A main limitation of this solution is that appointments are arranged only for a single agency. The solution does not support multiple agencies.

Two cases were analyzed from Singapore. The first case is related to the Immigration and Checkpoints Authority (ICA) [6], an agency from the Ministry of Home Affairs. The service [7] arrange appointments for citizens to: collect identity cards and passports; for residents to apply for permanent residence, renew or transfer re-entry permit or certificate of identity and complete permanent residence formalities; and for visitors to complete visit pass and secure Trade Partnership formalities. The main features of the service include: (1) authentication of applicants based on different data depending on the service for which the appointment is requested; (2) the provision of a calendar based user-interface, in which available and non-available dates, holidays and the applicant's choice are highlighted with different colors; (3) provision of different validation rules for making appointments for different services, like the time in advance for being able to modify an existing appointment; and (4) issuing receipts for appointments made for some of the services - the applicant is later required to scan the receipt in the Self Service Ticketing Kiosk when attending the appointment for getting a queue ticket. Although the solution enables the management of appointments for various services, the main limitation is that all such services are provided by the same unit.

The second case from Singapore is related to the Labour Relations and Workplace Division (LRW) [8], a government unit under the Ministry of Manpower of the Government of Singapore. The service [9] enables a person to book an appointment for consulting the Division advisory officers on the Employment Act. Main features of the solution are: (1) provision of terms and conditions for using the service that must be accepted by applicants before accessing any information related to it; (2) applicants are not authenticated for accessing the service; (3) availability of on-line demo explaining the process for obtaining an appointment; (4) the use of Singapore contact phone as the only requested data for validation on the form; (5) the use of an appointment identifier for modifying or canceling an existing appointment; and (6) a survey is conducted after the appointment is agreed. The limitation of the solution is that it only manages appointments for one single service.

Collectively, the five solutions analyzed provide good basis for synthesizing concrete desirable features of an e-appointment system. However, none of these systems provide a one-stop e-appointment solution able to support multiple government agencies or service providers.

Before elaborating our proposed one-stop e-appointment solution, we examine concrete challenges that must be addressed by our solution and indeed any other similar solution.

4 One-Stop e-Appointment Challenges

In addition to common challenges faced while developing electronic public services, there are specific challenges associated with offering one-stop e-Appointment service supporting the delivery of various public services produced by different government agencies. These include the following four challenges:

o *Understanding the business process* [1] – Although arranging an appointment appears to be a simple task of negotiating or organizing a selection process, there are two main alternatives for its implementation, with possible variations: i) based on service provider options – the provider offers the available time slots and the consumer selects one; and ii) based on service consumer options – the consumer informs its available (or restricted) dates and times, the provider matches with its own schedule and presents possible options, and the consumer selects one. While the core phase of the appointment service is the negotiation process, the business process goes beyond the negotiation itself. Prior to arranging appointments, service consumers seek information about services for which appointments are requested, usually through various channels – like counters, phone, fax, etc. After the agreement, applicants may follow-up with different types of actions, like requesting other appointments, modifying or cancelling existing appointments, etc. The challenge to overcome is to select the best alternative for negotiating the appointment (see the Mediator model in Section 2) and to provide support for all stages of the business process.

o *Relying on software infrastructure* [1] – Offering a one-stop e-Appointment service requires retrieving data about the availability of service providers and updating them with data about requested appointments. Therefore, the solution needs to rely on software infrastructure enabling secure communications between various service providers and the one-stop government portal hosting the e-Appointment service.

o *Addressing organizational issues* – In addition to technical challenges highlighted above, some organizational issues and controls also need to be addressed including: i) Controlling Misuse – since e-Appointment services provided by public institutions are exposed to misuse such as multiple appointments arranged by a single customer, additional efforts should be dedicated to avoid such risks; and ii) Staff Resilience – front-office staff may present resilience since e-Appointment services may contribute to reducing corrupt practices; for instance, customers may not be able to choose the official who serves them.

o *Addressing regulatory issues* – Some regulatory issues to address are: i) Multi-Channel Delivery – applicants should be able to interact with the e-Appointment service through multiple channels; ii) Privacy – since specific services may require applicants authentication, customer personal data may be exchanged while making appointments, therefore, privacy issues must be considered. In fact, to provide advanced appointment services such as in the Mediator model, access to information on other appointments made by the customer should be provided.

These challenges which provide good benchmarks for e-appointment solutions in general are used later in Section 8 in evaluating our solution.

5 The Solution – Business Process

The underlying business process of an e-Appointment service comprises three major activities: (i) Pre-Application, (ii) Application and (iii) Post-Application, each of them comprising various tasks. The tasks for each activity are specified in Table 1.

Table 1. Activities and Tasks of the e-Appointment Business Process

Activity		Service Provider – Tasks		Service Consumer - Tasks
Pre-Application	P1	Announcing e-Appointment service in support of a public service (S)	S1	Searching for the required service (S)
			S2	Finding e-Appointment service for S
	P2	Defining places for S-related appointments	S3	Finding information related to S, like: application form, supporting documents, eligibility criteria, delivery channels, delivery centers other relevant information
	P3	Defining time for appointments related to S		
	P4	Registering performance measures for S, like: number of consumers served at a time; mean time for serving each consumer; etc.		
Application	P5	Negotiating place for appointments related to S	S4	Negotiating place for appointments related to S
	P6	Negotiating time for appointments related to S	S5	Negotiating time for appointments related to S
	P7	Providing pre-defined requirements for attending the appointment	S6	Receiving pre-defined requirements for attending the agreed appointment
			S7	Notifying the service provider about special conditions
Post-Application	P8	Notifying consumer about agreed appointment	S8	Fulfilling requirements for attending the appointment
	P9	Assuring resources are available for providing S on the agreed place at the agreed time	S9	Being present at the place and time agreed
			S10	Modifying existing appointment
	P10	Reminding consumer about agreed appointment	S11	Canceling existing appointment

The Pre-Application phase comprises tasks that parties execute before the negotiation of the appointment takes place. For instance, the service provider announces the e-appointment service for a public service - called S (P1); defines the place (P2) and time (P3) where appointments regarding S can take place; and registers some performance measures related to S (P4) – like number of customers that can be served at a time; mean time for serving a customer; and how much time in advance the service provider would like to remind applicants about the agreed appointment. Service consumers can search for the required service (S1) on the government portal, find the e-appointment service supporting the delivery of the required service (S2), and find information about the service (S3) – like application form, eligibility criteria, required supporting documents, delivery channels and centers, etc.

The Application phase involves those interactions between parties that enable the parties to arrive at an agreement. For instance, both parties need to negotiate the place (P5, S4) and time (P6, S5) for interacting. The service provider supplies information about requirements that the consumer needs to fulfill before the meeting (P7); while service consumers receive such information (S6). In addition, service consumers may notify the service provider about its constraints before interacting (S7).

The Post-Application phase comprises all possible actions that parties can execute after the agreement is established. For example, service providers notifies the consumer about a confirmed appointment (P8), ensures that all the required resources will be available for the interaction (P9), and reminds the service consumer some time in advance of the agreed appointment (P10). The service consumer fulfills the

Table 2. Implementing Appointment Tasks

Activity	Service Provider – Tasks		Service Consumer - Tasks	
Pre-application	P1	Making available the e-Appointment service through the Government Portal (GP)	S1	Search service of GP
			S2	Search service of GP
	P2	e-Appointment application	S3	Search service of GP
	P3	e-Appointment application		
	P4	e-Appointment application		
Application	P5	e-Appointment application	S4	e-Appointment application and optionally Authentication service of software infrastructure (SI)
	P6	e-Appointment application	S5	e-Appointment application and optionally Authentication service of SI
	P7	e-Appointment application and/or search services of GP	S6	out of scope
			S7	e-Appointment application
Post-application	P8	e-Appointment application and Notification service of SI	S8	out of scope
	P9	Organizational procedure	S9	e-Appointment application
			S10	e-Appointment application
	P10	e-Appointment application and Notification service of SI	S11	out of scope

requirements before attending the appointment (S8) and ensures its availability at the time and place agreed (S9). In addition, the consumer can also modify (S10) or cancel (S11) an existing appointment.

These tasks can be implemented through the Government Portal (GP), e-Application Service and the supporting Software Infrastructure (SI) providing notification and authentication services as shown in Table 2. Informational tasks are done through the portal, appointment requests and negotiation are done through the e-appointment service while authentication and notification services are provided by the underlying software infrastructure. Features not supported in the presented solution are marked as out of scope.

6   The Solution - Software

This section introduces the software solution to implement the business process presented in Section 5. The requirements are presented in Section 6.1 while Section 6.2 describes the design and implementation of the software.

6.1 Requirements

Functional Requirements: Three basic actors are considered: i) portal administrator – responsible for the administration of the government portal; ii) service provider – responsible for operating the e-Appointment service in each of the agencies delivering services supported by e-Appointment; and iii) service consumers – persons requesting appointments. Functional requirements are grouped by actors as shown in Table 3.

The portal administrator needs to manage data related to the services for which appointments can be requested (supported services), the agencies providing such services and public holidays.

Table 3. Functional Requirements for e-Appointment Service

Portal Administrator	F1	Manage supported services
	F2	Manage agencies
	F3	Manage public holidays
Service Provider	F4	Manage supported service-related data
	F5	Manage centers
	F6	Manage non-working days
	F7	Manage working hours
	F8	View appointments
	F9	Export appointments
Service Consumer	F10	Make appointment
	F11	Modify appointment
	F12	Cancel appointment
	F13	Receive notification
	F14	Receive reminder

Service providers maintain data related to the supported services, for instance mean time for serving a customer and time in advance for reminding applicants about appointments. In addition, for each supported service they need to maintain information about centers where appointments take place, non-working days and working hours. They should also be able to view and export appointment information.

Consumers need to make, modify or cancel an appointment, receive notifications when one of such actions takes place, and be reminded about appointments.

Non-Functional Requirements: Three non-functional requirements are defined: i) Reliability – information about all appointments confirmed, modified and cancelled through the portal should be received by the provider agencies; and an agency should only receive appointment-related information for the services it produces; ii) Security – users should be authenticated for accessing the system functionality, and data used for authenticating applicants should be minimal and should also be exchanged and maintained securely; and iii) Interoperability – the system shall be able to interact with other software components, part of software infrastructure for e-Government.

6.2 Design and Implementation

As depicted in Figure 2, the system presents a layered architecture comprising the following five main packages: UI-Portal, UI-Agency, CoreBusiness, Entities, and Database. UI-Portal and UI-Agency comprise all the web pages providing the user interface. Web pages are grouped in three components: i) Common – set of common pages required at the government portal and provider agencies; ii) Portal – pages providing functions to the portal administrator and service consumers, and iii) Agency – pages offering functions to service providers. The Core Business package implements the e-Appointment business logic; for instance, it comprises classes implementing methods for making, cancelling and modifying an appointment (Service), for sending and receiving messages between the government portal and the agencies providing services (Communication) and for storing some

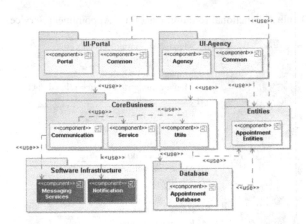

Fig. 2. e-Appointment Architecture – Static View

system parameters (Util). The Entities package implements the system entities. Finally, the Database package is responsible for managing data persistence through the database. The system relies on services provided by the software infrastructure [6], like the Messaging Gateway [12] enabling secure communications between the government portal and agencies, and the Notification service for notifying applicants.

The service was implemented using open-source technologies and open-standards. All components were implemented in Java. MySQL was used for database management with Hibernate for the object-relational mapping. Messages were written using XML, and composed and decomposed using XMLBeans. The exchange of messages was supported by the e-Macao Messaging Gateway. Log4J API was used for logging messages and JavaMail for sending e-mails. The development framework used is Apache Wicket 1.3.4 with Apache Tomcat 6 for the web server and Spring 2.5 as the container for instantiating objects. Details are provided in [12].

7   Assessing the Solution

Our solution addresses the challenges described in Section 4 as explained below.

o   *Understanding the business process* – The underlying business process for the proposed solution was explained in Section 4 and an implementation approach was highlighted for each of its tasks. The negotiation process is dissolved by our implementation by adopting the service provider option.

o   *Relying on software infrastructure* – The service fully relies on a Messaging Gateway for communications between the portal and agencies providing the supported services. For instance, at least six messages are exchanged for making an appointment – request (1) and response (2) for obtaining centers where appointments can take place, request (3) and response (4) for obtaining available times, and confirming the appointment by consumer (5) and provider (6). In addition, the e-Appointment service relies on the Notification and Authentication components of the software infrastructure.

o *Addressing organizational issues* - two concrete measures can prevent the risks of misuse: authenticating applicants for accessing the e-Appointment service and the adoption of a policy that ensures that an applicant cannot make more appointments than the maximum number allowed for a service. In terms of staff resilience, procedures for change management are expected to accompany the introduction of e-appointment implementation.

o *Addressing regulatory issues* - since the e-Appointment service is one more service offered through the one-stop portal, the same multi-channel delivery strategy applied to other electronic public services should be applied to it. In the area of privacy, in addition to the technical features implemented (e.g. use of minimal data for authentication) and secure data exchange, administrative procedures ensuring data protection of stored data are required.

8 Conclusions

The paper introduced the concept of one-stop e-Appointment service and elaborated on the organizational and technical features of a concrete solution which could be considered part of software infrastructure for e-Government.

Existing solutions for e-Appointments were analyzed and shown to lack support for appointments booking in a multi-service provider environment required for delivering one-stop e-appointment service. Challenges inherent in providing one-stop e-Appointment services were identified as a basis for benchmarking solutions. Subsequently, the business process underlying the service and the details of the implementing software solution were presented. Finally, remarks on how our solution addresses identified challenges were provided.

The main contribution of the paper lies in the provision of a detailed solution for e-Appointment service, which can be offered as a one-stop service and at the same time delivered as part of software infrastructure for e-Government. It also contributes to addressing the paucity of scholarly literature in this area.

References

1. Klichevski, R.: The Challenges of e-Appointment: Process Modeling, Infrastructure, and Organizational Context, http://citeseer.ist.psu.edu/681167.html
2. StormSource Software, Inc., Appointment-Plus,
   http://www.appointment-plus.com/
3. YouBookIn, You Book In – Online Appointment Scheduling,
   http://www.youbookin.com/index.htm
4. National Organization for Medicines (EOF), Ministry of Health, Government of Greece,
   http://www.eof1.eof.gr/eof_en/enhome.html
5. Giannakou, S.: Providing e-Appointment System to Pharma-ceutical Companies for Licensing Applications and Guidance. In: 5th Quality Conference for Public Administration in the EU (October 2008),
   http://www.5qualiconference.eu/bib_res/364.pdf
6. Immigration and Checkpoints Authority (ICA), Singapore Government,
   http://www.ica.gov.sg/index.aspx

7. ICA, e-Appointment Service,
   https://eappointment.ica.gov.sg/ibook/index.do
8. Labour Relations and Workplace Division (LRW), Singapore,
   http://www.mom.gov.sg/publish/momportal/en/home.html
9. LRW, e-Appointment Service,
   http://app.etools.mom.gov.sg/eindex.aspx
10. Estevez, E., Douwe, V., Janowski, T.: e-Appointment Service, Development Report,
    http://www.emacao.gov.mo
11. Janowski, T., Ojo, A., Estevez, E.: Rapid Development of Electronic Public Services.
    Software Infrastructure and Software Process, dg.o 228, 294–295 (2007)
12. Douwe, V., Estevez, E., Janowski, T.: Extensible Message Gateway, Development Report.
    Software Infrastructure for e-Government Project, e-Macao Program (2008)

QoS Management in EPC Network and Heterogeneous Digital Home Network

Yao-Chung Chang and Po-Wei Huang

Department of Computer Science and Information Engineering,
National Taitung University, Taiwan
ycc@nttu.edu.tw

Abstract. According to the International Organization EPC global Inc. which leads EPC network framework standard, EPC combines Internet and Radio Frequency Identification (RFID) technology with a rapid development in recent years. At the same time, with a variety of communications and network technology, the diversity and heterogeneity of the intercommunication technologies flourish in the digital home environment. However, variety of network architectures and protocols are different in digital home space; there are several important research issues in heterogeneous home network. In order to enhance the quality of service for heterogeneous home network, this paper constructs the EPC network architecture and performs QoS management through the EPC Framework. Also, this paper explores QoS issues in EPC network and heterogeneous home network environment. This paper accelerates the integration of heterogeneous networks in digital home environment. Finally, the EPC network and the heterogeneous home network will reach the effective management and assure the service quality.

Keywords: EPC Network, Quality of Service, Heterogeneous Digital Home Network.

1 Introduction

EPC code is the most important design for the EPC system. Each EPC code is a unique code in the information system, so the relevant information of objects can be accessed in the global EPC network and built up information exchange standards. In current applications, the EPC codes have the greatest opportunity to be the next generation of coding system. The coding structure extends the existing traditional Barcode. The Barcode and the EPC have the advantages and disadvantages: Barcode is lower-cost, but EPC is more expensive; Barcode needs be operated by human, hence it is easy to make mistakes by human; EPC is an automatic identification technology without requiring human operation. Hence, EPC code marks targets not only traditional barcode items, but also a single small object, boxes, large containers, trucks and even expanding the goods and services.

Figure 1 shows the global EPC network framework which is combined by a series of Local EPC network [4]. The composition unit in EPCglobal network includes EPC code, RFID Tag and Reader, Middleware, EPC IS, EPC ONS. We can contrast the

D. Ślęzak et al. (Eds.): UNESST 2009, CCIS 62, pp. 153–160, 2009.

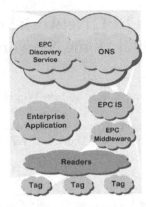

Fig. 1. Global EPC Network Framework

composition unit in EPCglobal network with Internet. The EPC IS is like websites on the Internet, and the EPC ONS is similar to DNS. EPC end users use various Enterprise Applications that joined inside enterprises EPCglobal network to look up EPC information.

Accelerate the integration speed of heterogeneous communication network technology in digital home is the main objective of this paper. In this research, we use the EPC network architecture to reach effective management and guarantee the service of quality in heterogeneous digital home network. The remainder of this paper is organized as follows: Section 2 provides a survey of heterogeneous digital home network. Section 3 describes the QoS issues. The system architecture is proposed in section 4. Experimental results and discussions are presented in section 5. Finally, section 6 concludes this paper.

2   Heterogeneous Digital Home Network

In recent years, with the flourishing development of different communication and network technology, the relevant devices of the network used in homes and Small and Medium-Sized Enterprises (SMEs) grow with each day. The concept of Information Appliance rises [5], the electrical household supplies with handy, convenient, and informative and internet accessible will appear in homes and small and medium-sized enterprises. Besides, varietal and heterogeneous interconnection communication technologies will coexist in the digital home environment, as shown in figure 2. It includes the HAVi (Home Audio Video Interoperability), IrDA (Infrared Data Association), IEEE 802.3, IEEE 802.11, Jini [6], UPnP (Universal Plug and Play) [7], USB (Universal Serial Bus) [8], Bluetooth [9], IEEE 1394 [10], PowerLine over Ethernet, Sensor Network, RFID Network, Home Plug and HomePNA, etc.

Under the environment of complicated and heterogeneous digital home network, the management of homes and small and medium-sized enterprises will be a serious challenge for users, electrical home appliances designers and service providers. At the same time, how to manage network and diagnose the mistake effectively under the environment of complicated digital home network is a major challenge to users, electrical home appliances designers and service providers.

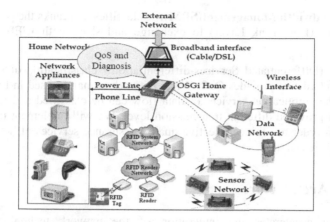

Fig. 2. Management Framework of Heterogeneous Remote Home Network

Under the standard of network management at present, the most popular is SNMP (Simple Network Management Protocol) in the local area network in IP-based [11-15] environment, but the standard is not unified in other heterogeneous home networks. The shortcomings are listed as followings:

1. SNMP polling may cause the emergence of the congested situation of network communication in a large network or step out the wide area network (WAN). The burden of collection information in SNMP put on the management client.
2. SNMP Agent is unable to offer the records of a certain devices and information.
3. SNMP protocol cannot keep all management information such as the identification, state of the device and dispose with the unified form.

The combining interfaces will be emerged in the future digital home environment to manage varietal and heterogeneous interconnection communication technology. Users are interesting only in the service that they can use; they will not mind how the communication protocols are operated. In order to realize various kinds of devices of communication with each other in digital home environment, each device must be able to automatic find other devices inside the same family and make communication with it, offer an integration service that can cross different technologies and protocols.

3   Quality of Service (QoS)

In order to meet the different needs of QoS mechanisms, QoS protocol and algorithm are listed as following:

1. **Resource Reservation Protocol (RSVP):** It offers the letter order that resources reserve of network.
2. **Differentiated Services (DiffServ):** It offers a simple classification and network aggregate flow to get the priority.
3. **Multi-Propocol Label Switching(MPLS):** It controls bandwidth management of network through the network path and aggregates data flow according to the marked network traffic dividing into groups.

4. **Subnet Bandwidth Management(SBM):** It classifies and ranks the priority to the OSI Layer 2(Data Link Layer) to exchange and share with IEEE 802 Series network.

The DiffServ (Differentiated Services-differentiation / classification of services), is the IETF standard that provides QoS. WAN network is mainly used in business, the principle is that application services or data flow can be classified and marked with the rules, and provided different transmission level. We will implement the DiffServ Framework in order to achieve effective quality assurance services of heterogeneous network in this research.

4 System Architecture

This research accelerates the integration of the network technology for the heterogeneous communication in the digital home through EPC network framework. We probe related topics of QoS in EPC network and heterogeneous digital home network. It includes management structure and mechanism of QoS in EPC network and heterogeneous network to reach effective management and guarantee the service of quality in heterogeneous digital home network.

4.1 Construct the EPC Network Gateway

During this stage, we construct standard services of different EPC specifications when implementing the digital home gateway system [16].

4.2 QoS in Heterogeneous Digital Home Network

Figure 3 and figure 4 show two modes of QoS: DiffServ Framework and DiffServ Region-wide Framework.

QoS in heterogeneous digital home network relative topics are as the followings:

- Internetworking: The existing network must link each other.
- Heterogeneity: It must consider various networks that contain broadcast, satellite, wireless network, broadcast network and other networks.
- Distributed Management: It allows the distributed management of the resource distribution.

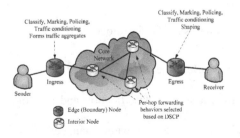
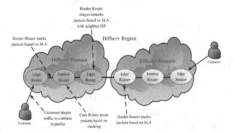

Fig. 3. DiffServ Framework   **Fig. 4.** DiffServ Region-wide Framework

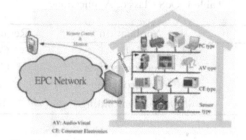

Fig. 5. Integration of EPC Network Framework with heterogeneous digital home network

- Easy Attachment: It allows the host to connect in a lower power mode.
- Accountability: It must be effective when resources are distributed.

Figure 5 shows the framework of heterogeneous digital home network integration with EPC Network Framework.

4.3   QoS Analysis in EPC Network and Heterogeneous Digital Home Network

Figure 6 shows the NS2 simulation of EPC Network and the QoS analysis in digital home network. Home network links different IP-Based devices in the simulation environment, such as the refrigerator, the microwave, the videophone and the web phone. The user can connect the internet through these IP-Based devices. Suppose the bandwidth resources that in home network are 2Mbps and the bandwidth that videophone in video conference and web phone need are 500kbps and 350kbps. In order to analyze the differences between QoS support and Non-Qos support, we gradually increase the bandwidth requirement of the video conference and web phone.

Table 1 shows the QoS classification according to the characteristic of the necessary service.

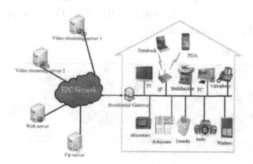

Fig. 6. Simulation Environment of QoS Analysis in Digital Home Network

Table 1. QoS Class of Applications

Device	Application	Required QoS Class
Web phone	VoIP	Conversation
Videophone	Videoconference	Conversation
Refrigerator	Web browsing	Interactive
Microwave	Data downloading	Background

Table 2 shows the start and stop time of application programs in the simulation environment.

Table 2. Start and Stop Time of Applications

Device	Start Time	Stop Time
Web phone	1.0	9.0
Videophone	2.0	9.0
Refrigerator	3.0	6.0
Microwave	4.0	7.0

5 Experimental Results

The figure 7 (a) and figure 7 (b) show the case of unsupported the bandwidth requirements. Non-QoS support web phone, video conference and interactive program of refrigerator join the resource competition successively. After it causes insufficient resources, the delay time rises from 0.05 milliseconds to 0.25 milliseconds and throughput drops about 320-325 kbps by 350 kbps, as shown in figure 9 (a) and figure 9 (b). By contrast, delay time is maintained at about 0.05 milliseconds with QoS support, as shown in figure 8 (a) and figure 8 (b). The throughput also maintains at about 350 kbps, as shown in figure 10 (a). The same situation shows in the video conference service, as shown in figure 9 (b) and figure 10 (a). The figure shows the different delay time between Non-QoS Support and QoS Support, the results can be sure with the QoS Support is better for heterogeneous digital home network.

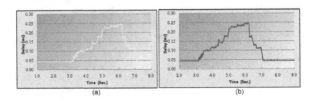

Fig. 7. Delay time of 350kbps Non-QoS Support videophone (a) and 500kbps Non-QoS Support video conference (b)

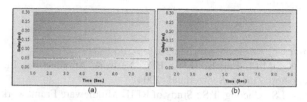

Fig. 8. Delay time of 350kbps QoS Support videophone (a) and 500kbps QoS Support video conference (b)

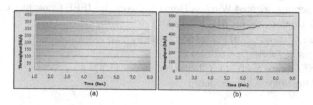

Fig. 9. Throughput of 350kbps Non-QoS Support videophone (a) and 500kbps Non-QoS Support video conference (b)

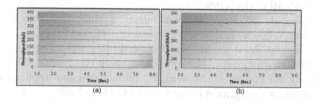

Fig. 10. Throughput of 350kbps QoS Support videophone (a) and 500kbps QoS Support video conference (b)

6 Conclusion

Minimize network delay, transfer different traffic packet and analyze network performance in EPC Network gateway are the key issues of this paper. QoS can efficiently partition bandwidth based on different parameters, and provide lower network delay and higher throughput. Hence, we construct the EPC Network through RFID/EPC framework to reach effective management and guarantee the service of quality in heterogeneous digital home network environment. This paper proposed the differentiated services mechanism with QoS control for EPC network framework and heterogeneous digital home network. The proposed QoS mechanism provides better performance and higher levels of administrative control over congested EPC network and heterogeneous digital home network.

Acknowledgements. The authors would like to thank the National Science Council of the Republic of China, Taiwan for financially supporting this research under Contract No. NSC 97-2221-E-143 -001 and NSC 98-2815-C-143 -003 -E.

References

1. Auto-ID Labs, http://www.autoidlabs.org
2. Leong, K.S., Ng, M.L., Engels, D.W.: EPC Network Architecture. In: Auto-ID Labs Research Workshop, Zurich, Switzerland (2004)
3. Kim, Y.I., Park, J.S., Cheong, T.S.: Study of RFID Middleware Framework for Ubiquitous Computing Environment. In: International Conference Advanced Communication Technology, vol. 2, pp. 825–830 (2005)
4. EPC Global, http://www.epcglobalinc.org/home
5. Ngo, C.: A Service-oriented Wireless Home Network. In: IEEE Consumer Communications and Network Conference, pp. 618–620 (2004)
6. Jini, https://wwws.sun.com/software/jini
7. UPnP, https://www.upnp.org
8. USB, http://www.usb.org/home
9. Bluetooth, https://www.bluetooth.org
10. IEEE1394, http://standards.ieee.org/reading/ieee/std_public/description/busarch/1394-1995_desc.html
11. Case, J.D., Fedor, M., Schoffstall, M.L., Davin, C.: A Simple Network Management Protocol (SNMP). RFC 1157 (1990)
12. Case, J., McCloghrie, K., Rose, M., Waldbusser, S.: Introduction to Version 2 of the Internet-standard Network Management Framework. RFC 1441 (1993)
13. Case, J., McCloghrie, K., Rose, M., Waldbusser, S.: Coexistence between Version 1 and Version 2 of the Internet-standard Network Management Framework. RFC 1452 (1993)
14. Case, J., Mundy, R., Partain, D., Steward, B.: Introduction and Applicability Statements for Internet Standard Management Framework. RFC 3410 (2002)
15. Presuhn, R., Case, J., McCloghrie, K., Rose, M., Waldbusser, S.: Management Information Base (MIB) for the Simple Network Management Protocol (SNMP). RFC 3418 (2002)
16. Chang, Y.C., Fan Chiang, C.T., Huang, P.W.: Secure Mobile RFID/EPC Network with AAA Mechanism. In: The 2009 International Conference on e-Technology (e-Tech 2009), pp. 2998–3014 (2009)

On the Security of an Attribute-Based Signature Scheme

Syh-Yuan Tan[1], Swee-Huay Heng[1], and Bok-Min Goi[2]

[1] Faculty of Information Science and Technology, Multimedia University
Melaka, Malaysia
{sytan,shheng}@mmu.edu.my
[2] Faculty of Engineering and Science, Tunku Abdul Rahman University
Kuala Lumpur, Malaysia
goibm@utar.edu.my

Abstract. In ISA 2008, Guo and Zeng proposed an attribute-based signature (ABS) scheme. They claimed that their ABS scheme is existentially unforgeable under adaptive chosen-message attack based on the strong extended Diffe-Hellman (EDH) assumption. In this paper, we show that Guo and Zeng's attribute-based signature scheme is vulnerable to the partial key replacement attack.

Keywords: attribute-based, signature, cryptanalysis.

1 Introduction

Background. The concept of identity-based (ID-based) cryptography was introduced by Shamir in 1984 [11] where the public key is the user's public identity string (e.g. email, ID number, name, etc.). A trusted third party called private key generator (PKG) is required to generate private key for every user based on their public identity. In year 2005, Sahai and Waters introduced an extension of ID-based cryptography, namely attribute-based cryptography [9]. In attribute-based cryptography, identity is viewed as a set of descriptive attributes instead of a single identity string. Thus, we can view ID-based cryptography as a special case of attribute-based cryptography where the attribute set contains only one value.

Attribute-based encryption (ABE) allows a private key corresponding to an identity set ω to decrypt ciphertext encrypted with a public identity set ω', if and only if the identity sets ω and ω' are at least intercepted by some distance metric d [9]. A year later, the notion of ABE is further defined by Goyal et al. [3], namely key-policy attribute-based encryption (KP-ABE) scheme. In KP-ABE, a policy (access structure) is attached to the decryption key and a user can decrypt any ciphertext encrypted with attributes that satisfy the policy. In year 2007, Khader adopted the access structure from KP-ABE and proposed an attribute-based group signatures (ABGS) scheme [5]. The verification is successful if the verifier's attribute set ω' satisfies the user private key's access structure $\mathcal{T}_\omega$. Soon after that, by injecting the revocation algorithm into the previous work, the same author proposed a new ABGS [6] which allows revocation. Inspired by the ABGS schemes, Guo and Zeng proposed an attribute-based signature (ABS) scheme [4] which shares the same nature as Khader [6]. Some other ABS schemes appeared in [8,7,10].

D. Ślęzak et al. (Eds.): UNESST 2009, CCIS 62, pp. 161–168, 2009.

In this paper, we show that the ABS scheme proposed by Guo and Zeng [4] is vulnerable to the partial key replacement attack. In particular, we show that an adversary can always generate a valid signature on any message from the view of any verifier by replacing or creating part of the components of public key and private key of an user.

Organization. The rest of the paper is constructed as follows. Firstly, we provide some preliminary background information and definitions in Section 2. Next, we present the flaw of the Guo and Zeng scheme and provide the proposed solution in Section 3. Finally, we conclude in Section 4.

2   Preliminaries

2.1   Bilinear Pairings

Definition 1. *Let $\mathbb{G}$ and $\mathbb{G}_T$ be groups of prime order p and let g be a generator of $\mathbb{G}$. The map $e : \mathbb{G} \times \mathbb{G} \to \mathbb{G}_T$ is said to be an admissible map if it satisfies the following conditions:*

1. *Bilinearity. $e(g^a, g^b) = e(g, g)^{ab}$ for all $a, b \in \mathbb{Z}_p$.*
2. *Non-degeneracy. $e(g, g) \neq 1$.*
3. *Efficiently Computable.*

2.2   Extended Diffie-Hellman Assumption (EDH) [4]

Definition 2. *Let $\mathbb{G}$ be groups of prime order p and let g_1, g_2 be the generators of $\mathbb{G}$. Let $\mathcal{O}_x(\cdot)$ take as input $c \in \mathbb{Z}_p^*$ and produce output $(g_1^v, g_2^{\frac{1}{(x+v)}}, g_2^{\frac{1}{(c+v)}})$ for random values $x, v \in \mathbb{Z}_p^*$. For all probabilistic polynomial-time adversaries $\mathcal{A}$, the advantage in solving the EDH is:*

$$\Pr[x \xleftarrow{R} \mathbb{Z}_p^* : \mathcal{A}^{\mathcal{O}_x}(g_1, g_1^x, g_2, g_2^x) = (c, a, a^x, a^r, g_2^{\frac{1}{(x+r)}}, g_2^{\frac{1}{(c+r)}} \wedge c \notin Q)] \leq \frac{1}{poly(k)}$$

for $r, c \in \mathbb{Z}_p^*$ and $a \in \mathbb{G}$ such that $a \neq 1$ where Q is the set of queries adversaries $\mathcal{A}$ make on oracle $\mathcal{O}_x(\cdot)$.

2.3   Strong Extended Diffie-Hellman Assumption [4]

Definition 3. *Given generators $g_1, g_2 \in \mathbb{G}$, and $x, y \in \mathbb{Z}_p^*$, let $\mathcal{O}_{x,y}(\cdot)$ be an oracle that take as input $m \in \mathbb{Z}_p^*$ and output $(g_1^r, g_2^{\frac{1}{(x+r)}}, g_2^{\frac{1}{(m+r)}}, g_2^{yr})$ for a random $r \in \mathbb{Z}_p^*$. For all probabilistic polynomial-time adversaries $\mathcal{A}$, the advantage in solving the strong EDH is:*

$$\Pr[x \xleftarrow{R} \mathbb{Z}_p^* : \mathcal{A}^{\mathcal{O}_{x,y}}(g_1, g_1^x, g_2, g_2^y) = (m, a, a^x, a^r, g_2^{\frac{1}{(x+r)}}, g_2^{\frac{1}{(m+r)}}, g^{yr} \wedge m \notin Q)] \leq \frac{1}{poly(k)}$$

for $m, c \in \mathbb{Z}_p^*$ and $a \in \mathbb{G}$ such that $a \neq 1$ where Q is the set of queries adversaries $\mathcal{A}$ make on oracle $\mathcal{O}_{x,y}(\cdot)$.

2.4   Lagrange Coefficient

Let $q(\cdot)$ be a random $(d-1)$-degree polynomial and $q(i) = s_i$, the polynomial $q(\cdot)$ can be reconstructed by having the knowledge of d-pair values of (i_η, s_{i_η}):

$$q(\cdot) = \sum_{\eta=0}^{d-1} s_{\iota_\eta} \triangle_{\iota_\eta, S}(\cdot)$$

where $S = \{i_0, i_1, \ldots, i_{d-1}\}$.

Definition 4. *The Lagrange coefficient $\triangle_{i,S}$ is defined as:*

$$\triangle_{i,S}(x) = \prod_{j \in S, j \neq i} \frac{x - j}{i - j}$$

where i and j are elements in the set S.

2.5   Definition of the ABS Scheme

The general definition of an ABS scheme is given below. It consists of the following algorithms [4]:

– **Setup.** Setup is a randomized algorithm. It takes a security parameter as input. It generates a set of parameters $Spara$ that will be used in the KeyGen algorithm.
– **KeyGen($Spara$).** KeyGen is an algorithm that takes the parameters of the Setup, then it generates public key pk, and private key sk for the user. Here, the private key is created using the public attribute set γ that the user owns.
– **Sign(pk, sk, M).** Given a public key, a private key of a user i and a message M, output a signature S, which is composed of σ and γ. The set γ describes the set of attribute that satisfies the tree.
– **Verify($pk, M, S, \gamma, \gamma'$).** Given a message M, a public key pk, a signature S, and a user's attribute set γ, output either an acceptance or a rejection for the signature based on the verifier's attribute set γ'.

2.6   Access Tree Construction [3]

Every non-leaf node of the access tree, $\mathcal{T}$, represents a threshold gate, owns its children and also a threshold value. If num_x is the amount of children of a node x and k_x is its threshold value, then $0 < k_x \leq num_x$. The threshold gate is an OR gate if $k_x = 1$, and it is an AND gate if $k_x = num_x$. Each leaf node x of the tree is an AND gate of one threshold value, $k_x = 1$ and x owns an attribute.

We first define a few functions for $\mathcal{T}$. $parent(x)$ returns the parent of a node x while $attr(x) = i$ and $node(i) = x$ are used to associate the node x with attribute i. The function $attr(x)$ and $node(i) = x$ is defined if and only if x is a leaf node. $\mathcal{T}$ defines an ordering for the children of every node, from 1 to num. The function $index(x)$ returns the ordering number associated with the node x. The index values are uniquely assigned to nodes in $\mathcal{T}$ in an arbitrary manner.

Let $\mathcal{T}_x$ be the subtree of the root access tree $\mathcal{T}_r$ at node x. If a set of attributes ω satisfies $\mathcal{T}_x$, we denote it as $\mathcal{T}_x(\omega) = 1$. If x is non-leaf node, $\mathcal{T}_x(\omega)$ is computed recursively by evaluating every $\mathcal{T}_{x'}(\omega)$ where x' is one of the children of x. $\mathcal{T}_x(\omega)$ returns 1 if and only if at least k_x children return 1. If x is a leaf node, then $\mathcal{T}_x(\omega)$ returns 1 if and only if $i = attr(x) \in \omega$.

3   Cryptanalysis on the Guo and Zeng ABS Scheme

Since attribute-based cryptography is an extension of ID-based cryptography, similar to identity-based signature, ABS does not need a key storage as well as key management where the user public key is the user public identity. However, since the verifier has no access to key storage, it does not know if a public key presented during verification process is a valid public key or not.

3.1   The Guo and Zeng ABS Scheme [4]

We describe the scheme as follows:

Setup. Define the universe for attributes $\mathcal{U} = \{1, 2, \ldots, n\}$. Choose $t_i \in \mathbb{Z}_p$ randomly for each attribute $i \in \mathcal{U}$. Next, choose $w \in \mathbb{Z}_p$ and the generators $g_1, g_2 \in \mathbb{G}$. The master public key will be the set $\{T_1 = g_1^{t_1}, \ldots, T_n = g_1^{t_n}, W = g_2^w\}$, and the master secret key will be the set $\{t_1, \ldots, t_n, w\}$.

KeyGen. The algorithm outputs a user private key that enables the user to sign a message M under a set of attributes γ, with the access structure $\mathcal{T}_\gamma$, if and only if $\mathcal{T}_\gamma(\gamma') = 1$ where γ' is the verifier's attribute set. In order to construct such an access structure, choose a polynomial q_x in a top-down manner starting from the root node r for each node x (including the leaf nodes) in $\mathcal{T}_\gamma$. For each node x in this tree, set the degree d_x of the polynomial q_x to be one less than the threshold value k_x. Now, for the root node r, set $q_r(0) = w$ and set d_r other points randomly to complete q_r. For any other node x, set $q_x(0) = q_{parent(x)}(index(x))$ and choose d_x other points randomly to complete q_x. Once the polynomials have been decided, for each leaf node x, we set the user private key as $J_x = g_2^{\frac{q_x(0)}{t_i}}$ where $i = att(x) \in \gamma$. The set of the above secret values is the private key $J = \{J_x\}_{x \in leaf nodes}$. The algorithm also generates another parts of the user private key by choosing $y \in \mathbb{Z}_p$ randomly. The user public key is the set $\{Y = g_1^y\}$ while the user private key is the set $\{J, y\}$.

Sign. The user computes $\sigma = (A, B, C, D) = (g_1^r, g_2^{\frac{1}{y+r}}, g_2^{\frac{1}{M+r}}, g_2^{wr})$ where r is chosen randomly from $\mathbb{Z}_p$. For every $i \in \gamma$, compute $ED_i = J_x^r = g_2^{\frac{rq_x(0)}{t_i}}$ and output the signature $S = (\sigma, \{ED_i\}_{i \in \gamma})$.

Verify. On input $(\gamma', g_1, Y, g_2, M, S)$, accept if and only if $e(g_1^y A, B) = e(g_1, g_2)$, $e(Ag_1^M, C) = e(g_1, g_2)$, and $e(g_1, D) = F_x$. We first define a recursive algorithm $VerNode(ED, x)$ which outputs a group element of $\mathbb{G}_2$ or $\bot$:

$$VerNode(ED, x) = \begin{cases} e(T_i, ED_i) = e(g_1^{t_i}, g_2^{\frac{rq_x(0)}{t_i}}) = e(g_1, g_2)^{rq_x(0)} & \text{if } i \in \gamma' \\ \bot & \text{otherwise} \end{cases}$$

If x is not a leaf node, there exist some nodes z which are children of x. x calls the algorithm $VerNode(ED, z)$ and stores the output as F_z. Let S_x be an arbitrary k_x-sized set of child nodes z such that $F_z \neq \bot$. If no such set exists then the node is not satisfied and the function returns $\bot$. Otherwise, compute $F_x = e(g_1, D)$. This can be seen as follows:

$$F_x = \prod_{z \in S_x} F_z^{\triangle_{i,S'_x}(0)} \quad \text{where } i = index(z), S'_x = index(z) : z \in S_x$$

$$= \prod_{z \in S_x} (e(g_1, g_2)^{rq_z(0)})^{\triangle_{i,S'_x}(0)}$$

$$= \prod_{z \in S_x} (e(g_1, g_2)^{rq_{parent(z)}(index(z))})^{\triangle_{i,S'_x}(0)}$$

$$= \prod_{z \in S_x} (e(g_1, g_2)^{rq_x(i)})^{\triangle_{i,S'_x}(0)}$$

$$= e(g_1, g_2)^{rq_x(0)}$$

If finally $e(g_1, D) = F_x$, the verifier accepts the signature, else rejects.

3.2 Cryptanalysis

The master secret key in the Guo and Zeng ABS scheme consists of two components: $\{t_i\}_{i \in \mathcal{U}}$ and w, but they are not bound together. Moreover, the user public key Y is not co-related with the user attribute set. These problems lead to the partial key replacement attack that we are going to present below. We show that an adversary $\mathcal{A}$ can create a valid signature S on any message M, from the view of any verifier by creating a new user public and private key pair (or replacing an existing user public and private key pair) based on the knowledge of partial master public key which is $\{g_1, g_2, T_1 = g_1^{t_1}, \ldots, T_n = g_1^{t_n}, \mathcal{U}\}$. However, this attack will not be successful if the verifier is the public key generator (PKG) which runs the **Setup** algorithm.

$\mathcal{A}$ begins the attack by creating a new user for the ABS scheme. It first chooses a suitable user attribute set before creating the new user public and private key pair. Obviously, $\mathcal{U}$ will be the best choice for an user attribute set as it includes all the attributes used in the system; intuitively, if the attribute set chosen is belong to an existing user, $\mathcal{A}$'s action is actually replacing an existing user public and private key pair.

After selecting the desired user attribute set, $\mathcal{A}$ chooses $y \xleftarrow{R} \mathbb{Z}_p$ and sets the user public key $Y = g_1^y$. It is able to do so because Y is not co-related with the master secret key. $\mathcal{A}$ then constructs a random polynomial, $q(\cdot)$ with degree 0 (this indicates threshold value $k = 1$) and sets $q(0)$ to a number $r' \xleftarrow{R} \mathbb{Z}_p$. $\mathcal{A}$ sets $index(i)$ for $i \in \mathcal{U}$ and computes $q(index(i))_{i \in \mathcal{U}}$ to complete the construction of the access structure $\mathcal{T}_\mathcal{U}$. The setting of $q(\cdot)$ makes $\mathcal{T}_\mathcal{U}$ behaves as an one level access structure which uses OR gate as the root node. Until here, $\mathcal{A}$ holds a fake user public key Y and a fake access structure $\mathcal{T}_\mathcal{U}$.

$\mathcal{A}$ then proceeds to sign a signature S on a message M, by computing $\sigma = (A, B, C, D) = (g_1^r, g_1^{\frac{1}{y+r}}, g_2^{\frac{1}{M+r}}, \prod_{i \in \mathcal{U}} T_i^{r'})$ where $r \xleftarrow{R} \mathbb{Z}_p$ and $\mathcal{U}$ is the universe of attributes. Next, $\mathcal{A}$ computes $ED_i = g_1^{q_x(0)} = g_1^{q(index(i))}$ and outputs the forged signature, $S = (\sigma, \{ED_i\}_{i \in \mathcal{U}})$. In the case of $\mathcal{A}$ makes replacement on the existing user public and private key pair, the partial key replacement attack still follows as above. It is not hard to see that S is always being verified successfully by a verifier, which holds an attribute set γ'. The verification conditions are as follows:

- $e(g_1^y A, B) = e(g_1^{y+r}, g_2)^{\frac{1}{y+r}} = e(g_1, g_2)$
- $e(Ag_1^M, C) = e(g_1^{r+M}, g_2^{\frac{1}{M+r}}) = e(g_1, g_2)$
- $F_x = e(g_1, D)$

Correctness:

$$VerNode(ED, x) = \begin{cases} e(T_i, ED_i) = e(g_1^{t_i}, g_1^{q_x(0)}) = e(g_1, g_1)^{t_i q_x(0)} & \text{if } i \in \gamma' \\ \perp & \text{otherwise} \end{cases}$$

$$F_x = \prod_{z \in S_x} F_z^{\triangle_{i, S_x'}(0)} \quad \text{where } i = index(z), S_x' = index(z) : z \in S_x$$

$$= \prod_{z \in S_x} (e(g_1, g_1)^{t_i q_x(0)})^{\triangle_{i, S_x'}(0)}$$

$$= \prod_{z \in S_x} (e(g_1, g_1)^{t_i r'})$$

$$= e(g_1, g_1)^{r' \sum_{i \in index(z)} t_i}$$

Finally, $e(g_1, D) = e(g_1, \prod_{i \in \gamma} T_i^{r'}) = F_x$ and the verifier accepts the signature. $\mathcal{A}$ is then successful in forging a signature S on a message M. If the verifier is not going to check the signature, i.e. check if D and/or ED match the value of any element in the master public key before verifying it, $\mathcal{A}$ can just set $r' = 1$ and the signature is still valid. Anyway, if the verifier is the PKG, the partial key replacement attack will fail because the PKG knows every user's public and private key pair.

In order to overcome this attack, the verifier needs to change the last verifying condition from checking if $e(g_1, D) = F_x$ to checking if $e(A, W) = F_x$. This ensures the master secret key w is bound inside ED_i. Since the value of the master public key W is fixed, $\mathcal{A}$ can only perform key replacement attack by producing a fake A but this attack will fail. This is due to $\mathcal{A}$ does not know the master secret key t_i for all corresponding $i \in \mathcal{U}$ and thus it cannot pass through the last verification condition.

3.3   ABGS Scheme

On the other hand, the ABGS scheme in [6] does not suffer from the attacks stated above as the user public and private keys are well formed. Besides, the values inside the signature are bound by hash functions. Although the partial key replacement attack still works on the ABGS's $VerNode(\cdot)$ function, the adversary will fail when finally the verifier requests the knowledge of exponents used. This is done by verifying the values of $\overline{R_2}$. Due to page limit, we are not giving the full description of the ABGS scheme. Reader may refer to [6] for the details.

We show how the attempt on the ABGS is going to fail as follows. Recall that the partial key replacement attack replaces or creates part of the components of public and private key pair of an user. With the knowledge of the master public key $\{g_1, g_2, w = g_2^y, \mathcal{U} = \{1, 2, \ldots, m\}, D_{leaf_1}, \ldots, D_{leaf_m}\}$ of the ABGS scheme, $\mathcal{A}$ chooses $r', \alpha \xleftarrow{R} \mathbb{Z}_p$, $(\hat{u}, \hat{v}) \leftarrow H_0(gpk, M, r')$ and sets $A_{\mathcal{A}} = g_1^{\frac{1}{r'}}, C_2 = A_{\mathcal{A}} v^\alpha, CT_1 = \{\beta_{(0,\mathcal{A},1)}, \beta_{(1,\mathcal{A},1)}\}, \ldots, CT_m = \{\beta_{(0,\mathcal{A},m)}, \beta_{(1,\mathcal{A},m)}\}$ where $\beta_{(0,\mathcal{A},j)} = A_{\mathcal{A}} v^\alpha$ and $\beta_{(1,\mathcal{A},j)} = e(\beta_{(0,\mathcal{A},j)}, D_{(0,j)})$.

$\mathcal{A}$ generates $R_1, R_2, R_3, c, s_\alpha, s_x, s_\sigma$ exactly the same way as in the original $Sign$ algorithm [6]. For those values $\mathcal{A}$ does not know, it will replace them with random values. Finally, $\mathcal{A}$ sends the fake signature $\sigma = (r, C_1, C_2, c, s_\alpha, s_x, s_\sigma, CT_1, \ldots, CT_m)$ to the verifier. It is not hard to see that σ is always being verified successfully by a verifier which holds an attribute set γ':

$$VerNode(leaf) = \begin{cases} \frac{e(\beta_{(0,\mathcal{A},j)}, D_{(0,j)} D_{(1,j)})}{\beta_{(1,\mathcal{A},j)}} = e(A_{\mathcal{A}} v^\alpha, g_2)^{q_{leaf_j}(0)} & \text{if } (j \in \zeta) \\ \perp & \text{otherwise} \end{cases}$$

where $j \in \gamma'$.

$$\begin{aligned} F_x &= \prod_{z \in S_x} F_z^{\Delta_{i,S_x'}(0)} \quad \text{where } i = index(z), S_x' = index(z) : z \in S_x \\ &= \prod_{z \in S_x} (e(A_{\mathcal{A}} v^\alpha, g_2)^{q_z(0) \Delta_{i,S_x'}(0)} \\ &= \prod_{z \in S_x} (e(A_{\mathcal{A}} v^\alpha, g_2)^{q_{parent(z)}(index(z)) \Delta_{i,S_x'}(0)}) \\ &= e(A_{\mathcal{A}} v^\alpha, g_2)^{q_{root}(0)} \\ &= e(C_2, w) \end{aligned}$$

The attack of $\mathcal{A}$ will stop here. The verification will fail when the verifier verifies the values of $\overline{R_2}$.

4 Conclusion

We have presented a partial key replacement attack on the Guo and Zeng ABS scheme. The flaw is due to that the two components of master secret key are not bound together and the user public key and private key are not co-related. We proposed the solution by changing the last verifying condition.

References

1. Bethencourt, J., Sahai, A., Waters, B.: Ciphertext-policy attribute-based encryption. In: IEEE Symposium on Security and Privacy, pp. 321–334 (2007)
2. Cheung, L., Newport, C.: Provably secure ciphertext policy ABE. In: ACM - CCS 2007, pp. 456–465 (2007)
3. Goyal, V., Pandey, O., Sahai, A., Waters, B.: Attribute-based encryption for fine-grained access control of encrypted data. In: ACM - CCS 2006, pp. 89–98 (2006)
4. Guo, S., Zeng, Y.: Attribute-based signature scheme. In: ISA 2008, pp. 509–511. IEEE Computer Society, Los Alamitos (2008)
5. Khader, D.: Attribute based group signatures, http://eprint.iacr.org/2007/159.pdf
6. Khader, D.: Attribute based group signature with revocation, http://eprint.iacr.org/2007/241.pdf
7. Li, J., Kim, K.: Attribute-based ring signatures, http://eprint.iacr.org/2008/394.pdf
8. Maji, H., Prabhakaran, M., Rosulek, M.: Attribute-based signatures: achieving attribute-privacy and collusion-resistance, http://eprint.iacr.org/2008/328.pdf
9. Sahai, A., Waters, B.: Fuzzy identity-based encryption. In: Cramer, R. (ed.) EUROCRYPT 2005. LNCS, vol. 3494, pp. 457–473. Springer, Heidelberg (2005)
10. Shahandashti, S.F., Safavi-Naini, R.: Threshold attribute-based signatures and their application to anonymous credential systems. In: Preneel, B. (ed.) AFRICACRYPT 2009. LNCS, vol. 5580, pp. 198–216. Springer, Heidelberg (2009)
11. Shamir, A.: Identity-based cryptosystems and signature schemes. In: Blakely, G.R., Chaum, D. (eds.) CRYPTO 1984. LNCS, vol. 196, pp. 47–53. Springer, Heidelberg (1985)
12. Waters, B.: Ciphertext-policy attribute-based ecnryption: an expressive, efficient, and provably secure realization, http://eprint.iacr.org/2008/290.pdf
13. Yang, P., Cao, Z., Dong, X.: Fuzzy identity based signature, http://eprint.iacr.org/2008/002.pdf

A Proposal on an Edu-Game Mechanism for Effectively Knowledge by Using Hierarchical Configuration

Eun-Young Park and Young-Ho Park

Department of Multimedia Science, Sookmyung Women's University,
Hyochangwon-gil 52, Yongsan-Gu, Seoul, Korea
parkey@sookmyung.ac.kr, yhpark@sookmyung.ac.kr

Abstract. An on-line game is growing up very fast through characters of the interactive computing and internet environment. In addition, an edu-game combining the advantages of the game and the education increase gradually. The paper proposes an edu-game system for providing knowledge through the hierarchical structure. The system differs from existing ones that combine a game and an on-line education. There are three different goals as follows. First, the paper proposes three levels of knowledge hierarchies. The method enables users to understand more easy and systematic and interesting education. Second, the graphic interface of a puzzle type is able to contact more conveniently and it provides beauties and functionalities. Third, among them, specifically the knowledge hierarchy is not forced to users and the method also can study in detail and users can enjoy systematically e-education by using the general type of a puzzle game.

Keywords: Edu Game, Interface Design, Puzzle Game.

1 Introduction

A basic instinct of humans for perfect completion usually drives us happy. Basically, humans purchase a certain complete match for scattered facts. The satisfaction of completing the scattered pieces gives us great pleasure. Thus many people put in their time and effort in the puzzle, and they gain strong satisfaction[1].

The paper focuses on the importance of the general effects of a puzzle in building the edu-game design. Legacy online education has following problems. First, educational effects became weaker than original text education since the physical guide for the study is absent. Second, students can lose interests in study since there are no interactions or dynamics like the real education atmosphere.

To overcome the above problem, an edu-game formation has been popularly used in general[2]. The edu-game harmonically combines the 'fun' effect of a game and the 'learning' effect of education.

However, the edu-game typically puts weight on only combining the two formations of the game and the education. Simply combining two areas indicates a problem which does not focus on real educational effects since the balance of the weight is biased to the interest and formation of the game whereas education focuses

D. Ślęzak et al. (Eds.): UNESST 2009, CCIS 62, pp. 169–176, 2009.
© Springer-Verlag Berlin Heidelberg 2009

on logical consequences and knowledge acquisition for the given problems. Thus the paper presents the educational effects as main issues.

Especially, the online game lacks systematic consistency. The paper focuses on the problems in above and presents a new stepwise method. The presented method follows general learning phases, which guide users the top-down steps for understanding any knowledge. For this, the paper proposes a new educational mechanism and web interface design method to gain improved effects for certain knowledge.

Thus, the paper makes the following contributions:

- The paper proposes a new game structure organized as three-hierarchical-steps, which are well matched to the human thinking process.
- Thus, the method can enforce the knowledge to the user gracely with interests of games. The interface of the presented method is organized as a form of a puzzle, which has various pieces. These can be easily accessed and arranged as a component among the puzzle pieces.
- The paper applies human's desire purchasing perfectness to the edu-game in borrowing the game formation. The idea can indicate a good result improving delivery effects for any knowledge.

Thus, the structure of the paper is as follows in section 2, the paper explains the edu-game through a comparative analysis. In section 3, the paper explains the hierarchies of edu-game, in section 4, presents the design of the puzzled game interface. Lastly, in section 5, the effect of the paper and in section 6, the conclusive future direction for the research is thought upon respectively.

2   Related Work

The first phase deals with related researches that are similar with the one we propose and through the comparison we explain the distinct features of Edu-game.

2.1   Edu-Game Research

Feature of games that could be applied to address the increasing demand for high quality education are already identified[3]. Edu-game is a new term made from combining Education and Game. The word literally means that the user can enjoy the online game while acquiring various kinds of knowledge.

Edu-game is different from other online games in that it draws interest by making the contents of the game experience more detailed and fun[4]. Moreover, it creates the notion that education is a kind of a play which enforces the educational effects and offers desires of accomplishment by setting goals for oneself[5].

2.2   Puzzle Games

Originally, puzzle games are made without computers, Yet, at present, digital puzzle games can be found on the web[1].

2.2.1 Jigsaw Puzzle

Jigsaw puzzle is a tiling puzzles in which players need to put discrete pieces together on a board to form a complete picture where each piece is interlocking with others[6].

2.2.2 Magic Square

Magic square is a number square in which the sums in each row, column and diagonal line must be equal, and at the same time the number of each entry cannot be repeated[7].

The existing online games make users, normally among the range of elementary and middle school students, solve problems online through appropriate puzzle games offered by site managers. When the user completes puzzle games the scores are presented in interesting ways, thus providing an interesting learning method that enforces effective learning through fun learning. The paper covers each related research as well as the one on new systematic paradigm.

3 Hierarchical Edu-Game

The first phase explains the definition of the three levels Knowledge hierarchy and the second phase explains the control methods of the puzzle edu-game proposed in the paper.

3.1 Three-Level Architecture

The core proposal of the paper is the three-level knowledge hierarchy that is divided according to encyclopedia levels. The reason of this division is that it corresponds to the human thought process which understands the upper structure and then the next. This kind of knowledge acquisition process can inspire interest and enable systematic knowledge transmission.

3.1.1 Schema Level

Schema, which is already defined in various studies, refers to the process that sorts or organizes general contents according to a certain format. Also, schema comprises a big portion of knowledge as it is based upon perceptions on human life experience. The crown of this kind of knowledge is called the Skeleton level or the Schema level. In this game, schema level can be taken as the skeleton level which makes up the whole knowledge structure.

3.1.2 Instance Level

Instance refers to the objects that belong to the same class among many. Instance level in this study means the level where all selectable objects are gathered. Let's look at Fig. 1. There are many species of butterflies that are under the group insects and the attempt of gaming happens in order to explain these objects selectively.

3.1.3 Atomic Level

Atomic level refers to the level where each atom is understood well enough to be combined into a new object. Atomic level in this game denotes a collection of games that have broken down the above instance level and have specifically and realistically realized it.

Here, we have defined the levels that comprise each hierarchy. In order to systematically deliver this hierarchical knowledge, the new notion of puzzle has been imported. Through the puzzle, attempts to acquire partial knowledge tend to shape into a holistic picture and at the same time detailed and systematic learning is possible through the introduction of an external factor, game, which is emphasized more than mere education.

3.2 Puzzle Edu-Game Control Methods

3.2.1 Contents

The puzzle game proposed in the paper follows the form of an encyclopedia. While the existing educational games are ineffective in depth education due to unhelpful interface and heavy focus on the mere combination of game and education, the puzzle game proposed in the paper has a hierarchical structure based on the encyclopedia and thus enables broad and systematic learning regardless of the age group.

3.2.2 The Structure of the Contents

The contents of the puzzle game suggested in the paper are consisted of a hierarchical structure as in Fig. 1. The user can select the contents to be learnt at the beginning stage and this selection can be made in step approaches with down grade movements. Factors of same Instance level are positioned horizontally and each factor is comprised of sub Atomic level structures so that detailed and in-depth learning of each factor is feasible.

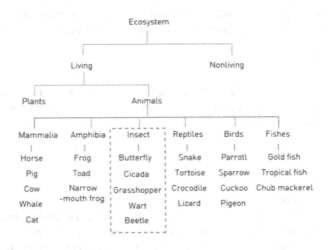

Fig. 1. Selection of the Interface Layout

3.3 Selection of Learning Method

The learning method can be described into two methods in our presentation and these are pre-learning after-game and pre-game after-learning. The former is a method where knowledge regarding the contents is acquired beforehand and the comprehension level is test and the contents are revised through quizzes, while the latter is a method where the user first plays a game to arouse interest in the parts that he does not know of and then studies those particular parts intensively. Users can select whichever method before starting the game.

3.4   Control Methods of the Game

This phase explains the method to start the game in order of precedence after logging in. The game is subject to changes in plan, thus the general structure of core contents is presented instead of the whole system.

3.4.1   The Goal of the Game

The first goal of the game is to change the black and white puzzle board located in the center into a colorful board using the pieces around the board. Upon drag-and-drop of a piece in a specific location on the puzzle board, a transparent box appears asking a question about an object that belongs to the Atomic level chosen when opening the game room.

When given the correct answer, the piece will turn colorful but when the wrong answer is given, the piece will bounce off the board, returning a different question each time of selection.

3.4.2   Rough Description of the Game

After completing the first goal, a screen appears and allows selection for another category depending on the option of the room. Moreover, the option of the room can be set so that there is a time limit for completing the puzzle and so when time is up, the game automatically ends and the user who has completed the most puzzles gets the highest points.

3.4.3   Moving between Categories

Fig. 2. shows the interface screen where the moving steps between categories can be fixed. While the first game allows learning through objects that have been set by the

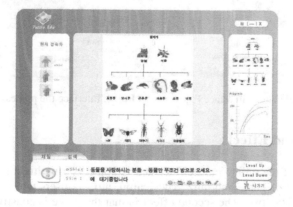

Fig. 2. Layout Moving between Categories

captain of the room, games after that offer puzzles at atomic levels shown in section 3.1.3 that suit personal standards of upper, lower and same levels, according to the options of the room.

4 Puzzle Game Interface Design

This phase presents the interface design of the puzzle Edu-game proposed in the paper. Fig. 3. is the puzzle game interface. Center left part of the interface shows the avatars of users who are participating in the game by selecting the same factors and offers detailed information on participants and respective game process status of all users. This provokes competition for the user just like in a real learning environment.

Shortcut icons are placed in the upper left corner and a mini map that contains the hierarchical structure of the educational contents comprising the whole game is located below to allow users convenient navigation. Below the mini map is brief information on personal information, learning levels, levels and scores of all participants in the game.

Fig. 4. shows the process of solving the problem in a puzzle game interface. The user drag-and-drops a small piece from the edge of the screen to a particular spot on the board. Then quizzes enable learning of the particular contents. When the correct answer is given, the piece turns colorful. The learning and game of the particular contents is completed when the whole puzzle image turns from black and white into colors.

The chatting box situated in center bottom enables information exchange and boosts educational and communicational effects through conversations between users. Lastly, there is an 'invite' button in the bottom right corner to invite users in the waiting room into the learning space and the 'exit' button in the right closes the game.

Fig. 3. Puzzle Game Interface Fig   **Fig. 4.** Interface the process of solving

5 Analysis and Effects

The first effect of the online puzzle interface is that it is a multiple game that allows simultaneous use of game and quiz. The feature attracts users who are only familiar with only one of the two. The second effect is that the game is constructed according to the human thought process based on the 3-step architecture proposed in the paper.

This enables systematic knowledge delivery mechanism through the hierarchy structure. The third effect is that the proposed puzzle interface makes use of the strong points of existing puzzle games whose effects have been proved, in order to develop intelligence, prevent dementia, improve concentration and arouse interest. The fourth effect is important in that by giving the impression that learning is another kind of play educational effect is enforced and users gain desires of accomplishment, in accordance to the intention of educational games.

This effect of the puzzle game fulfills the contents proposed in the paper. Along with these effects, the paper proposes the three-step game hierarchy structure adapted from the thought process and comprehension format of humans. The interface that emphasizes the aesthetics of the puzzle game is expected to offer various kinds of interesting educational effects.

6 Conclusion and Future Research

The paper proposes a game that significantly enforces educational effects by grafting the existing puzzle game to online education. The proposed education method is comprised of a hierarchical knowledge transmission system in a three-level-architecture and is novel in that acquiring knowledge supposedly happens naturally through puzzle games.

This kind of education has merits as it supports detailed and systematic learning through a free and interesting environment under the basic human desire of accomplishment. In addition, an easy-to-use interface has been suggested to offer not only educational effects but functionality and beauty.

This research currently divides the contents of learning in the game according to Creatures and inanimate objects. But this composition will be able to expand systematic learning of various fields including geography, history, astrology, medicine, etc. Besides, combinations of different kinds of puzzles are expected to make edu-game even more interesting. Future of edu-game should focus on development that can be quantitatively proved.

Acknowledgments. This work was supported by the Korea Research Foundation(KRF) grant funded by the Korea government(MEST) (No. 2-0905-0012).

References

[1] Huang, O.W.S., Cheng, H.N.H., Chan, T.-W.: Number Jigsaw Puzzle: A Mathematical Puzzle Game for Facilitating Players's Problem-Solving Strategies. In: DIGITEL 2007 (2007)
[2] Jovanovic, M., Starcevic, D., Stavlijanin, V., Minovic, M.: Surviving the Design of Educational Games:Borrowing from Motivation and Multimodal Interaction. In: HSI (2008)
[3] Federation of American Scientists, R&D Challenges in Games for Learning, Tech. Rep., Washington, DC (2006)
[4] Rodriguez, S.D., Cheng, I., Basu, A.: Multimedia Games for Learning and Testing Physicsi. In: ICME 2007, p. 1838 (2007)

[5] Choi, I.-K., Kim, E.-J.: In the Study of Theoretical Formation Process of Edutainment. Proceedings of the Korea Multimedia Society 5(2), 1–8 (2002)
[6] Puzzle, J.: (n. d.) (retrieved October 1, 2006), http://en.wikipedia.org/wiki/Jigsaw_puzzle
[7] Magic Square (n. d.) (retrieved October 1, 2006), http://en.wikipedia.org/wiki/Magic_square

Author Index